DATE DUE

OC 3 '96			
MY 28'98			
JE 18 00			
AR 28'01			
JE 11'01			

DEMCO 38-296

HAPPY
as a
CLAM

and 9,999 Other Similes

Larry Wright

Prentice Hall General Reference
New York   London   Toronto   Sydney   Tokyo   Singapore

PRENTICE HALL GENERAL REFERENCE
15 Columbus Circle
New York, New York, 10023

PRENTICE HALL is a registered trademark and colophon is
a trademark of Prentice-Hall, Inc.

Library of Congress Cataloging-in-Publication Data

Happy as a clam : and 9,999 other similes / [compiled by] Larry
  Wright.
      p.   cm.
    Includes index.
    ISBN 0-671-87918-9 — ISBN 0-671-87474-8 (pbk.)
    1. Simile.   I. Wright, Larry, 1935–
  PN6084.S5H36   1994
  423'.1—dc20   93-32548

Designed by Richard Oriolo
Manufactured in the United States of America

First Edition

Dedication

· · · · · · · · · · · · · · · · · · · ·

To Margaret, Sara, and Alison,
whom I love like a cat loves cream.

Acknowledgments

I am grateful to the following people for providing similes: Juanita Adams, IL; Matt Adams, IL; Scott Adams, IL; Edward Amburg, IL; Fred Armstrong, IL; Dick & Katy Baalmann, MO; Carl & Donna Badgett, TX; Kyle & Joan Boldt, MO; Randy Bollinger, IL; Churny Bradfisch, IL; Peyton Burford Harris*, MO; Dennis Burnham, CA; Willis & Linda Bywater, IO; Lew Cady, CO; Phil Carney, MO; Tom Carrico, KS; Barry & Susan Chase, TN; Dick & Jan Chedister, MO; Fred Coble, MO; Traci Cothran, NY; Joyce Cross, MA; Dick Davis, TX; Irving & Kay Diamant, MO; Tom Diel, MO; L. D. Douglas, IL; Dick Drury, MO; Jennifer Duffy, MO; Jerry Ersland, TX; Susie Feaster, IL; Jim Featherston, MO; Mrs. Wm. Fellenz, NB; Denny & Judy Flowers, IL; Amy Flowers & Rebecca Flowers, IL; Forrest Gill, KS; Mark & Nancy Gilman, KS; Frank Goodson, GA; Leo Graham, IL; Ruth Gregory, AL; Phil Hamilton, OK; Sheba Hancock, MS; Allen Harper, FL; Ed* & Evelyn Harper*, MO; Paul Harper*, MO; Richard Larry Harper, MO; Ed Harper, VA; Doug Haufe, IL; Joe Haufe, IL; Billy & Carole Hill, MO; Iola Hollowood, MO; Gary & Marge Holmes, MO; Rod Jackson, IL; Dee & Paul Jaenicke, MO; Clarence R. Keathley, MO; Debbie Fellenz Kelly, MO; Alan Klitzner, RI; Dan Knoll, IL; Bob & Paul Kraus, PA; Philip LeBow, CA; Dave Leroux, MO; Ed & Laura Lester, IL; Herb Levy, NJ; Joe & Joan Lipic, MO; George & Karen Matteson, MO; Brenda McAfee, MO; LeRoy McCoy, IL; Nancy McDow, IL; John McNeer, IO; Jerry & Sara Meyers, MO; Matthew & Catherine Meyers, MO; Rod Miller, OK; Bill & Debbie Mixon, MO; Michael Montgomery, IL; Tom Moore, AL; Marc & B. J. Morris, GA; Gerald "Windy" Nairn, IL; Ed & Vicki Nemec, MO; Ted Olson, TX; Cindy Pasley, IL; Bob Pecher, MO; Candy Peck, OH; Dathine Reed, MO; Mark & Alison Rohan, MO; Kelly & Brooke Rohan, MO; Richie Rohan, MO; Emmett & Peggy Ross, AR; James Roten, TX; The Rowling brothers, IL; Dick Rulo, IL; Claudia Ruso, NM; Tom & Peggy Ryder, IL; Chuck & Ann Schaffer, MO; Harold "Dutch" Schoultz, MO; Finis Schultz, IL; Rodney & Darlene Seidler, IL; Gloria Shealy, AL; Eddie Sholar, IL; Daryl Sorrell, MO; Marvin Spike, PA; Layton Stewart, MO; Bill Stubbs, GA; Mark Tynes, TX; Wanda Watson, IL; Jo Wilhelmi, MO; Cal Wofford, CA; Charles & Peggy Wright, MO; Denver M. Wright*, MO; Denver M. Wright, Jr.*, MO; Ed Wright, FL; Helen Wright, MO; Jack Wright, Sr.*, AZ; Jack Wright, Jr., CA; James R. Wright, Sr.*, MO; Lester & Lenore Wright, MO; Lois Wright, MO; Mellie Mae Wright*, MO.

I am also indebted with deepest gratitude to countless other relatives, friends, and strangers for their many contributions.

* = Deceased

Contents

Definition of Simile

simile (sim' ə lē) **n.** a figure of speech in which one thing is likened to another, dissimilar thing by the use of *like, as,* etc. (Ex.: a heart as big as a whale, her tears flowed like wine): distinguished from metaphor.

—*Webster's New World Dictionary,*
Third College Edition, 1994, Prentice Hall

Introduction

. . . .

I've been an avid collector of similes since 1948 when I was 13 years old. I spent that summer at our family's summer home in the Missouri Ozarks near the town of Doniphan. At that time I didn't know what a simile was!

An Ozark native, Arthur Brooks, was helping with the many chores around the place. One hot day he wiped his brow and said "I'm as busy as a tick in a tar barrel," and I laughed at this humorous comparison. During that summer I jotted down dozens of similes that Arthur said. I'm not sure that even Arthur knew he was a fount of similes, he was merely repeating expressions he'd heard over the years from his parents, grandparents, and others.

Later I bought a notebook and began to seriously record the similes. I was on the alert for them. They popped up in novels, commercials, old movies (especially Westerns), newspapers, talk shows, old books, sports programs, and in conversations with rural and city folk. By 1970, my notebook contained more than 5,000 similes, so I purchased a personal computer and entered my growing collection on floppy disks.

I've collected similes for enjoyment like other people collect stamps, coins, baseball cards, or beer cans (although simile collecting is less profitable than the collecting of just about anything else). My goal in publishing this book is to encourage people to use similes and to preserve their popularity and prevent their extinction. If you have any similes that should be included in this book's next printing, please send them to me and I will include your name on the acknowledgments page. Write to: Larry Wright, Box 640, Grafton, IL 62037.

I hope you like reading the similes as much as I've enjoyed collecting them!

About This Book

"Happy as a clam" is one of the oldest similes in the United States. But who ever saw a clam smile or laugh? This simile is actually a shortened version of the original, "happy as a clam at high tide." As clams are gathered when the tide is out, it seems clams are happy when it's high tide and there are no diggers around.

Similes are often humorous and lighthearted; some are ironic, nasty, and even vulgar. They enhance language to make points more vivid and clear as they colorfully express an idea or description. Similes build mental pictures in the reader's or listener's mind and increase the importance and clarity of the thought being expressed. They heighten persuasiveness, bring thoughts to life, and add spice to language to make it more interesting and entertaining.

For the sake of simplicity and consistency I've used the masculine pronoun when a pronoun is needed. For the most part, past tense has been used since most similes that are written down are recorded in this manner. The entries are arranged in alphabetical order by adjective (or noun). To avoid repetition and save the reader time in locating a simile, the first few words of each sentence have been deleted. For example, if the commonly known sentence was "He was as mad as a bear," the entry is found under **Mad** and reads "Mad as a bear."

Although some of the similes listed here are a bit racy, sexist, racist, and otherwise offensive, and probably unfit as pieces of conversation at dinner, they are included as a record of the language and to make this reference complete. Also, many of the similes included do not follow standard grammar rules, but they make delightful reading nonetheless.

A Note About Sources

The sources of many similes are provided. They do not necessarily represent that author's or speaker's view on the subject (the similes are taken from fiction and nonfiction works), and it would be erroneous to make any implication of the author's intent based on the simile attributed to him or her. Rather, the sources are listed because they are thought to be the originators of the similes. In some cases, it is obvious that the simile is an original one created by the author; in other instances, it isn't quite as clear, but the author listed is probably the originator or the first one to publish the simile. Many others are commonly used and have been handed down for many years, thus making it nearly impossible to find the originator, so there is no source listed.

Abandoned
Abandoned as a drive-in theater at noon.—Dan Rather
Abandoned as a ghost town.
Abandoned like a babe at a doorstep.
Abandoned like a one-pump gas station.
Also see Desolate.

Ablaze
Ablaze like poppies in the sun.—Ouida
Ablaze like a firebombed bamboo hut.
Also see Blazed, Burned, Flamed.

Abrupt
Abrupt as a guillotine.
Abrupt as a scissor cut.—T. C. Boyle
Abrupt as an axe chop.
Also see Sudden.

Absurd
Absurd as a Hottentot marooned on an iceberg.
Absurd as to expect a harvest in the dead of winter.—Robert South
Absurd as to instruct a rooster in the laying of eggs.—H. L. Mencken
Absurd as using a guillotine to cure dandruff.—Clare Booth Luce
Absurd as trying to put out a fire with applications of kerosene.
    —Tallulah Bankhead
Also see Crazy, Foolish, Funny, Mad, Nutty, Silly.

Abundant
Abundant as air and water.
Abundant as dandelions.
Abundant as the light of the sun.—Thomas Carlyle
Also see All over, Plentiful.

Abysmal

Abysmal as death.—Stephen R. Donaldson
Abysmal as deep depression.
   Also see Deep.

Ached

Ached like a broken rib.
Ached like a freshly stubbed toe.
Ached like a rotted tooth.
   Also see Hurt, Painful, Sore.

Acted

Acted like a bad-mannered schoolboy.
Acted like a committee.
Acted like a five-year-old.
Acted like a fool.
Acted like a love-starved calf at feeding time.
Acted like a ninny.
Acted like a scared rabbit.
Acted like he had no training.
Acted like its going out of style.
   Also see Behaved.

Active

Active as a beehive.
Active as a Chinese fire drill.
Active as a fire department during a conflagration.
Active as a hornet's nest.
Active as a pea on a griddle.
Active as a squirrel in a cage.—Aphra Behn
Active as an anthill.
Active and strong as a little lioness.—William James
About as active as a leftover fly in January.
About as active as the town drunk on Sunday morning.
   Also see Busy.

Adored

Adored him like a champ.
Adored him like an idol.
Adored him like a schoolgirl with a crush.

Advanced

Advanced like Grant through Richmond.
Advanced like the shadow of death.—John Ruskin
Advanced like Sherman's army.

Adventuresome

Adventuresome as a bee.—*Old Testament*
Adventuresome as a puppy.
About as adventuresome as a sick hound dog.—T. C. Boyle
   Also see Bold.

Advice
Advice is like castor oil—easy enough to give, but dreadfully uneasy to take.
Advice is like kissing; it costs nothing and is a pleasant thing to do.
    —Josh Billings

Ageless
Ageless as a South Sea idol.—James Wilcox
Ageless as the mountains.
Ageless as the sun.—A. C. Swinburne

Agile
Agile as a ballet dancer.
Agile as a cat.
Agile as a monkey.—Alexandre Dumas
Agile as a pickpocket.—Richard Harding Davis
Agile as an otter.—John Wingate
About as agile as a fat, old-maid washwoman in the change of life.
About as agile as a walrus.—Terry Ganey
    Also see Lively, Nimble, Spry.

Agreeable
Agreeable as an uninvited guest.—Abe Martin
Agreed like pickpockets at a fair.
Agreed about like Lent and fishmongers.—John Marston
Agreed about like the clocks of London.—*Partridge's*
Agreed about like the Three Stooges.

Alert
Alert as a coyote at hunt.
Alert as a child.
Alert as a fox.
Alert as a prowling cat.
    Also see Careful, Cautious, Wary.

Alien
Alien as a cockroach in an anthill.—Hank Searles
Alien as a whore in church.

Alike
Alike as a row of trees.
Alike as birds of a feather.
Alike as eggs.—William Shakespeare
Alike as flakes of snow.—Josh Billings
Alike as one pea is to another.—Edward Bulwer-Lytton
Alike as twins.—Robert Browning
Alike as two burrs in a mule's tail.
Alike as two halves of an apple.
Alike as two pins.
Alike as if the same mule kicked the whole family.
Alike as if they were split from the same piece of kindling.
    —F. Hopkinson Smith

About as alike as an apple and an oyster.
About as alike as Mutt and Jeff.
    Also see Go together, Similar.

All over

All over like shit in a pig yard.
All over him like a cape on a vampire.
All over him like a cheap suit.
All over him like city birds on stale bread crumbs.—James Patterson
All over him like a rainstorm.
All over him like an iguana on a sand beetle.—Dean R. Koontz
All over him like body lotion.—Lee Smith
All over him like scum on a pond.
All over him like stink on a skunk.
All over him like stink on shit.—Bob Leuci
All over him like ugly on an ape.
    Also see Abundant, Came down on him, Plentiful, Scattered.

Alluring

Alluring as a ripe peach.—Guy De Maupassant
Alluring as the apple of Eden.
    Also see Appealing, Attractive, Charming, Enticing.

Alone

Alone as a jilted bridegroom.
Alone as a leper.
Alone as a lost ship at sea.
Alone as a scarecrow.—Truman Capote
Alone as Crusoe.—Edward S. Martin
    Also see Forlorn, Lonely.

Aloof

Aloof as a lottery winner.
Aloof as a thumb in a mitten.—Susan T. Cromartie
Aloof as Lady Nevershit.—Arnold Wesker
    Also see Arrogant, Cool, Indifferent, Remote.

Ambitious

Ambitious as a salmon in the falls.—George Garrett
Ambitious as a Baltimore pimp.
Ambitious as Lady Macbeth.—James G. Huneker

Ambled

Ambled like a lame beggar.
Ambled like a lawnmower out for a stroll.—T. C. Boyle
Ambled like a man with the gout.
    Also see Walked.

American

American as a catcher's mitt.—George Jean Nathan
American as the World Series.

American as apple pie.
American as baseball.
American as corn on the cob.
American cities are like badger holes ringed with trash. —John Steinbeck

Amiable
Amiable as a cookie lady.
Amiable as a fruit merchant.
Amiable as a tarantula with its belly full. —John Crosby
    Also see Kind.

Amorous
Amorous as a pair of lovebirds.
Amorous as a warm spring day.
Amorous as the first of May. —Alfred Tennyson
    Also see Horny, Passionate, Randy.

Amusing
About as amusing as a boil on your butt.
About as amusing as breaking your leg.
About as amusing as sitting on a tack.
About as amusing as a groin injury.

Ankles
Ankles like Chianti bottles. —George Jean Nathan
Ankles small and curved like axe handles and they looked as tough.
    —F. Hopkinson Smith

Anonymous
Anonymous as a railroad bum.
Anonymous as the assistant purchasing agent of a one-saw sawmill.

Anxious
Anxious as a bull at a gate.
Anxious as a hen with one chick. —Mary Stewart
Anxious as a taxpayer with an audit notice from the IRS.
Anxious as an investor watching his stock go down.
Anxious as high school love.
    Also see Edgy, Frightened, Nervous, Restless, Scared, Tense,
    Touchy, Uneasy.

Appalling
Appalling as a great fat mother-in-law. —R. S. Surtees
Appalling as a murder scene.

Appealing
Appealing as apple pie à la mode.

About as appealing as a hooded cobra. —George MacDonald Fraser
   Also see Alluring, Attractive, Charming, Enticing.

Appetite

Appetite like a farmhand at hay time.
Appetite like a hungry bear.
Appetite like a long-hunted hound.
Appetite like a longshoreman.
Appetite like a lumberjack.
Appetite like an elephant.
   Also see Ate, Hungry.

Arched

Arched like a bow with a hundred-pound pull.
Arched like a cat's back at a dog show.
Arched like a mule's back in a hailstorm.
   Also see Bent, Drooped.

Arms

Arms as thin as pencils.
Arms like a mule's hind legs. —Tom Wicker
Arms like gateposts. —Leslie Thomas
Arms like ham hocks.
Arms like legs of mutton. —W. Somerset Maugham
Arms like logs. —James Crumley
Arms like sledgehammers. —F. Hopkinson Smith
Arms like thighs.
Arms looked like buggy whips with fingers. —Fred Allen

Arrogant

Arrogant as a sergeant major in the Foreign Legion. —Charles Willeford
Arrogant as Caesar. —Stephen King
   Also see Aloof, Cool.

Ascended

Ascended as the smoke of a furnace. —*Old Testament*
Ascended like a gas-filled balloon.

Ate

Ate like a bird.
Ate like a bull. —Robert Louis Stevenson
Ate like a cart horse.
Ate like a church mouse.
Ate like a dray horse.
Ate like a famished wolf. —Louisa May Alcott
Ate like a fat lady in an ice cream shop.
Ate like a hog.
Ate like a horse.
Ate like a lumberjack.
Ate like a one-man army. —Ivan Doig
Ate like a pig.

Ate like a sailor saved from an island. —Robert Lewis Taylor
Ate like a trucker.
Ate like a vacuum cleaner. —Tom McEwen
Ate like a well man and drank like a sick one. —Benjamin Franklin
Ate like he was going to the chair.
Shoveled in food like a stoker at the boiler fare. —Charles Gidley
　　Also see Appetite, Hungry.

Attacked

Attacked like a wild animal.
Attacked like something gone mad. —Max Crawford
Attacked like Teddy Roosevelt at San Juan Hill.
Attacked like the Indians at Little Big Horn.
　　Also see Came down on him, Charged.

Attracted

Attracted like a bitch in heat.
Attracted like a lofty oak tree attracts lightning. —Jack Matthews
Attracted like a moth to a flame.
Attracted like bees to honey.
Attracted like old people to day-old bread. —Tom McEwen
Attracted attention about as much as a dirty fingernail in the third grade.
　　—Ring Lardner
　　Also see Drawn.

Attractive

About as attractive as a dead toad.
About as attractive as a sump pump.
About as attractive as a truck-struck weasel. —TV show "Bob Newhart"
　　Also see Alluring, Appealing, Charming, Enticing, Handsome, Pretty.

Avoided it

Avoided it like a beast avoids a fire. —Ridley Wills
Avoided it like a dead cow. —Owen Ulph
Avoided it like a dog turd on the sidewalk.

Awkward

Awkward as a baby's first steps.
Awkward as a bear.
Awkward as a blind dog in a butcher shop.
Awkward as a bull in a china shop.
Awkward as a cow on ice.
Awkward as a cow with a wooden leg.
Awkward as a cub bear with an armload of shelled corn.
Awkward as a fish out of water.
Awkward as a lame elephant.
　　Also see Clumsy.

Babbled

Babbled like a bunch of guinea hens.
Babbled like hyenas.
Babbled like women at a bridge club.
    Also see Chattered, Jabbered, Prated.

Back and forth

Back and forth like a Ping-Pong ball.
Back and forth like a shuttlecock.
Back and forth like a tennis ball.
Back and forth like arguing fruit peddlers.
Back and forth like timed metronomes. —Richard Bachman
    Also see To and fro.

Backbone

About as much backbone as an angleworm. —Rex Beach
About as much backbone as a chocolate eclair. —Theodore Roosevelt
About as much backbone as an eel.
About as much backbone as wet spaghetti.

Bad

Bad as a dig in the eye with a blunt stick. —*Partridge's*
Bad as a jab in the ass with a sharp stick.
Bad as a kick in the ass.
Bad as a kick in the balls with a frozen boot.
Bad as a kick in the pants.
Bad as a slap in the belly with a wet fish. —*Partridge's*
Bad as a witch.
Bad as holding a horse in the rain.
Bad as old King Kong. —Jim Croce, "Bad, Bad Leroy Brown."
Bad as standing in the rain.
Bad as stepping on a rake.
    Also see Mean.

Bald

Bald as a baby. —Doris Leslie
Bald as a baby's bottom.
Bald as a balloon.
Bald as a bat.
Bald as a billiard ball.
Bald as a cannonball. —William M. Thackeray
Bald as a light bulb.
Bald as a new marine.
Bald as a peeled onion.
Bald as a stone.
Bald as an eagle.
Bald as an egg.
Bald as the belly of a bullfrog. —Jack Matthews
Bald as the palm of your hand. —R. H. Barham

Bare

Bare as a babe.
Bare as a birch at Christmas. —Sir Walter Scott
Bare as bones. —J.R.R. Tolkien
Bare as January. —Robert Armin
Bare as Mother Hubbard's cupboard.
Bare as the back of my hand.
Bare as winter trees. —William Wordsworth
Bare like a carcass picked by crows. —Jonathan Swift
Bare-assed as Eve in Eden. —George Garrett
    Also see Barren, Empty, Naked.

Barren

Barren as a desert.
Barren as a tavern after closing time.
Barren as death. —John Ruskin
Barren as the ground around a cabin door. —William Allen White
    Also see Bare, Empty.

Beamed

Beamed like a bishop.
Beamed like a doting grandfather. —T. C. Boyle
Beamed like a new father.

Beard

Beard like a brushfire. —John Gould
Beard like a matted buffalo robe. —James Goldman
Beard like Santa.
Beard like steel wool.

Beat

Beat like a drum.
Beat like a tom-tom.
Beat like dirty linen on the washing board. —Robert Louis Stevenson

Beat like the wings of an angel.
Beat him like a borrowed mule.
Beat him like a redheaded stepchild.
Beat him like a slave.
Beat him like a yard dog.

Beautiful
Beautiful as a flower in a seed catalog.—Robert H. Davis
Beautiful as a sunset.
Beautiful as day.—Lord Byron
Beautiful as God's hand.—John Ehle
Beautiful as May.—Henry W. Longfellow
Beautiful as Mona Lisa.
Beautiful as nature in the spring.—O. S. Wondersford
Beautiful as sky and earth.—John Greenleaf Whittier
Beautiful as the dawn.
Beautiful as the face of a young Greek god.
Beautiful like a dream of youth.—Oliver Wendell Holmes
Beautiful and freckled as a tiger lily.—O. Henry
About as beautiful as a boxcar on a desert siding.—Thomas Thompson
    Also see Attractive, Fair, Lovely, Pretty.

Begged
Begged like a child for candy.
Begged like a cripple at a cross.—Robert Whittington
Begged like a dog at a fair.
Begged like a dog for a bone.
Begged like a hungry dog.
    Also see Prayed.

Behaved
Behaved like an honor student at a military academy.—Peter Jenkins
Behaved like a child.
Behaved like a cross child.
Behaved like a pissed-off tennis pro.
Behaved like a sore loser.
Behaved like an old woman.
    Also see Acted.

Behind
Always behind, like a cow's tail.—Ancient proverb
Always behind, like a donkey's tail.—English proverb
Always behind like the runt of the litter.

Bellowed
Bellowed like a bull.—Mark Twain
Bellowed like a foghorn.—Robert R. McCammon
Bellowed like a Mississippi towboat.
Bellowed like a swamp alligator.—Douglas C. Jones

Bellowed like an auctioneer.
>   *Also see* Hollered, Howled, Screamed, Yelled.

Belly
Belly like a barrel.
Belly like a giant breast hanging over his belt.

Bent
Bent as a boat hook.—George MacDonald Fraser
Bent like a bow.—Robert Service
Bent like a broken flower.—A. C. Swinburne
Bent like a rainbow.—Robert Southey
Bent like a runover hat.
Bent like a soldier at the approach of an assault.—Victor Hugo
Bent like a washerwoman.—Stephen King
Bent like a whip.
Bent like a willow in the wind.
Bent like violets after rain.—T. B. Aldrich
Bent out of shape like a crushed beer can.
>   *Also see* Arched, Drooped.

Big
Big as a barn.
Big as a barn door.
Big as a bear.
Big as a blimp.
Big as a boxcar.
Big as a breadbox.
Big as a bulldozer.
Big as a bus.
Big as a circus strongman's fist.—Stephen King
Big as a church.—Mark Twain
Big as a church debt.—George Ade
Big as a circus tent.
Big as a hothouse cucumber.
Big as a house.—Rex Beach
Big as a moose.
Big as a palace.
Big as a tank.
Big as a whale.—Gene Stratton-Porter
Big as all outdoors.
Big as an ocean liner.
Big as Brooklyn.
Big as life.
Big as Texas.
Big as the ass-end of a gasoline truck.
Big as the deck of an aircraft carrier.
Big as the whole state of Texas.
About as big as a mosquito's eye.

About as big as gnat shit.
   Also see Fat, Immense, Large, Vast.

Binding
Binding as a contract.
Binding as a handshake.
Binding as a wedding ring.

Bitter
Bitter as a disappointed Democrat.—Abe Martin
Bitter as a sucked lemon.
Bitter as bile.
Bitter as home-brewed ale.—Henry W. Longfellow
Bitter as quinine.
Bitter as truth.—Victor Hugo

Black
Black as a back alley in Chelsea.
Black as a burned stump.—Opie Read
Black as a black cat.
Black as a chimney sweep.—F. P. Northall
Black as a chunk of coal.—F. Hopkinson Smith
Black as a coalpit.—Henry Ward Beecher
Black as a coal miner's neck.
Black as a country church at midnight.—Margaret Burnham
Black as a crow.—Geoffrey Chaucer
Black as a highwayman's boot.
Black as a mineshaft.
Black as a raven.—*Old Testament*
Black as a raven in a coal mine.—O. Henry
Black as a raven's neck.
Black as a raven's wing.
Black as a rotted tooth.
Black as a stack of black cats.
Black as a stove.
Black as a top hat.—Robert Bausch
Black as a wolf's mouth.—Arthur Conan Doyle
Black as an anvil.
Black as an elephant's asshole.—Stephen King
Black as blindness.
Black as coal.
Black as death.—Lord Byron
Black as ebony.—Alexandre Dumas
Black as Egypt's night.
Black as Hades.
Black as hell.
Black as india ink.
Black as ink.—William Shakespeare
Black as kiln-baked cork.—Wallace Irwin

Black as mahogany.
Black as midnight. —A. C. Swinburne
Black as midnight in a mineshaft. —Stephen King
Black as midnight in Nairobi.
Black as pitch. —Thomas Sackville
Black as rich farmland.
Black as satan.
Black as sloe. —Philip J. Bailey
Black as soot. —Francoise Voltaire
Black as tar. —Mark Twain
Black as the ace of spades.
Black as the duke of hell's riding boots.
Black as the grave.
Black as the inside of a chimney. —Alice Walker
Black as the inside of a fountain pen.
Black as the ninth plague of Egypt at midnight. —Thomas Hardy
Black as the Styx.
  Also see Dark.

Blank
Blank as a blackboard.
Blank as a slab of marble. —Robert Houston
Blank as a stone Buddha. —Stephen Wright
Blank as a wall.
Blank as a washed blackboard. —Stephen King
Blank as death. —Alfred Tennyson
Blank as the eyeballs of the dead. —Henry W. Longfellow
Blank and bare and still as a polar wasteland. —George Garrett

Blazed
Blazed like a wheat field fire in a strong wind.
Blazed like a barn afire.
Blazed like coals in a forge. —Erskine Caldwell
Blazed up like dry kindling in a woodstove. —Stephen King
  Also see Ablaze, Burned, Flamed.

Bleated
Bleated like a lamb.
Bleated like a ruptured choirboy. —George MacDonald Fraser
Bleated like a stuck pig.

Bled
Bled like a fountain.
Bled like a stuck hog. —Ferrol Sams

Blind
Blind as a bat.
Blind as Mr. MaGoo.
Just like a blind man I wandered along, just like a blind man that God gave his
  sight, praise the Lord, I saw the light. —Hank Williams, "I Saw the Light"

Blubbered

Blubbered like a baby. —Mark Twain
Blubbered like a crying drunk.
Blubbered like a seal. —C. S. Calverley
   Also see Cried, Wailed, Whimpered.

Blue

Blue as a Montana sky.
Blue as a cross-eyed carpenter's thumb.
Blue as a rain-washed forget-me-not. —J.R.R. Tolkien
Blue as a turkey's snout.
Blue as azure.
Blue as cobalt.
Blue as indigo.
Blue as October skies.
Blue as the eyes of a saint. —Francis S. Saltus
Blue as the Pacific.
Blue as the sea.
Blue as the sky.
Blue as your nose on a cold day.

Blundered

Blundered about like a fly in a thunderstorm.
Blundered into each other like two drunks on a dark night. —Tom Wicker

Blunt

Blunt as a mallet.
Blunt as a hammer.

Blushed

Blushed like a black dog. —William Shakespeare
Blushed like a blue dog.
Blushed like a bride. —Samuel T. Coleridge
Blushed like a June bride.
Blushed like a kid trying to get into a kootch show with his big brother's draft
   card. —Stephen King
Blushed like a schoolboy.
Blushed like a schoolgirl. —Harold Bell Wright
Blushed like a sunset. —Alfred Henry Lewis
Blushed like a virgin. —Richard Lovelace
Blushed like a young virgin on her wedding night. —Bayard Taylor
Blushed like a well-trained sunrise. —Margaret Halsey
Blushed like an opal.
Blushed like crimson dogwood in October. —George Meredith
Blushed like lads of seventeen. —James Whitcomb Riley

Bold

Bold as a bandit.
Bold as a blind horse. —Greek proverb
Bold as a cat at a mouse hole. —Tom Wicker

Bold as a general who is about to order an assault. —Guy de Maupassant
Bold as a hawk. —Samuel Lover
Bold as a life insurance salesman.
Bold as a lion. —*Old Testament*
Bold as a miller's shirt.
Bold as a used car salesman.
Bold as an unhunted fawn. —Percy B. Shelley
Bold as barbed wire. —Douglas C. Jones
Bold as brass. —Arthur Conan Doyle
    Also see Adventuresome.

Bolted

Bolted like a deer before hounds.
Bolted like a rabbit.
    Also see Jumped, Leaped, Sprang up.

Bony

Bony as a gar. —James Wilcox
Bony as a poor man's mule.
    Also see Gaunt, Lean, Skinny, Slender, Slim, Thin.

Boomed

Boomed like a cannon.
Boomed like loud speakers at a rock concert.
    Also see Loud, Roared.

Bored

Bored as a bankruptcy jury.
Bored as a plane passenger on a three-hour delay.
Bored as an eel sorter in a fish market.
Boring as a biology lecture.
Boring as waiting for school to let out.
Boring as watching grass grow.
Boring as watching trees grow.
    Also see Dull, Enticing, Exciting, Interest.

Bounced

Bounced around like a pauper in a pay toilet. —Movie, *Brian's Song*
Bounced around like a wasp looking for a window. —Lee Smith
Bounced around like rocks in a cement mixer. —Owen Ulph
Bounced back like a billiard ball.
Bounced back like a yo-yo.
Bounced like a ball.
Bounced like a berry off a buffalo. —Ivan Doig
Bounced like a Dutch girl's breasts. —Tom Wicker
Bounced like a paddle ball on a rubber string.
Bounced like a rubber ball.
Bounced like Silly Putty.
Bounced up and down like the head of a rag doll. —Richard Bachman

Bountiful

Bountiful as a good harvest.
Bountiful as April rains.

Bowed

Bowed like a dancing master.
Bowed like a poppy in the breeze.—Ogden Nash
Bowed like a snow-covered sapling.—T. C. Boyle

Bowlegged

Bowlegged as a cowboy.
Bowlegged as a hockey goalie.
Bowlegged as a pin setter in a bowling alley.

Bragged

Bragged like a new boxing champ.
Bragged like a new grandmother.
Bragged like the father of twins.

Brave

Brave as a barrel of bears.—Ogden Nash
Brave as a bull.
Brave as a lion.—Robert Louis Stevenson
Brave as a tiger in a rage.—Ogden Nash
Brave as Achilles.
Brave as David.
Brave as Lancelot.
Brave as winds that brave the sea.—A. C. Swinburne
    Also see Fearless.

Brayed

Brayed like a calliope.—T. C. Boyle
Brayed like a donkey.
Brayed like a jackass.—Mark Twain

Breasts

Breasts as big as healthy eggplants.—Ridley Pearson
Breasts as firm as melons.
Breasts bounced like a Dutch girl's.
Breasts bounced like a jersey cow's making it for home at sundown.
    —H. Allen Smith
Breasts drooped like an old woman's.
Breasts heaved as if from a swift run.—Rex Beach
Breasts jutted forward like the prow of a ship.—Margaret Mitchell
Breasts like a fat lady's knees.—Stephen Longstreet
Breasts like an avalanche of bowling balls.
Breasts like bruised lard.—Bernard Shrimsley
Breasts like cantaloupes.
Breasts like giant cabbages.—W. Somerset Maugham
Breasts like kettledrums.—Henry Fielding
Breasts like lemons.

Breasts like melons.
Breasts like raspberry popovers.
Breasts like two boys fighting under a blanket.
Breasts like two puppies fighting in a sack.
Breasts sagged like moist clay.—Gary Jennings
    Also see Built, Stacked.

Breath

Breath like a sewer draught.—Richard Bachman
Breath like spoiled dogfood.—Stephen King
Breath like stale cabbage.—Stephen King
Breath rattled like October wind in dead cornstalks.—Stephen King
Breath smelled like a buzzard's.—Mark Twain
Breath smelled like a leper's armpit.
Breath smelled like he'd been eating soft food for a month.
Breath smelled like rotten food sitting in a cat's basket.
Breath sour as a dragon's.
    Also see Smelled.

Breathed

Breathed like a packhorse with emphysema.
Breathed like a second-hand bicycle pump.—O. Henry
Breathed like an escape valve.—Joseph C. Lincoln
Breathed like the bellows of a forge.—Lord De Tabley
    Also see Gasped, Panted, Puffed, Wheezed.

Bred

Bred like rabbits.
Bred like rats.
Bred like rats on a grain ship.—Li Hung Chang
Bred bastards like jackrabbits.—George MacDonald Fraser

Brief

Brief as a sinner's prayer.
Brief as the twinkling of an eye.
Brief as time.—Ben Jonson
Brief as the Z column in a pocket dictionary.—Irvin S. Cobb
    Also see Abrupt, Quick, Sudden, Swift.

Bright

Bright as a banner.
Bright as a beacon.—Victor Hugo
Bright as a bugle.
Bright as a butterfly.
Bright as a button.
Bright as a carrot.—Stephen King
Bright as a copper penny.—Robert Elegant
Bright as a dozen suns.
Bright as a facet-cut diamond scattering light.—Charles Tupper
Bright as a neon sign in downtown Memphis.

Bright as a new dollar.
Bright as a new penny.
Bright as a new pin.
Bright as a silver dollar.
Bright as a thousand-watt bulb. —James Patterson
Bright as a widow's new window.
Bright as brass in the sunshine.
Bright as day. —Geoffrey Chaucer
Bright as hope. —A. C. Swinburne
Bright as light. —Alfred Tennyson
Bright as new silver.
Bright as sunshine on the sea.
Bright as the glaring sun.
Bright as the rising sun on a summer's day. —Alexander Pope
Bright as the sun.
Bright and cheerful as a chocolate box. —Derek Robinson
Brightened up like a pine cone fire. —Owen Ulph
About as bright as a small appliance bulb.
About as bright as a ten-cent shine.
   Also see Brilliant, Lustrous, Radiant, Shined, Smart.

Brilliant
Brilliant as a dream.
Brilliant as a star. —Ouida
Brilliant as an Indian summer.
Brilliant as diamonds. —Lee Smith
Brilliant as the colors of the rainbow.
   Also see Bright, Lustrous, Radiant, Shined, Smart.

Brisk
Brisk as a bee. —Frederic S. Isham
Brisk as a bee in a tar pot.
Brisk as a flea.
Brisk as a morning breeze.
Brisk as a southwester. —Thelma Strabel
Brisk as bottled ale. —John Gay

Bristled
Bristled like a constipated porcupine. —James Sherburn
Bristled like a gamecock. —Margaret Mitchell
Bristled like a panther. —Victor Hugo

Brittle
Brittle as a dead tree in the wind. —George Garrett
Brittle as an old bone.
Brittle as coral. —James Wilcox
Brittle as glass.

Broad
Broad as a barn.
Broad as an aircraft carrier.
Broad as barn doors.—John Heywood
Broad as the sea.—*Old Testament*
   Also see Wide.

Broke (without money)
Broke as a dog.—Rex Beach
Broke as an out-of-work beggar.
Broke as a sailor on his second day of shore leave.
Broke as a virgin whore.
Broke as seven people.
   Also see Poor.

Brooded
Brooded like a dove for its mate.
Brooded like a hen over a chalk egg.—Edward Bulwer-Lytton
Brooded like an owl.
   Also see Pouted.

Brown
Brown as a berry.
Brown as a bun.—Thomas Hood
Brown as a cacao bean.—J.R.R. Tolkien
Brown as a gypsy.—Jeffery Farnol
Brown as a hazel nut.—William Shakespeare
Brown as a nut.—Henry W. Longfellow
Brown as a pine nut.—Robert R. McCammon
Brown as a pineapple.—Alphonse Daudet
Brown as a turd.—T. C. Boyle
Brown as a vixen's tit.—Patrick McGinley
Brown as an Indian.
Brown as Bosco.—Robert R. McCammon
Brown as umber.—Robert Louis Stevenson

Bruised
Bruised as a hammered thumb.
Bruised as a hockey goalie.—David Letterman, "Late Night"
Bruised like a halfback in a football game.—F. W. Crowninshield

Bucked
Bucked like a bronco.
Bucked like a colt.
Bucked like a rodeo bronco.
Bucked like a mule with a wasp on his nose.—Tom Wicker
Bucked like a wasp-stung deer.—Gary Jennings
Bucked like there was a bobcat on his back.—Owen Ulph

Built (erected)
Built like a demented beaver. —Robert Adelman

Built (strong physique)
Built like a bear.
Built like a bouncer. —Derek Robinson
Built like a brewery dray. —Max Hennessey
Built like a brick outhouse.
Built like a buffalo.
Built like a bull.
Built like a fullback.
Built like a government mule. —Jerry Clower
Built like a greyhound. —T. C. Boyle
Built like a Mack truck.
Built like a mahogany stump. —Lawrence Sanders
Built like a moose.
Built like a redwood stump. —H. Allen Smith
Built like a smith. —Tom Dehaven
Built like a truck.
Built like a young bull.
Built like the back end of an elephant.
Built like the side of a house.
Also see Big, Breasts, Strong.

Bumbled
Bumbled like a bee.
Bumbled like a bee in a tar tub.
Also see Buzzed, Hummed.

Burned
Burned like a brand. —Alfred Noyes
Burned like a hot iron. —Robert Louis Stevenson
Burned like fire.
Burned like molten jewels. —W. W. Story
Burneth like a flaming fire. —*Old Testament*
Also see Ablaze, Blazed, Flamed.

Burrowed
Burrowed like a mole.
Burrowed like a prairie dog.
Burrowed like a weasel. —R. D. Blackmore

Burst
Burst like a balloon.
Burst like a barrel dropped off a cart.
Burst like a firecracker.
Burst like a lightning flash. —Johann Schiller
Burst like a mortar shell.
Burst like a surf. —Westland Marston
Burst like a thunderbolt. —Alfred Tennyson

Burst like an overdone potato.—Arthur Conan Doyle
Burst forth like a covey of frightened quail.—George Garrett
Also see Burst, Exploded.

Bustled
Bustled like a flea market.
Bustled like a railway station.—Derek Robinson

Busy
Busy as a bandycoot.—*Brewer's*
Busy as a barber on Saturday night.
Busy as a battlefield.—C. L. Skelton
Busy as a beaver.
Busy as a bee.—John Lyly
Busy as a bee in a molasses barrel.—Thomas Jefferson
Busy as a beehive attacked by a bear.
Busy as a boilsucker at a leper colony.
Busy as a boy killing snakes.
Busy as a box of kittens.—Griffin Smith, Jr., *National Geographic*
Busy as a buzz saw in a pine knot.
Busy as a cat covering up shit after a buffalo stampede.
Busy as a cat in a mess of guitar strings.—Stephen King
Busy as a cat trying to bury droppings on a hardwood floor.
Busy as a cat with eleven kittens that won't stay in the box.
Busy as a chimpanzee looking for fleas.
Busy as a cow's tail at fly time.—James Fenimore Cooper
Busy as a cross-eyed boy at a three-ring circus.—James Fenimore Cooper
Busy as a dentist in Hershey, Pennsylvania.—Calvin Trillon
Busy as a dog with fleas.
Busy as a fart in a whirlwind.
Busy as a fiddler's elbow.
Busy as a fly.
Busy as a freeway at rush hour.
Busy as a hen with one chick.
Busy as a long-tailed cat in a roomful of rocking chairs.
Busy as a moth in a mitten.—Dan Rather
Busy as a mouseburger stand at a cat picnic.
Busy as a one-armed paper hanger.
Busy as a one-armed paper hanger with crabs.
Busy as a one-eyed hunting dog in tall grass.
Busy as a one-eyed terrier in a sausage shop.
Busy as a one-legged ballerina.
Busy as a one-legged man in a forest fire.
Busy as a one-legged man in an ass-kicking contest.
Busy as a paper hanger with a prickly itch.
Busy as a pigeon at a shooting match.
Busy as a pointer at a duck farm.
Busy as a settin' hen with one chick.
Busy as a squirrel in a wheel.

Busy as a streetwalker when the fleet's in. —Vincent Bugliosi
Busy as a stumpful of ants.
Busy as a tenor's eyebrows. —Angie Papadakis
Busy as a three-headed cat in a fish market.
Busy as a tick in a tar barrel. —Arthur Brooks
Busy as a ticking clock.
Busy as a two-dollar whore on dollar night.
Busy as an accountant at tax time.
Busy as an undertaker in Arizona. —Walt Mason
Busy as ants at a family picnic.
Busy as ants at a picnic.
Busy as Broadway. —Ivan Doig
Busy as Daytona Beach at spring break.
Busy as Grand Central Station.
Busy as jumper cables at a used car lot.
Busy as the Green Stamp redemption center a week before Christmas.
    —Stephen King
Busy as the hooks on a bra in a whorehouse.
About as busy as a Swiss admiral.
    Also see Active.

Buzzed
Buzzed like a blue-assed fly.
Buzzed like a fly.
Buzzed like a swarm of flies caught in a bottle.
Buzzed like bees when they swarm. —Thomas Hood
    Also see Hummed.

Cackled

Cackled like a hen that just laid an egg.
Cackled like a loon.
Cackled like an overworked clock.—T. C. Boyle

Calloused

Calloused as a donkey's butt.
Calloused as shark's skin.—Mark Twain
Calloused as the sea.—Robert Louis Stevenson

Calm

Calm as a bathtub.—George Garrett
Calm as a Buddhist.—Elizabeth Taylor
Calm as a child in its soft slumber lying.—E. M. Kelly
Calm as a convent.
Calm as a cucumber.—Beaumont and Fletcher
Calm as a day in June.
Calm as a deeply sheltered mountain lake.—John Ruskin
Calm as a field of snow.—Bliss Carman
Calm as a frozen lake when ruthless winds blow fiercely.
    —William Wordsworth
Calm as a gliding moon.—Samuel T. Coleridge
Calm as a heifer in clover.—Thomas Thompson
Calm as a knitting party.
Calm as a lonely shepherd's song.—Thomas Moore
Calm as a Mandarin sipping his tea.—Richard Covey
Calm as a May morning.—Shelby Foote
Calm as a midnight sea.
Calm as a mirror.—Alexandre Dumas
Calm as a Quaker.—William M. Thackeray
Calm as a sister's kiss.
Calm as a slumbering babe.—Percy B. Shelley

Calm as a summer sea.—Louisa May Alcott
Calm as a virgin discussing flower arrangements.
　—George MacDonald Fraser
Calm as beauty.—Robert Browning
Calm as dawn.—Walt Whitman
Calm as death.—Percy B. Shelley
Calm as dewdrops.—William Wordsworth
Calm as if he were attending a funeral and weren't related to the corpse.
　—Mark Twain
Calm as if nothing had happened.—Harold Bell Wright
Calm as if she were sitting for her portrait.—Henry James
Calm as lakes that sleep.—William Wordsworth
Calm as night.—Victor Hugo
Calm as old Nelly pulling the plow.—Tom Wicker
Calm as the sky after a day of storm.— Francoise Voltaire
Calm as though he had been to church.—Robert Louis Stevenson
Calm as though he were discussing the weather.—Margaret Mitchell
Calm as virtue.—William Shakespeare
Calm and composed as a choirboy.—George Garrett
Calm and deliberate as a tax collector.—T. C. Boyle
Calm like the deep sleep which follows an orgy.—Mark Twain
　Also see Composed, Peaceful, Placid, Serene, Tranquil, Unruffled.

Came

Came like a shot.—Rex Beach
Came like a swift river.—Michael Doane
Came like the cavalry in light fiction.—Shelby Foote
Came and went like apparitions.—Jack Fuller
Came and went like the lighthouse gleam on a black night at sea.
　—Robert Buchanan
Came and went like weather.—John Updike
　Also see Arrived, Came in.

Came back

Came back like a boomerang.
Came back like a fox to a henhouse.
Came back like shooflies on a summer day.—Keith Korman
Came back like summer mosquitoes.—Stephen King
Came back like swallows to Capistrano.
Came back like tourists to watch the swallows come back to Capistrano.
　Also see Returned.

Came down

Came down like a butterfly with sore feet.
Came down like a California mud slide.
Came down like a cat upon a mouse.—Robert Louis Stevenson
Came down like a clap of thunder.—Douglas C. Jones
Came down like a karate chop.—Patrick Buchanan
Came down like a rock.

Came down like a thousand bricks.—Charles Dickens
Came down like a ton of bricks.
　　Also see Fell.

Came down on him

Came down on him like a benediction.—Margaret Mitchell
Came down on him like a duck on a June bug.
Came down on him like a duck on popcorn.
Came down on him like a fox on a henhouse.
Came down on him like a hammer on an anvil.—Mark Twain
Came down on him like a locomotive.—Stephen King
Came down on him like a new Republican president on a Democratic
　　postmaster.—George W. Peck
Came down on him like a pigeon on breadcrumbs.
Came down on him like a prostitute on a prospective client.—Margaret Mitchell
Came down on him like a rooster on a June bug.—Lewis W. Green
Came down on him like a shot.
Came down on him like a swarm of hornets.
Came down on him like a top sergeant.
Came down on him like a vulture.—Stephen King
Came down on him like a wolf on a flock of sheep.
Came down on him like a wolf on the fold.
Came down on him like flies on a rib roast.—Tom DeHaven
Came down on him like flies on green meat.—Robert Houston
Came down on him like shit in a privy. —Terry C. Johnston
Came down on him like the fall of night.—C. L. Skelton
Came down on him like the Great Wall of China.—Stephen King
Came down on him like the wrath of God.—Derek Robinson
Came down on him like ugly on an ape.
　　Also see Attacked, Charged.

Came in

Came in like a bat out of hell.
Came in like a herd of elephants.
Came in like a pack of hungry wolves.—William M. Raine
Came in like a storm.—Pete Dexter
Came in like a whirlwind.—Olive Wadsley
　　Also see Came.

Came on

Came on like a maddened, hungry tiger.
Came on like fury.
Came on like Gangbusters.

Carefree

Carefree as a drunken lord.
Carefree as children.
Carefree as teenage love.
　　Also see Careless.

Careful

Careful as a man disarming a bomb.
Careful as a mule eating briars.
Careful as if walking through a tornado with a quart jar of
    nitroglycerin. —Peter Jenkins
Careful as mice in a house with a hundred cats. —Dean R. Koontz
Careful as porcupines making love.
    Also see Alert, Cautious, Wary.

Careless

Careless as a child at play. —William Winter
Careless as the wind. —William J. Linton
Careless and happy as children. —George Garrett
    Also see Carefree.

Carried on

Carried on like the last act of Hamlet. —George MacDonald Fraser
Carried on like they lost the twelve disciples. —Mark Twain
Carried on like wildcats. —Mark Twain

Casual

Casual as a falling leaf. —Cecelia Holland
Casual as a hired gunslinger. —Stephen Longstreet
Casual as a man waiting for eternity. —Ivan Doig
    Also see Calm, Cool, Informal.

Caught

Caught like a moth in a mitten.
Caught like a nut between two stones. —George MacDonald Fraser
Caught like a possom in a poke.
    Also see Trapped.

Cautious

Cautious as a banker. —Malcolm Bosse
Cautious as a burglar walking over a tin roof in cowhide boots. —Wallace Irwin
Cautious as a lion trainer trainee.
Cautious as a squirrel. —Robert Houston
Cautious as a tightrope walker. —C. H. Spurgeon
    Also see Alert, Careful, Wary.

Certain

Certain as a gun. —Samuel Butler
Certain as death and taxes. —Daniel Defoe
Certain as leaves falling in September.
Certain as lines at return counters after Christmas.
Certain as night succeeds the day. —George Washington
Certain as the sunrise.
    Also see Sure.

Chance

About as much chance as a cat at a Doberman convention.—Dean R. Koontz

About as much chance as a cat in hell without claws.—*Partridge's*

About as much chance as a dishfaced chimpanzee in a beauty contest.
—Arthur Baer

About as much chance as a dog with tallow legs chasing an asbestos cat in hades.—Elbert Hubbard

About as much chance as a fart in a windstorm.

About as much chance as a fat june bug would have in the pathway of a road roller.—Grantland Rice

About as much chance as a grasshopper in a henhouse.

About as much chance as a hot-house in a hailstorm.—Arthur Baer

About as much chance as a keg of cider at a barn raising.
—Alfred Henry Lewis

About as much chance as a lamb in Mr. Armour's slaughter house.
—George Ade

About as much chance as a man with a wooden leg in a forest fire.
—George Broadhurst

About as much chance as a one-legged man in a football game.
—Elbert Hubbard

About as much chance as a rat's ass.—Robert R. McCammon

About as much chance as a snowball in hell.

About as much chance as a stump-tailed cow at fly time.

About as much chance as selling a British flag in Ireland.

About as much chance as the hunchback of Notre Dame finding a suit off the rack.

Changeable

Changeable as a baby's diaper.

Changeable as a fickle teenager.

Changeable as the sea.

Changeable as the weather.

Changeable as the wind.—John Gay

Charged

Charged like a bull.

Charged like a mad steer on a rampage.—Zane Grey

Charged like a Sioux.—Rex Beach

The angry rhino charged like a demented express train.

Also see Attacked, Came down on him.

Charming

Charming as a Southern girl.—Ridley Pearson

About as charming as a cobra.

About as charming as a defecating elephant.—William Pearson

About as charming as a fox in a henhouse.—Tom Wicker

Also see Alluring, Appealing, Attractive, Enticing.

Chaste

Chaste as an angel.—Aphra Behn

Chaste as an Easter lily.
Chaste as ice. —William Shakespeare
Chaste as flowers. —Rosemary H. Jarman
Also see Pure, Virtue.

Chattered

Chattered like a dozen gray squirrels.
Chattered like a flight of starlings. —Michael Carreck
Chattered like a jay. —Robert Browning
Chattered like a lunatic chimpanzee. —Truman Capote
Chattered like a mob of sparrows. —J. K. Jerome
Chattered like a shipload of monkeys in a storm.
Chattered like bone castanets. —Lewis Carroll
Chattered like jaybirds drunk on chinaberries. —Patrick Smith
Chattered like magpies. —C. G. Rossetti
Also see Babbled, Jabbered, Prated, Talked.

Cheap

Cheap as air.
Cheap as dirt.
Cheap as dog's meat.
Cheap as indifference.
Cheap as Jack Benny.
Cheap as lies. —William Shakespeare
Cheap as stinking mackerel. —William Shakespeare
Cheap as water.
Also see Frugal, Tight.

Cheeks

Cheeks as brown as oak leaves.
Cheeks as brown as the sun could kiss them. —Alice Cary
Cheeks as fat as butter. —John Gay
Cheeks as pale as milk. —Richard Bachman
Cheeks as soft as July peaches. —W. C. Bennett
Cheeks blazed like a maid's on the marriage bed. —Cecelia Holland
Cheeks like a behind. —Stephen King
Cheeks like a burning rose. —Barry Cornwall
Cheeks like a chipmunk.
Cheeks like a trumpeter. —John Arbuthnot
Cheeks like apples. —John Updike
Cheeks like he had the mumps.
Cheeks like roses.
Cheeks like the dawn of day. —Henry W. Longfellow
Cheeks pale as turnips.
Cheeks round and red as a cherry. —David Garrick
Cheeks sagged like a bedspread. —Robert Bausch
Also see Face.

Cheerful

Cheerful as a carousel. —Ferrol Sams

Cheerful as a little bird. —Ridley Wills
Cheerful as tulips.
>*Also see* Gay, Happy, Merry.

Chin
Chin as naked as a heel. —Shelby Foote
Chin as sharp as a can opener.
Chin like a coffin. —George MacDonald Fraser
Chin like a rabbit.
Chin like a slab of granite. —Robert R. McCammon
>*Also see* Face.

Choosy
Choosy as an alley cat.

Circled
Circled like a flight of doves. —George Meredith
Circled like a gull in the wind. —Craig Thomas
Circled like a vulture.
Circled like buzzards waiting for a death.
Circled like gulls around a fishing boat. —George Garrett
Circled like moths inspecting a lightbulb.

Clammy
Clammy as death. —Owen Meredith
Clammy as the grave. —James Sherburn

Clanged
Clanged like a blacksmith's hammer.
Clanged like a boiler factory. —John Crosby
Clanged like a smithy shop. —Rudyard Kipling
Clanged like church bells.

Clawed
Clawed like a frightened cat.
Clawed like a parrot. —William Shakespeare

Clean
Clean as a bolt of summer lightning. —Scott C. S. Stone
Clean as a cat's ass.
Clean as a Dutch oven.
Clean as a hound's tooth. —Theodore Roosevelt
Clean as a new pin.
Clean as a New England kitchen.
Clean as a New England meadow.
Clean as a pearl. —Play, *Jacob and Esau*, 1586
Clean as a pebble.
Clean as a new penny. —John Gay
Clean as a pin.
Clean as a preacher's conscience.
Clean as a whistle. —Lord Byron

Clean as an old bone.
Clean as mushrooms in an unplowed field.
Clean as soap.
Clean and shining as a new sword.
Cleans like a white tornado. —Ajax cleanser slogan
About as clean as a pigsty.
    Also see Immaculate.

Clear

Clear as a bell. —Samuel T. Coleridge
Clear as a glass of spring water. —Patrick McGinley
Clear as a line drawn in the dirt. —Stephen R. Donaldson
Clear as a mountain stream.
Clear as a whistle.
Clear as an infant's eyes. —John Keats
Clear as air. —F. Hopkinson Smith
Clear as creek water.
Clear as crystal. —*New Testament*
Clear as day. —Arthur Conan Doyle
Clear as glass. —Ovid
Clear as mountain spring water.
Clear as noonday. —Robert Louis Stevenson
Clear as reality.
Clear as the air at 15,000 feet. —Peter Jenkins
Clear as the nose on your face. —Robert Burton
Clear as the sun. —*Old Testament*
Clear as the water in a trout pool. —O. Henry
Clear as well water. —Thomas Thompson
About as clear as mud.
    Also see Evident, Obvious, Plain, Stood out.

Clever

Clever as a bird dog.
Clever as a cat. —Anthony Forrest
Clever as a dog reading Shakespeare on a high wire. —Dean R. Koontz
Clever as a wagon load of monkeys.
Clever as paint.
Clever as the Indian rope trick.

Close

Close as a carriage dog's spots. —Arthur Baer
Close as a clam.
Close as a tomb.
Close as a vise.
Close as bark on a tree. —Charles Sedley
Close as clapboards on a house.
Close as dammit is to swearing.
Close as hand and glove.
Close as kin.

Close as kissing kin.
Close as lovers sitting on a sofa.
Close as paper on the wall.
Close as six in a bed.
Close as the fingernail is to the quick.—Hugh Clifford
Close as the numbers on a dollar bill.
Close as thorn is to the rose.—Robert Lloyd
Close as three in a bed with one kicked out.—Ivan Doig
Close as two peas in a pod.
Close as two ticks on a dog's tail.— TV show "Three's Company"
    Also see Near.

Closed up
Closed up like a bank vault.
Closed up like a coffin.
Closed up like a fist.—T. C. Boyle

Clumsy
Clumsy as a cow in a cage.
Clumsy as a cub bear handling his prick. —*Partridge's*
Clumsy as a dancing bear.—Barry Cornwell
Clumsy as a miller's mare.
Clumsy as an inebriated moose.
    Also see Awkward.

Clung
Clung like a chigger.
Clung like a drowning man.
Clung like a leech.
Clung like a magnet to steel.—T. B. Read
Clung like a sloth.—Rudyard Kipling
Clung like a shadow.
Clung like a tick.
Clung like a vine.
Clung like a wet towel to a nail.
Clung like a whore to a prospective client.
Clung like barnacles.
Clung like grim death.—Gene Stratton-Porter
Clung like moss to a stone.—Walter S. Landor
Clung like seaweed to a rock.—Ridley Pearson
Clung like swarming bees.—Lord Byron
Clung like the wicked stench of a harlot's room.—John Antrobus
    Also see Gripped, Held, Hung.

Clustered
Clustered like children afraid of the dark.—Rosemary H. Jarman
Clustered like flies around a jam pot.
Clustered like sheep when a wolf is near.

Coarse
Coarse as a steel file.

Coarse as a turnip field.—Henry James
Coarse as horse hair.—Eugene Sue

Coiled

Coiled like a snake.—W. S. Blunt
Coiled up like the letter *S*.—Damon Runyon
  Also see Twisted.

Cold

Cold as a banker's heart.
Cold as a barn.—F. Hopkinson Smith
Cold as a bartender's heart.
Cold as a block of ice.
Cold as a boxcar crossing the Dakotas.—Owen Ulph
Cold as a car show model.
Cold as a carp.
Cold as a cast iron commode on the shady side of an iceberg.
Cold as a Chicago bus stop in March.
Cold as a corpse.—Charlotte Brontë
Cold as a crypt.—Honore de Balzac
Cold as a cucumber.—Beaumont and Fletcher
Cold as a dead man's nose.—William Shakespeare
Cold as a diplomat's handshake.
Cold as a dog's nose.
Cold as a fish.
Cold as a frog.
Cold as a frog in an icebound pond.—James Wilcox
Cold as a frozen yak.
Cold as a grave.—Matthew Arnold
Cold as a gravedigger's handshake.—Thomas Thompson
Cold as a gravestone.
Cold as a hot water bag in the morning.
Cold as a Kelvinator.—Shelby Hearon
Cold as a mackerel.
Cold as a marble headstone.
Cold as a mother-in-law's kiss.—Robert L. Hunter
Cold as a Norwegian fjord.
Cold as a nun's kiss.—Rosemary H. Jarman
Cold as a parson's heart.—Bernard Cornwell
Cold as a pawnbroker's smile.—H. C. Witwer
Cold as a polar bear's pajamas.
Cold as a preacher's wife on her wedding night.—Terry C. Johnston
Cold as a Siberian toilet seat.
Cold as a snake.
Cold as a snowbank.—Louisa May Alcott
Cold as a stepmother's kiss.
Cold as a stone.—William Shakespeare
Cold as a ticket-taker's smile at the Avalon at a Saturday afternoon matinee.
Cold as a toad.—Rex Beach

Cold as a tomb.
Cold as a vault. —Margaret Mitchell
Cold as a wagon tire on a frosty morning.
Cold as a well. —Robert Louis Stevenson
Cold as a whale's backside. —George MacDonald Fraser
Cold as a welldigger's balls in Alaska.
Cold as a welldigger's belt buckle. —Stephen King
Cold as a welldigger's foot. —Robert L. Hunter
Cold as a whore's heart.
Cold as a winter sky. —J. A. Symonds
Cold as a witch's ear.
Cold as a witch's refrigerator. —Dean R. Koontz
Cold as a witch's tit.
Cold as a witch's tit in the Yukon. —John Madson
Cold as an I. R. S. audit.
Cold as an I. R. S. smile.
Cold as an ice cube.
Cold as an ice floe. —George MacDonald Fraser
Cold as an icicle.
Cold as an X-ray table. —Thomas Harris
Cold as Alaska in January.
Cold as boarding house soup. —Jack Buck
Cold as clay.
Cold as congealed grease. —Norman Mailer
Cold as creek water. —John Ehle
Cold as death. —Jeffery Farnol
Cold as dry ice.
Cold as granite.
Cold as Greenland's icy mountains.
Cold as ice. —Hans Christian Andersen
Cold as ice cream. —James Patterson
Cold as ice water. —Doris Leslie
Cold as if he had swallowed snowballs. —William Shakespeare
Cold as iron.
Cold as iron shackles. —George Garrett
Cold as Jack Frost. —Thomas Thompson
Cold as marble. —Leo Tolstoy
Cold as penquin droppings.
Cold as Presbyterian charity. —Sam Slick
Cold as slab ice.
Cold as snow.
Cold as steel. —Doris Leslie
Cold as the back coast of Ireland. —Norman Mailer
Cold as the balls on a brass monkey.
Cold as the bottom of a well. —Joan Samson
Cold as the bricks of Boston. —Tom McEwen
Cold as the center seed of a cucumber.
Cold as the embrace of death. —Cecelia Holland

Cold as the hair on a polar bear's ass.
Cold as the hot water in a truck stop john.
Cold as the North Pole.—Doris Leslie
Cold as the north side of a gravestone by moonlight in January.
Cold as the other side of the pillow.
Cold as the other side of your bed.
Cold as wind blowing over a glacier.—William M. Raine
Cold as yesterday's mashed potatoes.—Dorothy Fields
Cold as yesterday's toast.
Cold and indifferent as a judge.—Mary Stewart
Cold and raggedy as Lazarus.—George Garrett
    Also see Cool, Frigid.

Collapsed
Collapsed like a concertina.
Collasped like a gut-shot doe.—Gerald Duff
Collasped like a house of cards.
Collapsed like a heart-shot deer.
Collapsed like a paper bag.— T. C. Boyle
Collapsed like he'd been shot.
Collapsed like the cheeks of a starved man.—Charles Dickens
    Also see Fell.

Comfortable
Comfortable as a bug in a rug.—F. Hopkinson Smith
Comfortable as a feather pillow.
Comfortable as a litter of pups sleeping under a stove.
Comfortable as a saggy armchair.—Donald McCaig
Comfortable as a truck stop waitress.
Comfortable as an old shoe.
Comfortable as an old slipper.—Stephen King
Comfortable as floating on a cloud.
Comfortable as matrimony to an old woman.
Comfortable like sleeping on a cloud.—slogan, Sealy, Inc.
About as comfortable as a hairbrush in bed.—W. L. George
About as comfortable as a roller coaster.
About as comfortable as a rooster in a pond.—E. N. Westcott
About as comfortable as a toothache.—Mark Twain
Comfy as a goosedown pillow.—Stephen King

Common
Common as a back-fence cat.
Common as a bad debt.—Vincent Bugliosi
Common as a hedge.
Common as a weed.
Common as an old shoe.—Dolores Fellenz
Common as boiled cabbage.
Common as cat shit and twice as nasty.—*Partridge's*
Common as coals from Newcastle.

Common as daisies. —Edward Bulwer-Lytton
Common as dirt. —Charles Reade
Common as ignorance. —Lee Smith
Common as lying.
Common as mud.
Common as pins.
Common as pig tracks. —Olive Ann Burns
Common as pig tracks in wet weather.
Common as poverty. —Elizabeth C. Gaskell
Common as pump water. —Joseph G. Baldwin
Common as rain. —Pierce Egan
Common as sawdust around a sawmill.
Common as white trash. —Margaret Mitchell
   Also see Familiar, Natural.

Complex
Complex as a hill of ants. —James Goldman
Complex as the *Iliad*. —Victor Hugo
   Also see Confused, Hard.

Complexion
Complexion like a pink rose. —Maurice Hewlett
Complexion like a pizza.
Complexion like a volcano. —Richard Bachman
Complexion like cheese. —Doris Leslie
Complexion like peaches and cream.
Complexion like the skin of a raw fowl. —John Oliver Hobbes
   Also see Face.

Composed
Composed as a statue. —Ivan Doig
Composed as heaven. —William Livingston
   Also see Calm, Cool, Peaceful, Placid, Serene, Tranquil, Unruffled.

Confident
Confident as a Christian holding four aces. —John Madson
Confident as a homing bird. —Doris Leslie
Confident as a Yorkshire terrier.
Confident as four aces. —Mark Twain
Confident as Hercules. —William Prynne
Confident as St. Peter out of a job.
   Also see Sure.

Confused
Confused as a baby raccoon.
Confused as a rabbit in a snare. —Stephen King
Confused as in a dream.
Confused and stunned like a duck hit on the head. —Abraham Lincoln
   Also see Complex, Hard.

Conscientious
Conscientious as a dog.—Robert Louis Stevenson
About as conscientious as a fox in a poultry farm.—George Bernard Shaw

Constant
Constant as the flowing river.
Constant as the Northern Star.—William Shakespeare
Constant as time passing.

Consumed
Consumed like a flame.—Matthew Arnold
Consumed like grasshoppers in a bean field.

Contagious
Contagious as a smile.—J. Benavente
Contagious as a yawn.
Contagious as wet paint.

Contemporary
Contemporary as a man lounging in a cafe.—James A. Michener
Contemporary as a newspaper.—William Lyon Phelps

Contented
Contented as a cow.
Contented as a fat cat.
Contented as a fat man at a feast.—Cecelia Holland
Contented as a fox when the hounds were drawn off and gone home.
    —Colley Cibber
Contented as a Holstein.—Peter Jenkins
Contented as an infant smiling through its dreams.—William Allingham
Contented as Borden's cow.
Contented as kittens before the fire.
    Also see Happy.

Contrary
Contrary as a child.
Contrary as a handful of coat hangers.—Phyllis Born
Contrary as a seventh-grader.
    Also see Inflexible, Stubborn, Unyielding.

Controlled
Controlled as a small dog on a short leash.—George Garrett
Controlled as a life-term prisoner.
Controllable as putty in his hands.

Convincing
Convincing as a gun.
Convincing as the multiplication table.

Cool
Cool as a butcher in a meat cooler.—Richard Bachman
Cool as a cave.

Cool as a chunk of ice.—F. Hopkinson Smith
Cool as a cube of cucumber on ice.—Carl Sandburg
Cool as a cucumber.—John Gay
Cool as a custard.
Cool as a grotto.
Cool as a minnow.
Cool as a November twilight.
Cool as a snowbank.—Louisa May Alcott
Cool as a trout.
Cool as an assassin.—T. C. Boyle
Cool as an undertaker at a hanging.—H. L. Mencken
Cool as aspen leaves.—John Keats
Cool as autumn.
Cool as the moist side of a dipper.—Tom Wicker
Cool as the other side of a pillow.—Angelo DiBernardo
Cool as well water.—Tom Wicker
    Also see Aloof, Arrogant, Calm, Cold, Indifferent, Remote.

Cordial

Cordial as a warm handshake.
Cordial as a prostitute.
Cordial as a smile.
Cordial as a welcome mat.
Cordial as an open door.—Owen Johnson
    Also see Amiable, Kind.

Corrupt

Corrupt as a political boss.
Corrupt as smugglers.
    Also see Crooked, Dishonest.

Costly

Costly as burning money.
Costly as eating money.
Costly as termite damage.

Coughed

Coughed like a prune juice drinker.—James Goldman
Coughed like a smoker with pneumonia.
Coughed like dice in a box.—T. C. Boyle
Coughed and sneezed like a performing seal.—Michael Carreck

Countless

Countless as lakes in Minnesota.
Countless as leaves on autumn's tempest shed.—Percy B. Shelley
Countless as locusts.
Countless as mayflies.
Countless as the desert sands.—Bayard Taylor
Countless as trees in the forest.

Covert

Covert as the birth of thought.—James Montgomery

About as covert as a brass band.—George F. Will
About as covert as a Saint Patrick's Day parade.
Also see Secret.

Cowered

Cowered like an often-kicked dog.
Cowered like quail.—Rex Beach

Cozy

Cozy as a bird's nest.—Phoebe Cary
Cozy as a nest.—Emile Zola
Cozy as a warm home.
About as cozy as standing on a bull's horns.—Herman Melville
Also see Comfortable.

Cracked

Cracked like a Brazil nut.—Nicholas Salaman
Cracked like a broken stick.—Howard Spring
Cracked like a whiplash.
Also see Snapped.

Crafty

Crafty as a fox.
Crafty as a snake.—John Keats
Crafty as the sea.—W. B. Yeats
Also see Cunning, Sly, Wily.

Crazy

Crazy as a bat.
Crazy as a bat in a henhouse.
Crazy as a bedbug.
Crazy as a blue goose.
Crazy as a coot.
Crazy as a cuckoo bird.
Crazy as a dog in a hubcab factory.—Stephen King
Crazy as a fish in a car wash.
Crazy as a hare.—Mary Stewart
Crazy as a latrine rat.
Crazy as a loon.
Crazy as a lord.
Crazy as a mad rooster.
Crazy as a March hare.—Richard Ewel, referring to Stonewall Jackson
Crazy as a monkey in itching powder.—Robert R. McCammon
Crazy as a mouse in a milk can.
Crazy as a parrot eating sticky candy.
Crazy as a pet coon.
Crazy as a pup on worms.—Owen Ulph
Crazy as a quilt.
Crazy as a rat in a drainpipe.
Crazy as a shithouse rat.

Crazy as a three-legged toad-frog.—Robert R. McCammon
Crazy as a waltzing mouse.—John Irving
Crazy as a waltzing pig.
Crazy as a waltzing pissant.
Crazy as a wild, wild western movie.—Joe Eyly
Crazy as a woodpecker drumming on a tin chimney.—Owen Ulph
Crazy as "Nebokoodneeser."—Mark Twain, *Huckleberry Finn*
Crazy like a fox.
    Also see Absurd, Mad, Nutty.

Creaked
Creaked like an old screen door.
Creaked like an old house in a thunderstorm.
Creaked like dry snow.
    Also see Squeaked.

Crept
Crept away like a whipped dog.
Crept like a hound dog kicked once too often.—Tom Wicker
Crept like a shadow.—William Shakespeare
Crept like a thief.—Doris Leslie
Crept like a thief in the night.

Cried
Cried like a baby.
Cried like a child.—Robert Louis Stevenson
Cried like a lost soul.—T. C. Boyle
Cried like an aunt at a funeral.
Cried like an eagle freed.—Victor Hugo
Cried like blue murder.
Scarlet cried all morning like a furious thwarted child.—Margaret Mitchell
    Also see Wailed.

Crisp
Crisp as a cracker.
Crisp as a head of young lettuce.
Crisp as a new bank note.—Charles Dickens
Crisp as a November oak leaf.—Douglas C. Jones
Crisp as an apple.—James Goldman
Crisp as ancient paper.—Dean R. Koontz
Crisp as notepaper.—Derek Robinson

Crooked
Crooked as a barrel of fishhooks.
Crooked as a coat hanger.
Crooked as a corkscrew.
Crooked as a country lane.
Crooked as a dog's hind leg.
Crooked as a gaff.
Crooked as a line of Russian infantry.—George MacDonald Fraser

Crooked as a pretzel.
Crooked as a ram's horn.
Crooked as a snake.—Robert Lewis Taylor
Crooked as a snake with the colic.—Samuel Hopkins Adams
Crooked as a worm writhing on a hook.—Herman Wouk
Crooked as an old man's teeth.—Stephen King
Crooked as the hairs in a gypsy's nose.
Also see Corrupt, Dishonest, False.

Cross

Cross as a bear.
Cross as a bear with a sore ass.
Cross as a bulldog.
Cross as a red donkey.—Honore de Balzac
Cross as a sitting hen.
Cross as a turkey gobbler with measles.—Jack Matthews
Cross as nine highways.
Cross as tongs.
Cross as two sticks.—Sir Walter Scott
Cross as X.
Also see Mad, Mean, Ornery, Sore.

Crouched

Crouched like a dog.—F. Hopkinson Smith
Crouched like a frightened animal.—Harold Bell Wright
Crouched like a tackle.
Crouched like a wild beast in its lair.—Henry W. Longfellow

Crowded

Crowded as a freeway at rush hour.
Crowded as chickens in a cluster.—John H. Frere
Crowded as herrings in a barrel.
Crowded as sardines in a can.
Also see Dense, Thick.

Cruel

Cruel as a cannibal chief.—George MacDonald Fraser
Cruel as a cat.
Cruel as a ghetto rapist.—Norman Mailer
Cruel as a switchblade.—Michael Doane
Cruel as loneliness.—W. L. George
Cruel as Medea.—Robert Burton
Cruel as the crack of a whip.—Margaret Mitchell
Cruel as the grave.
Also see Mean, Merciless, Vicious.

Crumbled

Crumbled like a run-over beer can.
Crumbled like a sand castle.—Dean R. Koontz
Crumbled like tissue paper.
Crumbled like wet cardboard.—Derek Robinson

Crushed

Crushed like a rotten apple. —William Shakespeare
Crushed like an empty beer can.
Crushed like old leather.

Cunning

Cunning as a demon. —Nicholas Salaman
Cunning as a fox. —George Garrett
Cunning as a wild animal. —Louis L'Amour
About as cunning as a dead pig.
        Also see Sly, Wily.

Curious

Curious as a cat.
Curious as a child.
Curious as a fish. —Johann Goethe
Curious as a monkey.
Curious as a rabbit. —Hank Searles
Curious as a squirrel. —Louis L'Amour

Curled up

Curled up like a cat.
Curled up like a dog by a fireplace.
Curled up like a fishing worm. —Mark Twain
Curled up like a shaving near a fire. —Zane Grey
Curled up like a writhing worm. —Robert R. McCammon
Curled up like paper on fire. —Pete Dexter

Cut

Cut like a knife. —Rudyard Kipling
Cut like soft butter.
Cut like the flick of a wet towel. —Stephen King
Cut like wire through cheese.

Cut off

Cut off like a circumcision.
Cut off like carrot stems.
Cut off like flowers for the vase.
Cut off like last year's hemline.

Cute

Cute as a bug.
Cute as a bug's ear.
Cute as a button.
Cute as a kitten.
Cute as a mouse's ear.
Cute as a pearl button. —John Ehle
Cute as a spotted puppy.
Cute and spunky as a basket of puppies. —Robert Adelman

Dainty

Dainty as a blushing violet.
Dainty as a doily.
Dainty as a quail.—Emile Zola
Dainty as Dresden china.
Dainty as ladies' underthings.—Owen Ulph
Dainty as thistledown.
    Also see Delicate, Elegant.

Danced

Danced like a cork upon the waves.
Danced like a flame.
Danced like a hen on a hot griddle.
Danced like a man in a swarm of hornets.
Danced like an elephant with a hernia.
Danced like an Indian putting out a camp fire.
Danced like drops of water on a hot skillet.
Danced like Fred Astaire.
Danced like he had two left feet.
Danced like popcorn over a hot fire.
Danced like witches in their maniac mirth.—Walter Malone
    Also see Pranced, Strutted.

Dangerous

Dangerous as a cornered wolf.—William M. Raine
Dangerous as a flamethrower.—Stephen King
Dangerous as a kicking horse.—Robert Louis Stevenson
Dangerous as a grizzly.—Evan S. Connell
Dangerous as a machine gun.
Dangerous as a mating gorilla.
Dangerous as a riled rattlesnake.
Dangerous as a shark.

Dangerous as a snake. —Malcolm Bosse
Dangerous as an open manhole.
Dangerous as half-scabbarded steel. —William M. Raine
Dangerous as hammering dynamite. —James G. Huneker
Dangerous as setting on a powder magazine. —Zane Grey
Dangerous as walking under a ladder.
About as dangerous as a canned peach. —Stephen King
    Also see Risky.

Dark

Dark as a cellar.
Dark as a closet. —Tim Rumsey
Dark as a coalhole.
Dark as a coal hopper. —John Ehle
Dark as a dug grave. —George Garrett
Dark as a dungeon.
Dark as a funeral scarf.
Dark as a mine pit.
Dark as a prison. —Stephen R. Donaldson
Dark as a stack of black cats.
Dark as a thief's pocket.
Dark as a thundercloud. —Steven Vincent Benet
Dark as a wall of slate. —Gary Jennings
Dark as a wolf's mouth. —Miguel de Cervantes
Dark as a womb. —T. C. Boyle
Dark as a yard up a black cow. —James Sherburn
Dark as death. —Alice Cary
Dark as fear. —A. C. Swinburne
Dark as gloom. —Zane Grey
Dark as ignorance. —William Shakespeare
Dark as ink.
Dark as midnight. —Thomas Hardy
Dark as pitch. —John Bunyan
Dark as sin. —Mark Twain
Dark as the bottom of a well. —W. C. Russell
Dark as the brooding thunderstorm. —John Greenleaf Whittier
Dark as the deep blue sea.
Dark as the devil's dishrag.
Dark as the devil's mouth. —Sir Walter Scott
Dark as the grave.
Dark as the inside of a cow. —Mark Twain
Dark as the inside of a pocket. —Mary J. Holmes
Dark as the inside of a tire.
Dark as the inside of a whale. —F. W. Thomas
    Also see Black.

Darted

Darted like a bat.
Darted like a bird. —Victor Appleton

Darted like a frightened hummingbird.—Margaret Mitchell
Darted like a serpent.—Alexandre Dumas
Darted like a swallow.—Henry W. Longfellow
Darted like an eagle.
Darted like thoughts.
Darted away like a scared rabbit.
  Also see Flitted.

Dazzling

Dazzling as a lightning storm.
Dazzling as a pawnbroker's wife.

Dead

Dead as a beaver hat.—John Wayne, *The Alamo*
Dead as a bedpost.
Dead as a brick.—Thomas Hood
Dead as a can of Spam.
Dead as a carp in a cup of spit.—Glendon Swarthout
Dead as a dodo.
Dead as a dog that lieth in a ditch.—Samuel Rowlands
Dead as a doorknob.
Dead as a doornail.—Charles Dickens
Dead as a dream.—William Watson
Dead as a duck.
Dead as a hammer.
Dead as a herring.—John Gay
Dead as a log.
Dead as a mackerel.
Dead as a man after two doctors have visited him.
Dead as a nail.—George Garrett
Dead as a nail in a coffin.
Dead as a radio with a blown tube.—Stephen King
Dead as a stone.
Dead as a stone marker.—Stephen King
Dead as a stump.—Lee Smith
Dead as a tent peg.
Dead as a turd.—Stephen King
Dead as a two-hour-old streetcar transfer.
Dead as a used fuse.—Stephen King
Dead as a wooden Indian.
Dead as Abe Lincoln.—James Sherburn
Dead as bilge.—Robert Louis Stevenson
Dead as charity.—Nathaniel Field
Dead as chunks of baled snake.—Owen Ulph
Dead as dog shit.—Stephen King
Dead as John Wilkes Booth.
Dead as Julius Caesar.—Joseph Conrad
Dead as last year's clothes in a fashionable fine lady's wardrobe.
  —George Meredith

Dead as Latin.—F. Paul Wilson
Dead as Napoleon.
Dead as Pharaoh.—Charles Dickens
Dead as Scrooge's partner.—Henry A. Clapp
Dead as stone.—Geoffrey Chaucer
Dead as the Roman Empire.
Dead as the wholesale district on Sunday.—A. C. Swinburne
Deadly as nightshade.—T. B. Aldrich
Deadly as the viper of Sumatra.—Edward Bulwer-Lytton
    Also see Fatal.

Deaf

Deaf as a brick.—Thomas Hood
Deaf as a door.—Nicholas Breton
Deaf as a doorknob.
Deaf as a fence post.
Deaf as a nail.
Deaf as a poker.
Deaf as a post.
Deaf as a stone.
Deaf as a stump.
Deaf as a white cat.
Deaf as an adder.—Ben Jonson

Deceitful

Deceitful as a crow.—Aeschylus
Deceitful as a magician.
    Also see Crooked, Dishonest.

Deep

Deep as a bottomless pit.—G. S. Viereck
Deep as a scar.
Deep as a well.
Deep as death.
Deep as despair.
Deep as first love.—Alfred Tennyson
Deep as grief.
Deep as hate.—A. C. Swinburne
Deep as hell.—William Shakespeare
Deep as hip pockets on a tall giraffe.
Deep as lust.—Craig Thomas
Deep as shark shit.
Deep as sin.
Deep as sullen quarry water.—Stephen King
Deep as the fountains of sleep.
Deep as the grave.—A. C. Swinburne
Deep as the ocean.
Deep as the pit of hell.—A. C. Swinburne
Deep as the sea.—William Shakespeare

About as deep as heavy dew.
About as deep as May frost. —George MacDonald Fraser
    Also see Abysmal, Intense.

Delicate

Delicate as a fairy's sigh. —Francis S. Osgood
Delicate as a lily.
Delicate as a silver strand of spider web. —Stephen King
Delicate as an eggshell.
Delicate as butterflies wings. —Thomas Hardy
Delicate as filigree. —Stephen R. Donaldson
Delicate as flowers.
Delicate as old Chinese pots.
About as delicate as an elephant in a swamp. —George MacDonald Fraser
    Also see Dainty, Elegant.

Delicious

Delicious as a banana split.
Delicious as forbidden fruit.
Delicious as homemade ice cream.

Delighted

Delighted as a child with a new toy. —Arthur Conan Doyle
Delighted as a gutter puppy finding a bone. —Robert Adelman
    Also see Happy, Pleasant.

Demure

Demure as a cat.
Demure as a nun.
Demure as a Quaker.
About as demure as an old whore at a christening. —*Partridge's*

Dense

Dense as darkness. —A. C. Swinburne
Dense as falling leaves in October.
Dense as Grandma's knitting. —Stephen Wright
Dense as London fog.
Dense as smog in Los Angeles.
Dense as the village idiot.
    Also see Crowded, Dumb, Ignorant, Stupid, Thick.

Descended

Descended as swiftly as the funnel of a tornado. —Evan S. Connell
Descended like a wolf on the fold.
Descended like locusts.
    Also see Came down.

Desolate

Desolate as a ghost town.
Desolate as a mausoleum.
Desolate as a summer resort in midwinter. —Richard Harding Davis

Desolate as a tomb.—Heinrich Heine
Desolate as death.—Francis S. Saltus
Desolate as the back side of the moon.—Shelby Foote
   Also see Abandoned.

Destructive
Destructive as a forest fire.
Destructive as a pipe bomb.
Destructive as a hurricane.
Destructive as a tornado.
Destructive as a two-year-old.
Destructive as grasshoppers.
Destructive as hail on wheat.
Destructive as moths in a woolens closet.
Destructive as the bite of a rattlesnake.
Destructive as the San Francisco earthquake.

Devoured
Devoured it like a hungry dog.
Devoured it like a ravenous wolf that had been starving a fortnight in the
   snow.—Daniel DeFoe
   Also see Ate.

Died
Died like a dog.—Arthur Conan Doyle
Died like a dog in a ditch.—Robert Service
Died like a grown man.
Died like a rat.
Died like a rat in a hole.—Ranger Gull
Died like flies.
   Also see Dead.

Different
Different as a lamb and a wolf.—Jeffery Farnol
Different as a sword and a toothpick.
Different as a whale and a tadpole.
Different as a yacht is to a coal barge.
Different as black and white.
Different as chalk and cheese.—John Masters
Different as crochet and oilcloth.—Ivan Doig
Different as dawn to dusk.—Gore Vidal
Different as day and night.
Different as fire and water.
Different as heaven and hell.—William Wordsworth
Different as mustard and custard.
Different as noses.
Different as peas and apples.—J. R. R. Tolkien
Different as salt and sugar.—Francis Bacon
Different as summer and winter.
Different as an elephant and a giraffe.

Dignified

Dignified as a dowager empress concluding an audience. —M. M. Kaye

Dignified as Julius Caesar.

Direct

Direct as a bullet.

Direct as a hammer. —Tom Wicker

Direct as the arrow of logic. —George Meredith

Direct as the crow flies.

Also see Blunt.

Disappeared

Disappeared as fast as a gallon of ice cream at a fat boys' convention.

Disappeared like a leaf in a windstorm.

Disappeared like a phantom.

Disappeared like a pickpocket.

Disappeared like a shadow.

Disappeared like an apple in an orphanage. —Arthur Baer

Disappeared like dew on a June morning. —Edward G. Buffum

Disappeared like magic.

Disappeared like smoke.

Disappeared like the blues on a warm spring day.

Also see Melted, Vanished.

Dishonest

Dishonest as a gas meter.

Dishonest as local elections. —Amy Leslie

Also see Corrupt, Crooked, Deceitful, False, Lied.

Dismal

Dismal as a bowling alley without beer. —James G. Huneker

Dismal as a defaced tombstone. —John Hay

Dismal as a funeral chorus. —Robert Lewis Taylor

Dismal as a hearse. —Nicolas Boileau

Dismal as a mute at a funeral. —William M. Thackeray

Dismal as a wet Derby Day. —A. E. Housman

Dismal as death. —Cleanthes

Also see Gloomy, Sad, Unhappy.

Dispersed

Dispersed like dandelion fluff on a brisk wind. —Dean R. Koontz

Dispersed like smoke from a bonfire. —Mary Stewart

Also see Scattered.

Disposition

Disposition as bright as a ten-cent shoe shine.

Also see Moody.

Distant

Distant as death. —Ivan Doig

Distant as dowagers in church. —George MacDonald Fraser

Distant as stars.—John Crosby
Distant as the horizon sail.—George Meredith
Also see Aloof, Far, Isolated, Remote.

Dizzy

Dizzy as a dervish.
Dizzy as a drunk on St. Patrick's Day.
Dizzy as a goose.
Dizzy as a moth that flutters 'round the flame.—H. H. Boyesen

Docile

Docile as a lamb.—Honore de Balzac
Docile as a nun.—D. Giardina
Docile as a pet spaniel.—Nathaniel Hawthorne
Also see Tame.

Drab

Drab as a dead man's hand.
Drab as a February day.
Drab as a storekeeper.—Robert Houston
Drab as unpolished pewter.—Howard Spring

Dragged

Dragged like a child to the first day of school.
Dragged like a lamb to a slaughterhouse.—Thomas Holcroft
Dragged himself like a World War II prisoner on a death march.—Peter Jenkins

Drank

Drank like a beast.
Drank like a caged bird.
Drank like a Christian.
Drank like a country parson.—George MacDonald Fraser
Drank like a fish.
Drank like a funnel.
Drank like a lord.
Drank like a man with a hollow leg.
Drank like a sieve.
Drank like a suction hose.
Drank like they were going to reinstate prohibition.—Stephen King
Drank like they were going to stop making it.
Also see Drunk.

Drawn

Drawn a crowd like a building on fire.
Drawn a crowd like a fistfight.
Drawn like a cat to fish.—Tom DeHaven
Drawn like a dogfight.—Mark Twain
Drawn like a fire truck.
Drawn like a magnet.
Drawn like a magnet to a needle.—T. S. Arthur
Drawn like a moth to a flame.

Drawn like a moth to a porch light.
Drawn like filings to a magnet.—T. C. Boyle
Drawn like flies to honey.
Drawn like molasses.—Erskine Caldwell
Drawn like raw meat draws jackals.—Dean R. Koontz
Drawn like the moon draws the sea.
Drawn like whores to a fraternal convention.
   Also see Attracted.

Dressed

Dressed like a Basque onion seller.—Doris Leslie
Dressed like a carnival barker.
Dressed like a Christmas tree.
Dressed like a maypole.—John Evelyn
Dressed like a Nebraska farmer on his way to church.
Dressed like a pimp.
Dressed like a Punjabe whoremaster.—George MacDonald Fraser
Dressed like a ragpicker's child.—Margaret Mitchell
Dressed like a scarecrow.
Dressed like a used car salesman.
Dressed like a walking garage sale.
Dressed like a whistle-stop town librarian.—Stephen Longstreet
Dressed like a whore on Saturday night.
Dressed like an ice cream man.
Dressed like an Italian sunset.
Dressed like charity girls.
Dressed like going to a ball.—Margaret Mitchell
Dressed like an Arabian bazaar.—T. C. Boyle
Dressed like an Easter egg.
Dressed up like a sore finger.

Drifted

Drifted like a somnambulist.—William Morris
Drifted like an unanchored ship.—Doris Leslie
Drifted like droppings from a cottonwood tree.
Drifted like flakes of snow.
Drifted like gossamer.—Robert Louis Stevenson
   Also see Floated.

Dripped

Dripped like an old faucet.—Lawrence Sanders
Dripped like a kid's nose.

Drooped

Drooped like a broken lily.
Drooped like a cheerleader whose team had lost.—Thomas Thompson
Drooped like a crippled zeppelin.—Tom McEwen
Drooped like a drunken dancing partner.—H. Allen Smith
Drooped like a flower in the frost.—John Greenleaf Whittier
Drooped like a shower-beaten flower.—D. G. Rossetti

Drooped like a wilted flower.—George Garrett
Drooped like an old man with a back problem.—T. C. Boyle
Drooped like an old woman's breasts.
Drooped like wash on the line.
   Also see Bent.

Dropped
Dropped like a bad habit.
Dropped like a beef animal falls under the blow of the butcher's killing maul.
   —Harold Bell Wright
Dropped like a bombshell.—Doris Leslie
Dropped like a flower cut down by a sickle.—Alexandre Dumas
Dropped like a full sack.
Dropped like a lead plummet.—Bernard Shrimsley
Dropped like a sack of cement.
Dropped like a sack of fertilizer.
Dropped like a shot buffalo.
Dropped like a spent horse.—George H. Boker
Dropped like a steer hit with a hammer.
Dropped like a stone.
Dropped like a stone falling into a chasm.
Dropped like a stunned ox.
Dropped like flies.
Dropped like he'd been shot.
Dropped like mercury on a cold day.
Dropped like needles from a Christmas tree.
Dropped it like a hot coal.—Doris Leslie
Dropped it like a hot potato.
Dropped her like a prom queen with a dose of clap.
Dropped off like leaves in autumn.—Robert Blair
   Also see Fell.

Drowned
Drowned like a rat.
Drowned like a rat in a rain barrel.—Stephen King
Drowned like a mouse in a trap.—George Bernard Shaw

Drowsy
Drowsy as a kitten.
Drowsy as a yawn.
Drowsy as the clicking of a clock.—William Cowper
Drowsy as the hum of a bagpipe.
   Also see Tired.

Drunk
Drunk as a badger.
Drunk as a bastard.
Drunk as a blind owl.
Drunk as a boiled owl.
Drunk as a brewer's fart.

Drunk as a bunghole.
Drunk as a coon on stump-likker. —Stephen King
Drunk as a fart.
Drunk as a fiddler. —The Puritan
Drunk as a fish. —Ben Jonson
Drunk as a fool.
Drunk as a hoot owl.
Drunk as a hillbilly at a rooster fight.
Drunk as a little red wagon.
Drunk as a loon.
Drunk as a lord. —George Coleman
Drunk as a piper. —John Gay
Drunk as a prohibition enforcement agent. —Bayard L. Taylor
Drunk as a sailor.
Drunk as a skunk.
Drunk as a skunk in a trunk.
Drunk as a tapster.
Drunk as a tinker.
Drunk as a waltzing pissant.
Drunk as an owl.
Drunk as eight hundred dollars. —Ivan Doig
Drunk as a hoot.
Drunk as seven earls. —Margaret Mitchell
Drunk as whiskey.
Drunk as Zeus.
     Also see Drank, High, Lit up, Out.

Dry
Dry as a Baptist picnic.
Dry as a bone.
Dry as a bundle of sticks. —George MacDonald Fraser
Dry as a chip. —Charles Dickens
Dry as a cinder. —Joseph Conrad
Dry as a covered bridge. —Arthur Baer
Dry as a dead man's scalp.
Dry as a document. —Thomas Harris
Dry as a drought. —Erskine Caldwell
Dry as a gourd. —H. Allen Smith
Dry as a pond in the summer.
Dry as a powder horn. —Mark Twain
Dry as a powder house.
Dry as a powder keg.
Dry as a prohibition fight in Vermont.
Dry as a prune.
Dry as a scoop of hot sand. —Robert Lewis Taylor
Dry as a sponge.
Dry as a stick. —Victor Canning
Dry as a wooly sock. —Stephen King

Dry as an ash.—Dean R. Koontz
Dry as an oatcake.—T. C. Boyle
Dry as an old saddle.—Rosemary H. Jarman
Dry as ash.—Rikki Ducornet
Dry as breadcrumbs.—John Ehle
Dry as chalk dust.
Dry as corn fodder in March.—David Grayson
Dry as Death Valley.
Dry as desert dust.—Stopford A. Brooke
Dry as Deuteronomy.
Dry as dust.—William Shakespeare
Dry as granny's tits.—William Dieter
Dry as leaves in the winter.
Dry as lizard skin.—Stephen King
Dry as lumber.—Robert R. McCammon
Dry as old snuff.
Dry as peanut shells.
Dry as sand.—Charles G. Leland
Dry as sandpaper.
Dry as sawdust.—Henry Higden
Dry as spice dust.—Mary Stewart
Dry as the Congressional Record.—James J. Monague
Dry as the crop report.—H. C. Witwer
Dry as the desert.—Charles Dickens
Dry as the Egyptian room in the museum.—Stephen King
Dry as tinder.
Dry as your grandaddy's scalp.
Dry and crowded as a dictionary.—John Irving

Dull

Dull as a banker.—Honore de Balzac
Dull as a boiled goldfish.—Sam Slick
Dull as a convent.
Dull as a country squire.—William Wycherley
Dull as a dog biscuit.
Dull as a donkey.—Thomas Hood
Dull as a lecture at the Royal Society.—Oscar Wilde
Dull as a London fog.—James G. Huneker
Dull as a platonic lover.
Dull as a post.—John Gay
Dull as a Quaker meeting.
Dull as a whetstone.—Robert Heath
Dull as an archdeacon.—G. K. Chesterton
Dull as an ass.
Dull as an obsolete almanac.—John Hay
Dull as an ox.—Henry Fielding
Dull as an oyster.—H. L. Mencken
Dull as books in a guest room.

Dull as catalogues.—R. B. Sheridan
Dull as fire ember's final glow.—Keith Korman
Dull as mutes at a funeral.
Dull as the doldrums.—Robert Louis Stevenson
Dull as the country in November.—Edward Bulwer-Lytton
   Also see Bored, Exciting, Interest.

Dumb

Dumb as a bat.
Dumb as a beetle.
Dumb as a board.—Robert R. McCammon
Dumb as a box of bent nails.
Dumb as a box of creek gravel.
Dumb as a box of rocks.
Dumb as a boy who can't park his bicycle.
Dumb as a brass spitoon.
Dumb as a can of worms.
Dumb as a carpenter who can't drive a nail into a bail of hay.
Dumb as a dodo.
Dumb as a doorknob.
Dumb as a feather mop.—George MacDonald Fraser
Dumb as a hay rake.
Dumb as a hubcap.
Dumb as a june bug.
Dumb as a man who can't find his butt with a stick and a map.
Dumb as a milkcow.
Dumb as a person who can't chew tobacco and ride a horse at the same time.
Dumb as a person who doesn't know his ass from a hole in the ground.
Dumb as a person who doesn't know shit from Shinola.
Dumb as a poet in search of a simile.—Thomas Holcroft
Dumb as a post.
Dumb as a rubbing post.
Dumb as a stage doorkeeper.
Dumb as a stone.—Robert Browning
Dumb as a tick on a dead dog.
Dumb as a tree.
Dumb as a yard dog.—Tom Wicker
Dumb as an ox.
Dumb as cement and as hard.—John Irving
Dumb as dirt.
Dumb as dog shit.
Dumb as one who thinks Scotland Yard is a place where they hang out kilts.
Dumb as one who thinks the Mexican border pays rent.
Dumb as shit.
   Also see Foolish, Ignorant, Stupid.

Eager

Eager as a beaver.

Eager as a bridegroom.

Eager as a cry for life. —George Meredith

Eager as a fine-nosed hound. —William Wordsworth

Eager as a ghoul for blood.

Eager as a greyhound on his game. —Sir Walter Scott

Eager as an understudy.

Eager as hunters pursuing their prey.

Eager as hunting dogs on a leash. —Wilbur Smith

Also see Anxious, Enthusiastic.

Ears

Ears like a hound dog. —Robert R. McCammon

Ears like a lynx.

Ears like a pickup truck with both doors open.

Ears like an elephant. —C. L. Skelton

Ears like bagels.

Ears like mangled donuts.

Ears like twin sails full of wind. —George Garrett

Easy

Easy as a dog can lick a dish.

Easy as a hot knife cuts through butter.

Easy as a mule breaking wind. —James Sherburn

Easy as a smile.

Easy as ABC.

Easy as ambition.

Easy as an old shoe.

Easy as biting a dentist.

Easy as breaking wind.

Easy as breathing.

Easy as cake.—Dean R. Koontz
Easy as child's play.—Victor Appleton
Easy as climbing a fallen tree.—Danish proverb
Easy as clockwork.—Doris Leslie
Easy as drawing a child's first tooth.—Johann Goethe
Easy as falling off a cable car.—Cutliffe Hyne
Easy as falling off a log.
Easy as falling off a wagon.
Easy as falling out of a canoe.
Easy as getting money in a letter.
Easy as kissing.—James R. Lowell
Easy as loving.
Easy as lying.—William Shakespeare
Easy as one, two, three.
Easy as ordering a drink.—Leonard Merrick
Easy as passing gas.
Easy as peeling a banana.
Easy as peeling a hard-boiled egg.
Easy as pie.
Easy as pissing in bed.
Easy as playing hooky.—Mark Twain
Easy as pointing your finger.—Colt Fire Arms Co. slogan
Easy as robbing a blind boy.
Easy as robbing a child's bank.
Easy as rolling off a log.—Mark Twain
Easy as saying "Jack Robinson."
Easy as selling beer at a picnic.—Guy Bolton
Easy as selling watermelons on June tenth.—Thomas Thompson
Easy as shelling peas.—Charles Reade
Easy as shooting birds on the ground.
Easy as shooting ducks in a pond.
Easy as shooting fish in a barrel.
Easy as shooting tame ducks in a pond.—William M. Raine
Easy as sinking your thumb into fresh dough.—Stephen King
Easy as spitting.—Anton T. Chekhov
Easy as stealing pennies from a blind man.
Easy as sucking a fresh egg.—Benvenuto Cellini
Easy as swallowing a Hershey bar.—Tom DeHaven
Easy as swallowing minute tapioca.—Tom DeHaven
Easy as swatting a fly.—Tom Wicker
Easy as taking a drink.—John Davidson
Easy as taking candy from a baby.
Easy as taking money from a child.
Easy as taking toffy from a child.
Easy as to set dogs on sheep.—William Shakespeare
Easy as turning the page in a book.
Easy as twice one is two.—Edward Eggleston
Easy as two plus two.

Easy as winking.
About as easy as dressing an elephant in panty hose.
About as easy as eating soup with a fork.
About as easy as licking honey off a thorn tree.
About as easy as nailing a glob of mercury to the wall.
About as easy as pouring California wine out of a French bottle.
About as easy as pulling teeth from an alligator. —Dean R. Koontz
About as easy as putting pants on a bull. —Ferrol Sams
About as easy as riding a tricycle through a field of molasses.
About as easy as shaking peaches out of a fruit jar.
About as easy as stealing kittens from a bobcat. —Owen Ulph
    Also see Simple.

Edgy
Edgy as a man badly in need of a drink.
Edgy as a terrier watching a rat hole. —Doris Leslie
    Also see Anxious, Nervous, Restless, Tense, Touchy, Uneasy.

Effective
Effective as a blackjack.
Effective as a bullet. —Edgar Saltus
    Also see Efficient.

Efficient
Efficient as a bear trap. —Warren H. Miller
Efficient as a can opener.
Efficient as a customs inspector.
Efficient as furniture movers. —Sam Koperwas
    Also see Effective.

Elegant
Elegant as a chesterfield.
Elegant as a five-star French restaurant.
Elegant as a rapier. —George MacDonald Fraser
Elegant as Cary Grant. —Robert R. McCammon
Elegant as poetry. —Cecelia Holland
    Also see Dainty, Delicate.

Eloquent
Eloquent as a queen's ball.
Eloquent as a rattlesnake's tail.
Eloquent as Cicero.

Elusive
Elusive as a fox.
Elusive as a sunbeam.
Elusive as an echo.
Elusive as quicksilver. —Garrett Mattingly
    Also see Intangible.

Embarrassed

Embarrassed as a preacher's child caught in a lie. —Ridley Wills
Embarrassed as a teen with new braces.

Embraced

Embraced like a lost lover. —T. C. Boyle
Embraced like old friends.

Empty

Empty as a bird's nest in winter. —Vincent Bugliosi
Empty as a broken bowl. —George Garrett
Empty as a church on Monday morning.
Empty as a church on payday. —Robert Houston
Empty as a cobbler's curse. —Thomas Dermody
Empty as a contribution box.
Empty as a dry shell on the beach. —Daphne Du Maurier
Empty as a gourd. —Michael Mewshaw
Empty as a gutted fish. —George Garrett
Empty as a moneylender's soul. —Robert Houston
Empty as a nun's hope chest. —Robert Houston
Empty as a piggy bank the day after Christmas.
Empty as a poor man's Christmas stocking. —Robert Houston
Empty as a reed. —G. Boccaccio
Empty as a robbed room. —John Ehle
Empty as a sewing basket at a nudist camp.
Empty as a sieve. —Doris Leslie
Empty as a skull. —Frances M. Trolloppe
Empty as a tin drum. —Steven Callahan
Empty as a winter rain barrel.
Empty as an author's pocket.
Empty as an Englishman's heart. —Douglas C. Jones
Empty as an office building at night.
Empty as an old bottle. —F. Scott Fitzgerald
Empty as an old shoe. —Doris Leslie
Empty as space. —Guy de Maupassant
Empty as the Kremlin's suggestion box. —Orben's *Current Comedy*
    Also see Bare, Barren, Hollow.

Enduring

Enduring as a camel. —John Keats
Enduring as eternity. —Joseph Conrad
Enduring as marble.
Enduring as the stars.
    Also see Eternal, Lasted, Permanent, Stable.

Energetic

Energetic as a convict on a one-day pass. —Norman Mailer
Energetic as a tugboat. —Howard Jacobson

Enthusiastic

Enthusiastic as a bride buying her trousseau.
Enthusiastic as a kid in a toy store.—Tom Clancy
Enthusiastic as a three-headed cat in a creamery.—H. C. Witmer
About as enthusiastic as a guy going to the chair.—H. C. Witmer
    Also see Eager.

Enticing

Enticing as a partly clad woman bent on seduction.—Ian St. James
Enticing as a riddle.—P. W. Shedd
Enticing as a summer's dip in the pool.—Robert Adelman
    Also see Alluring, Appealing, Attractive, Charming.

Erect

Erect as a battle flag.—Peter Bowman
Erect as a fence post.—James Sherburn
Erect as a hat rack.—T. C. Boyle
Erect as a lightning rod.—Mark Twain
Erect as a palace guard.
Erect as a pillar.—T. C. Boyle
Erect as a turkey gobbler.—Ferrol Sams
Erect as an aristocrat.—Ferrol Sams
Erect as an icon.—Stephen R. Donaldson
    Also see Straight.

Erection

Erection like a telephone pole.
Erection like a tire iron.—T. C. Boyle
    Also see Hard, Penis.

Erratic

Erratic as a dragonfly's flight.—John Masters
Erratic as a woman's whims.
    Also see Wandered.

Eternal

Eternal as life.
Eternal as mediocrity.—James G. Huneker
Eternal as the eternal God.—J. C. Guthrie
Eternal as the mountains.
Eternal as the sky.—John Greenleaf Whittier
    Also see Enduring, Immortal.

Even

Even as a row of corn.
Even as a row of telephone poles.
Even as a row of West Point cadets on parade.
    Also see Flat.

Evident

Evident as a light in dark.—George Meredith

Evident as the light of day.
Evident as the sun at noon.—Thomas Carlyle
   Also see Clear, Obvious, Plain, Stood out.

Exact
Exact as a blueprint.
Exact as clockwork.—Thomas Carlyle
Exact as mathematics.
   Also see Precise.

Examined
Examined it like a customs inspector.
Examined it like a pawnbroker's wife.—Derek Robinson
Examined it like the owner of a new car.
   Also see Inspected, Looked him/her over.

Excited
Excited as a cat at a mouse show.
Excited as a child in a candy store.—Peter Jenkins
Excited as a child on his first Christmas.—Peter Jenkins
Excited as a child on the last day of school.
Excited as a cop making his first pinch.—H. C. Witmer
Excited as a debutante at her first ball.
Excited as a dog with two tails.—Victor Canning
Excited as a girl at her first dance.—Shelby Hearon
Excited as a girl on her first date.
Excited as a kid seeing Santa for the first time.—Peter Jenkins
Excited as a summer child preparing for a camping trip.—Joan Samson
   Also see Eager, Enthusiastic.

Exciting
Exciting as a Chinese fire drill.
Exciting as five rattlers in a canoe.
Exciting as uncovering a barrel of snakes.—Mark Childress
Exciting as war.—Winston Churchill
About as exciting as a Quaker meeting.—George Ade
About as exciting as an account of a flower show.—Gertrude Atherton
About as exciting as constipation.
About as exciting as watching grass grow.
About as exciting as watching trees grow.
About as exciting as working a toll booth.
About as exciting as yesterday's newspaper.

Exhilarating
Exhilarating as a cold shower.
Exhilarating as love.—Honore de Balzac

Exotic
Exotic as fine perfume.

Exotic as profanity from Mars.—Ivan Doig
Also see Sexy.

Exploded

Exploded like a bomb.
Exploded like a Chinese firecracker.—Thelma Strabel
Exploded like a clay pigeon.
Exploded like clay ducks at a shooting gallery.—Stephen King
Explosive as a firecracker.—Peter Jenkins
Also see Burst.

Expressionless

Expressionless as a gravestone.
Expressionless as a lizard.—Peter Straub
Expressionless as a robot.—John Crosby
Expressionless as a rock.—Cecelia Holland
Expressionless as a side of mutton.—Robert Lewis Taylor
Expressionless as the night.
Also see Face.

Extinct

Extinct as the bison.—Finley P. Dunne
Extinct as the dodo.

Eye-catching

Eye-catching as a mooner.
Eye-catching as a streaker in a fine restaurant.
Eye-catching as Joan of Arc at the stake.
Also see Attractive, Stood out.

Eyes

Eyes as baleful as a boar's.—Ferrol Sams
Eyes as big as buckeye seeds.—John Ehle
Eyes as big as fried eggs.—Keith Korman
Eyes as big as pocket watches.—T. C. Boyle
Eyes as big as saucers.
Eyes as black as coal.
Eyes as black as gun bores.—Cormac McCarthy
Eyes as black as oil.—John Updike
Eyes as blank as the village idiot's.—Rosemary H. Jarman
Eyes as blue as a baby's blanket.—Robert R. McCammon
Eyes as blue as autumn mist.—Thomas Hardy
Eyes as bright as a button.
Eyes as bright as a coin.
Eyes as bright as the keenest lancet.—Samual Minturn Peck
Eyes as cold as gold coins dropped into a well.
Eyes as cold as an ascetic's.—Margaret Mitchell
Eyes as cold as fresh oysters.—James Sherburn
Eyes as cold as pebbles.—M. M. Kaye
Eyes as cold as water in a spring.—John Ehle

Eyes as colorless as rain.—Charles McCarry

Eyes as dark as caves with maybe a squirrel peeping out.—John Ehle

Eyes as dark as ripe olives.—V. G. Bortin

Eyes as dark as semi-sweet chocolate.—Dean R. Koontz

Eyes as dull as a fish in the market towards the end of the day.
   —Thomas Harris

Eyes as empty as a blind man's.—Jack Fuller

Eyes as evil as a snake's.

Eyes as fixed as a stone idol's.—George MacDonald Fraser

Eyes as fresh and clear as morning skies.—James Whitcomb Riley

Eyes as gentle as a collie dog's.—Margaret Mitchell

Eyes as glazed as skim ice in January.—Gerald Duff

Eyes as glazed as the eyes of a dead fish.—Stephen King

Eyes as green as the hills of Ireland.—Margaret Mitchell

Eyes as gray as a glacier on a cloudy day.—Stephen King

Eyes as gray as ice.—Doris Leslie

Eyes as hard and bright as marbles.—Lee Smith

Eyes as hard as pebbles.—George MacDonald Fraser

Eyes as honest and clear as a mountain pool.—Rex Beach

Eyes as keen as a hawk's.—Victor Appleton

Eyes as keen as those of a bird of prey.—Thomas Hardy

Eyes as lidless as snakes.

Eyes as pale as water in a china cup.

Eyes as pink as a hamster's.—Keith Korman

Eyes as remote as mountain lakes.—Margaret Mitchell

Eyes as sharp as bayonet points.

Eyes as shiny and blank as doorknobs.—Richard Bachman

Eyes as stars of twilight fair.—William Wordsworth

Eyes as teasing as a small boy's.—Margaret Mitchell

Eyes as transparent as a cloudless sky.

Eyes as wide as terror.—Jack Fuller

Eyes as wide as those of a child lost in the dark.—Margaret Mitchell

Eyes as wild as a spooked horse's.—Alan Hines

Eyes blinked like a vigilant lizard.—Owen Ulph

Eyes bloodshot and dull like those of a goaded, fly-maddened bull.
   —Rex Beach

Eyes bright and large like the eyes of a baby.—Robert R. McCammon

Eyes darted around like blips on a video game—John Lutz

Eyes darted every which way like a wild thing.—Mary Stewart

Eyes darted like gnats on a summer river.—Howard Jacobson

Eyes darted like little mice.—H. Allen Smith

Eyes darted like newts.

Eyes flashed like sapphires.—Theodore Watts-Dunton

Eyes glowed like lamps of hell.

Eyes glowed like twin coals.—Margaret Mitchell

Eyes large and brown like a spaniel.—Max Hennessey

Eyes light and bright as a bird's, blinking and winking strangely.
   —Robert Louis Stevenson

Eyes like a bat.—Robert W. Chambers
Eyes like a cat.—Louis L'Amour
Eyes like a sheep caught in a barbed wire fence.—Richard Bachman
Eyes like a suffering cat.—Doris Leslie
Eyes like an animal brought to bay.—Stephen King
Eyes like blue flowers seen through mist.—Doris Leslie
Eyes like cinders all aglow.—Lewis Carroll
Eyes like coals on the hearth of a winter midnight.—John Jakes
Eyes like dark blue pansies.—Norman Gale
Eyes like glass marbles.—Herman Wouk
Eyes like grottoes.—James Carroll
Eyes like open furnace doors.—George MacDonald Fraser
Eyes like pebbles.
Eyes like pissholes in the snow.
Eyes like quartz crystals.—James Sherburn
Eyes like Rasputin.
Eyes like rubies.—Howard Spring
Eyes like saucers.
Eyes like the Lakes of Killarney.—Richard Hovey
Eyes like two twinkling stars on a winter night.—Robert Greene
Eyes like violets by a river of pure water.—Oscar Wilde
Eyes limpid and still like pools of water.—Robert Louis Stevenson
Eyes lit up like a kid's at Christmas.
Eyes looked like a hungry cat's.—Margaret Mitchell
Eyes looked like two holes burned in a blanket.—Harold Bell Wright
Eyes looked like two pills.
Eyes puffed as a prizefighter's.—T. C. Boyle
Eyes red and lurid like furnace doors of hell.—Stephen King
Eyes rolled up as if he were in a fit.—Doris Leslie
Eyes sharp as a bobcat's.
Eyes sharp as a cat's.—Clare Francis
Eyes shone like diamonds.—Rex Beach
Eyes shone like knife blades.—George Garrett
Eyes shone like pieces of mica.
Eyes stabbed like an angry swan's.—Doris Leslie
Eyes stuck out like gooseberries.—Jeffery Farnol
Eyes swept toward me like prison searchlights.—Robert R. McCammon
Eyes twinkled like diamonds.—T. B. Aldrich
Eyes upraised like those of a dying saint.—F. Hopkinson Smith
Black eyes like moles in his head.—Margaret Truman
Blue eyes as bright as polished gems.—Dean R. Koontz
Bright eyed as a monkey—Tom McEwen
Dark eyes dull as charcoal.—Joan Samson
Eyeballs glowed like little lanterns.—Thomas Hardy
Two little eyes like gimlet holes.—Emile Zola

Face

Face as aloof and sulky as an old hound dog's. —M. M. Kaye
Face as big as a ham. —Robert Louis Stevenson
Face as black as an undeveloped photograph. —Michael Doane
Face as blank and stiff as a Halloween mask. —Tom Wicker
Face as blank as a billiard table.
Face as blank as a dinner plate. —Keith Korman
Face as blank as a milk bottle. —Tristan Jones
Face as brown and wrinkly as a walnut. —Doris Leslie
Face as dried and brown as the leaves that were blowing about the lawn of Tara. —Margaret Mitchell
Face as fair as a cloudless dawn. —Harry Romaine
Face as flat as a plate. —George MacDonald Fraser
Face as flawless as a child's complexion. —Tom DeHaven
Face as forlorn as a lost and motherless hound. —Margaret Mitchell
Face as friendly as a St. Bernard's. —Peter Jenkins
Face as gloomy as a thunderstorm. —Thomas Hardy
Face as grave as the face of a wooden Indian. —Harold Bell Wright
Face as gray as old snow. —James Sherburn
Face as grim as granite. —Robert Lewis Taylor
Face as hard and dark as old wood. —Jack Fuller
Face as hard as a nut. —Margaret Mitchell
Face as heavy as a bag of stones. —Robert R. McCammon
Face as lined as a river delta. —T. C. Boyle
Face as long and cold as a slate gravestone. —Stephen King
Face as long as a fiddler's.
Face as long as a hearse. —Rosemary H. Jarman
Face as long as a double bass. —Derek Robinson
Face as long as an undertaker's. —Edward Bulwer-Lytton
Face as pale as death. —Harold Bell Wright
Face as pitiful as a child's under a mother's disapproval. —Margaret Mitchell

Face as pitted as a waffle mold.—Mark Twain
Face as questioning as a student's.—Lewis W. Green
Face as red as a beet.
Face as red as a fall apple.—John Ehle
Face as red as a fireplug.—Robert R. McCammon
Face as red as a rose.—Thomas Hardy
Face as red as an angry turkey gobbler's.—Margaret Mitchell
Face as red as an innkeeper's.—T. C. Boyle
Face as red as though he'd been drinking.—Doris Leslie
Face as red as yesterday's rhubarb.—Ian St. James
Face as round as a tire.—John Irving
Face as sharp as a butcher's cleaver.—Daniel D. Emmett, song, "Dixie"
Face as smooth as satin.—Burma-Shave sign
Face as soft as cheese.—John Irving
Face as solemn and blank as the back of a tombstone.—Mark Twain
Face as sun-browned as a faun's.—Doris Leslie
Face as taut as a rat.—James Sherburn
Face as tight as if she'd had to pee for a week.—Mark Childress
Face as tired as a wrung-out rag.—Derek Robinson
Face as white as a sheet.
Face as white as a wax dummy.
Face as white as chalk.
Face as white as death.—Edward Bulwer-Lytton
Face as white as paste.—Doris Leslie
Face as white as pie dough.—Stephen King
Face as white as tallow candle.—Robert Louis Stevenson
Face as wrinkled as old parchment.—George Eekwood
Face afire like sunset.—Mark Twain
Face ashen like an executioner.
Face burnt like a brand.—Alfred Noyes
Face clenched like a fist.—George Garrett
Face creased like an often-read letter.—Laura Kalpakian
Face crumpled like a child's when it is going to cry.—M. M. Kaye
Face fell like a cookbook cake.—Joseph C. Lincoln
Face glowed like a lamp.—Cecelia Holland
Face heavy as a sack.—Honore de Balzac
Face like a bagful of wrenches.
Face like a bottle of warts.
Face like a busted sofa.
Face like a collapsed rubber ball.—Derek Robinson
Face like a demon king.—George MacDonald Fraser
Face like a fried ham.
Face like a gravestone.—T. C. Boyle
Face like a horse.
Face like a Lutheran preacher.—John Ehle
Face like a map of anger.—Anthony Forrest
Face like a painted doll.—Robert R. McCammon
Face like a pizza.—Stephen King

Face like a rock. —Margaret Mitchell
Face like a Roman senator, set and firm. —Frederic S. Isham
Face like a seaboot.
Face like a sheep. —Doris Leslie
Face like a squeezed orange. —Ben Jonson
Face like a three-day corpse. —George MacDonald Fraser
Face like a tragic mask carved out of stone. —H. S. Commager
Face like a walnut.
Face like a wayward saint.
Face like a wicked pixie. —Nicholas Salaman
Face like an abandoned parcel. —Derek Robinson
Face like an ancient lemon. —Joseph Conrad
Face like an old battered shoe. —Dean R. Koontz
Face like an open book. —F. Hopkinson Smith
Face like embalmed youth. —Peter Bowman
Face like pie out of the oven too soon. —William Faulkner
Face like the ass-end of a gasoline truck and a body to match. —Stephen King
Face like the back side of a jersey bull.
Face like the north end of a southbound cattle truck.
Face like the Wicked Witch of the West. —Ridley Pearson
Face looked like a wedding cake left out in the rain. —James Patterson
Face painted like a mask. —Doris Leslie
Face shone like a coin.
Face sweet and bland as a baby's. —Margaret Mitchell
Face sweet and youthful and fair as the moon at full. —Edwin Arnold
Face that looked like a sucked lemon. —Josh Billings
Face that looked like it had worn out four bodies.
Face that looked like the north end of a southbound mule.
Face weathered and homely as a plowed field.
    —Stephen Vincent Benet (describing Lincoln)
Face wrinkled up like a pecan. —Lee Smith
A beautiful face cut as clear and sharp as a cameo. —Jack London
An angular face sharp as the face of the knave in a deck. —George Garrett
    Also see Cheeks, Chin, Complexion, Eyes, Lips, Nose.

Faded

Faded like a bad radio signal. —Richard Bachman
Faded like a cloud which had outwept its rain. —Percy B. Shelley
Faded like a dream of youth. —Oliver Wendell Holmes
Faded like a shadow.
Faded like a thief. —T. C. Boyle
Faded away like a pound of soap in a hard day's wash.
Faded away like morning dew.
Faded away like vapor. —Percy B. Shelley
    Also see Disappeared, Faint, Pale.

Faint

Faint as a candle's last pulse.
Faint as a ghost.

Faint as a hum of distant bees.
Faint as a rising star struggling in heavy earthward mists.—J.R.R. Tolkien
   Also see Faded, Indistinct, Pale.

Fair

Fair as a flower.
Fair as a lily.—Diaphenia
Fair as a peach.—Miles O'Reilly
Fair as a star.—William Wordsworth
Fair as a virgin's vows.
Fair as a wild rose.
Fair as a woodland flower.—Mary Johnston
Fair as day.—William Shakespeare
Fair as is the rose of May.—Geoffrey Chaucer
Fair as marble.—Percy B. Shelley
Fair as spring flowers.—George Garrett
Fair as summer roses.
Fair as the daughter of Job.—*Old Testament*
Fair as truth.—Barry Cornwall
Fair as winter lilies.
Fair as youth.
   Also see Lovely, Pretty.

False

False as a dentist's smile.
False as a harlot's tears.—Thomas D'Urfey
False as his teeth.—Ferrol Sams
False as vows made in wine.—William Shakespeare
   Also see Corrupt, Crooked, Dishonest.

Familiar

Familiar as a popular song.
Familiar as the sun and moon.—Henry David Thoreau
Familiar as turning a key.—Steven Callahan
   Also see Common.

Far

Far as a bird can fly in a lifetime.—Ivan Doig
Far as a country mile.
About as far as one can throw a bull by the tail.
   Also see Distant, Isolated, Remote.

Farted

Farted like a fat baby.
Farted like a marching band.—Tom Wicker
Farted like a Mexican burro.
Farted like a mule.
Farted like a racehorse.

Farted like a shot from a gun barrel.
Dry-farted like the taster in a popcorn factory.—Ivan Doig

Fascinating

Fascinating as a cobra.—Dean R. Koontz
Fascinating as a fly struggling in a pot of glue.
Fascinating as a hanging or a dogfight.—H. L. Mencken
Fascinating as a loose tooth.
Fascinating as a seed catalog.
Fascinating as an ant farm.
Fascinating as the scene of a murder.

Fast

Fast as a cabbage bed produces snails.
Fast as a cat can pull its claws in.
Fast as a cat on wet stones.—John Ehle
Fast as a cheetah with a hotfoot.—Johnny Carson
Fast as a clipper.
Fast as a cockroach on casters.—Nicholas Salaman
Fast as a cowboy on Saturday night.
Fast as a derby winner in the last furlong.
Fast as a dog can lick a dish.
Fast as a dog picking up fleas.—Ian St. James
Fast as a fly can leave a flat surface.—Robert Bausch
Fast as a gust from the North.—Peter Jenkins
Fast as a hooker at a convention.—Dan Jenkins
Fast as a jackrabbit in front of a prairie fire.
Fast as a lottery winner making new friends.—Leda Silver
Fast as a lovesick sailor on a three-hour pass.
Fast as a maid can eat blackberries.—Thomas Hardy
Fast as a pig going downhill on roller skates.
Fast as a pig's wink.
Fast as a rabbit gets fucked.—Movie, *Scarface*
Fast as a scalded cat goes through a back window.
Fast as a speeding bullet.
Fast as a streak.—Ridley Wills
Fast as a striking serpent.—Rex Beach
Fast as a tornado.—Peter Jenkins
Fast as a turtle withdrew its head beneath its shell.—Margaret Mitchell
Fast as a whippet.—Robert R. McCammon
Fast as a wink.
Fast as an arrow.
Fast as an Omaha pig sticker.—H. Allen Smith
Fast as blue blazes.
Fast as greased lightning.
Fast as Houdini tied his shoelaces.—Ivan Doig
Fast as light.—Victor Hugo
Fast as lightning on a summer night.
Fast as small-town gossip.

Fast as the flash of a prayer.—John Ehle
Fast as the twinkling of an eye.
Fast as the wind.
Fast as three shakes of a sheep's tail.—Mark Twain
Fast as wildfire.
Fast as you can say Jack Robinson.—Edward Bulwer-Lytton
Fast as you can say William Howard Taft.—James Sherburn
Fast as you can say scat.—F. Hopkinson Smith
Fast as you can slap a tick.
About as fast as a constipated cracker taster.
About as fast as a crippled caterpillar.
About as fast as a gopher.—John Ehle
About as fast as a stone locomotive.
   Also see Brief, Fleeting, Flew, Off, Quick, Swift, Took off, Went.

Fat
Fat as a baby.—T. C. Boyle
Fat as a bacon pig.
Fat as a balloon.—Mark Twain
Fat as a boar before slaughter.—George Garrett
Fat as a butterball.
Fat as a cherub.
Fat as a distillery pig.—Scottish proverb
Fat as a gourd.—John Ehle
Fat as a hippo.—Dean R. Koontz
Fat as a hog.
Fat as a miller's horse.—Scottish proverb
Fat as a pig.
Fat as a sausage.
Fat as a sheep's tail.
Fat as a whale.—Geoffrey Chaucer
Fat as butter.—William Shakespeare
Fat as lard.
Fat and lazy like a fixed tomcat.
Fat and lean like a rabbit.
Fat, round and proud as a friar.—George Garrett
About as fat as a hen's forehead.
   Also see Plump.

Fatal
Fatal as a hangman.
Fatal as arsenic.
Fatal as death.
Fatal as the scythe of death.—William Cowper
   Also see Dangerous, Dead.

Fearless
Fearless as a drunkard.—Thomas Middleton
Fearless as a happy child too innocent to fear.—Robert Southey

Fearless as an eagle.
  Also see Brave.

Feet

Feet as bare as a yard dog's.—Margaret Mitchell
Feet as light as linden leaves.—J.R.R. Tolkien
Feet like clay.
Feet like hamburger.—Peter Jenkins
Feet like manhole covers.—James Herriot
Feet like nerveless stumps.—Peter Jenkins
Feet like sled runners.
Feet looked as big and fixed in place as tombstones in a cemetery.—Gerald Duff

Fell

Fell from the sky like a wounded bird.—Alistair MacLean
Fell like a bolt out of the blue.—Thomas Carlyle
Fell like a cookbook cake.—Joseph C. Lincoln
Fell like a dead bird.
Fell like a house of cards.
Fell like a limp rag doll.
Fell like a load of bricks.
Fell like a ripe plum.—H. S. Commager
Fell like a sack of mail.—Richard Bachman
Fell like a sand castle.
Fell like a side of beef.—T. C. Boyle
Fell like a spent bullet.—Clinton Scollard
Fell like a stone.
Fell like a ton of bricks.
Fell like a weed cut by the scythe of a mower.—Harold Bell Wright
Fell like an apple from a tree.—Doris Leslie
Fell like an axed tree.
Fell like an egg from a tall chicken.
Fell like dominoes.
Fell like fifty pounds of milled oats.—James Sherburn
Fell like grain before a hailstorm.—Margaret Mitchell
Fell like Humpty Dumpty.
Fell like lead.—Victor Canning
Fell like leaves in October.
Fell like raindrops.
Fell like ripe peaches from a tree.—Margaret Mitchell
Fell like tenpins.
Fell like twenty-nine-cent socks.
Fell like wheat before a reaper.
Fell like wildflowers underfoot.—Tom Wicker
Fell softly, like a snowflake.—Philip J. Bailey
  Also see Dropped.

Fell apart

Fell apart as fast as a ten-dollar suit.

Fell apart like a badly wound ball of wool. —Francoise Chandernagor
Fell apart like a broken blossom. —John Updike
Fell apart like a fifty-cent umbrella in a gale.
Fell apart like a two-dollar suitcase. —Dan Jenkins

Felt

Felt like a boiled rat.
Felt like a Christian in a pitful of lions. —Stephen King
Felt like a dog.
Felt like a half-dead goat the next morning. —Dean R. Koontz
Felt like a nickel waiting for change.
Felt like a penny with a hole in it.
Felt like a plugged nickel.
Felt like a wooden nickel.
Felt like he'd been chewed up and spit out.
Felt like he'd been eaten by a wolf and shit off a cliff.
Felt like he'd been hit in the face with a wet squirrel.
Felt like he'd been run over by a Mack truck.
Felt like homemade shit. —Stephen King
Felt like the apple on top of William Tell. —E. Y. Harburg
Felt like the devil.
Felt like the little boy the calf ran over. —Havilah Babcock
Felt like the symptoms of a medicine bottle. —George Ade

Ferocious

Ferocious as a hungry bear.
Ferocious as a wolf. —Francoise Voltaire
    Also see Fierce, Mean, Savage.

Fickle

Fickle as a changeful dream. —Sir Walter Scott
Fickle as a weather vane. —Robert Baldwin
Fickle as love. —Honore de Balzac
Fickle as the lightning.
Fickle as the weather.
Fickle as the wind. —Horace

Fidgeted

Fidgeted like a flea on a hot griddle.
Fidgeted like a rabbit's nose.
Fidgeted like he had swallowed a spring mattress. —Mark Twain
Fidgety as an old maid. —Honore de Balzac
    Also see Edgy, Nervous.

Fierce

Fierce as a bear. —Robert Service
Fierce as a blast of hate from hell. —A. C. Swinburne
Fierce as a famished wolf. —Robert Southey
Fierce as a mother bear.
Fierce as a mother bird.

Fierce as a rat-catcher's dog at a sinkhole. —Alfred Croquil
Fierce as a shark.
Fierce as a tigress protecting her young.
Fierce as a whirlwind. —Homer
Fierce as a wolf. —Leo Tolstoy
Fierce as Achilles. —Christopher Marlowe
Fierce as an eagle. —Lee Smith
Fierce as ten furies. —John Milton
    Also see Ferocious, Mean, Savage.

Figure
Figure like a beer barrel. —Oscar Wilde
Figure like a pillow.
Figure like an hourglass.

Final
Final as a broken mirror.
Final as a chapter's end.
Final as a hammer on coffin lumber. —Tom Wicker
Final as a sentence of execution. —Stephen R. Donaldson
Final as death.
Final as going to heaven. —Joseph Conrad

Fine
Fine as a cobweb.
Fine as a cow turd stuck with primroses.
Fine as a fiddle.
Fine as a spider's web. —Harold Begbie
Fine as baby hair.
Fine as bug dust.
Fine as cats hair to make you a pair of kitten britches.
Fine as frog hair.
Fine as frog hair split and twisted.
Fine as frog hair split up the middle and tied at both ends.
Fine as gossamer.
Fine as ground flour.
Fine as point lace.
Fine as silk.
Fine as silkworm's thread. —Robert Southey
Fine as snuff.
Fine as split silk.
Fine as tanned snakeskin. —Owen Ulph
Fine as wine. —John Inzer

Firm
Firm as a fortress. —Lord Byron
Firm as a mountain. —Mark Akenside
Firm as a pillar. —George Meredith
Firm as a rock.
Firm as a stone. —*Old Testament*

Firm as Atlas.—William Shakespeare
Firm as Plymouth Rock.
Firm as steel.—Virginia W. Johnson
Firm as the oak on rocky heights.—Edward Lovibond
Firm as the Rock of Gibraltar.
Rock firm as facts.—Thomas Hardy
Also see Fixed, Immobile, Immovable, Stiff.

Fit
Fit as a fiddle.
Fit as a flea.—Henry James
Fit as a pudding for a friar's mouth.
Fit like a banana skin.
Fit like a Brooks Brothers suit.
Fit like a glass eye.
Fit like a glove.
Fit like a kid glove.—George Meredith
Fit like a plug and socket.—Dean R. Koontz
Fit like a skin on a sausage.
Fit like feathers on a duck.
Fit like bark on a tree.
Fit like the paper on the wall.
Fit about like a saddle fits a sow.
Also see Hardy, Healthy.

Fixed
Fixed as a monument.—Rikki Ducornet
Fixed as a star.—William Wordsworth
Fixed as an oak.—Paul Whitehead
Fixed like a statue on a marble throne.—F. W. Faber
Also see Firm, Immobile, Immovable, Stiff.

Flamed
Flamed like a match.
Flamed like a torch.
Flamed like the jaws of hell.
Also see Ablaze, Blazed, Burned.

Flapped
Flapped like a flag in the wind.
Flapped like a torn flag.—Keith Korman
Flapped like wash in the wind.—T. C. Boyle

Flashed
Flashed like a firefly.—Thelma Strabel
Flashed like a jewel.—Robert Bridges
Flashed like a lighthouse.
Flashed like a meteor.

Flashed like a steel blade. —George M. Brandes
Flashed like lightning.

Flat

Flat as a batter cake. —Olive Ann Burns
Flat as a beaten coin. —Antar
Flat as a blade. —Cecelia Holland
Flat as a board. —Howard Spring
Flat as a book. —T. C. Boyle
Flat as a bullfrog on a four-lane highway.
Flat as a filet of sole. —Irvin S. Cobb
Flat as a flounder. —John Gay
Flat as a fried egg. —Derek Robinson
Flat as a fritter.
Flat as a mother-in-law's kiss.
Flat as a pair of chaps hangin' on the wall. —William M. Raine
Flat as a pancake. —Ludvig Holberg
Flat as a pewter platter. —Mary J. Holmes
Flat as a pizza.
Flat as a plate.
Flat as a rose that has long been pressed. —Oliver Wendell Holmes
Flat as a tortilla. —Gary Jennings
Flat as a toad frog on a West Texas highway.
Flat as a waiter's feet. —Arthur Baer
Flat as an anvil's face. —Robert Browning
Flat as an empty leather mail sack. —William M. Raine
Flat as day-old beer.
Flat as Kansas.
Flat as last night's beer. —Louis Untermeyer
Flat as ma's pancakes.
Flat as old cider.
Flat as your momma's chest.
Flat and bare as a tennis court. —Wilbur Smith
    Also see Even.

Fled

Fled like a dream. —William Cowper
Fled like a felon. —Oliver Wendell Holmes
Fled like a passing thought. —Robert Burns
Fled like rats from a sinking ship.
Fled like the company was about to go bankrupt.
    Also see Fast, Ran, Took off, Went.

Fleeting

Fleeting as a dream.
Fleeting as a ferryboat shoe shine. —Franklin P. Adams
Fleeting as a greyhound.
Fleeting as an antelope. —Zane Grey
Fleeting as joy of youth. —Edwin Arnold

Fleeting as the faces of the moon.—Robert R. McCammon
> *Also see* Fast, Swift.

Flew

Flew like a bat out of hell.
Flew like a dog that had burnt his paw.—Osmani proverb
Flew like a dream.—Jonathan Swift
Flew like a duck with a hernia.—Stephen Longstreet
Flew like spray from under a ship's bow.
Flew like wasps shaken from their winter sleep.
Flew about like a kite in the wind.—Emma Marshall
Flew up like a window shade.—Stephen King
> *Also see* Fast, Hurried, Off, Quick, Swift, Took off, Went.

Flickered

Flickered like a candle in the wind.—Henry James
Flickered like a lamp.—Sigmund Krasinski
Flickered like fire.

Flitted

Flitted like a deer.—Robert Louis Stevenson
Flitted like a ghost.—John Keats
Flitted like a june bug.—Tom Wicker
Flitted like a shadow.
Flitted like bats at dusk.—Derek Robinson
Flitted like purple martins.
> *Also see* Darted.

Floated

Floated like foam upon the wave.—Sir Walter Scott
Floated about like a stone.—Alistair MacLean
Floated aimlessly as a drowned soul.—Howard Jacobson
Floated around like milkweed in a strong breeze.
Float like a butterfly, sting like a bee.—Mohammed Ali
> *Also see* Drifted.

Flopped

Flopped like a fish out of water.
Flopped like a rag doll.
Flopped like the ears of a dog.—Edgar Allan Poe
Flopped around like a chicken with its head cut off.
Flopped around like a runover snake.—William Dieter

Flourished

Flourished like crabgrass.
Flourished like weeds.
Flourished like a young bay tree.—Jeffery Farnol
> *Also see* Grew, Thrived.

Flowed

Flowed like a waterfall.

Flowed like beer at a wedding.
Flowed like Niagara.
  Also see Poured.

Flung

Flung around like yesterday's laundry.—Robert R. McCammon
Flung aside like a discarded overcoat.—Tom Wicker
Flung aside like butcher's rags.
Flung aside like empty sacks.—Phoebe Gray
Flung himself down like a wet rag.—T. C. Boyle
Flung himself down like he'd just walked thirty miles.
  Also see Tossed.

Flushed

Flushed as one afire with wine.—A. C. Swinburne
Flushed like a zealot.—Ferrol Sams
Flushed like the cheeks of a schoolboy.—Harold Bell Wright
Flushed and happy as a bride.—Victor Canning

Fluttered

Fluttered like a hummingbird's wings.
Fluttered like a moth.—Lee Smith
Fluttered like a moth assailing a lighted window.—Owen Ulph
Fluttered like bats in daylight.—Robert R. McCammon
Fluttered like so many white pigeons around the cote at feeding time.
  —Frederic S. Isham
Fluttered like spent fire.
Fluttered like the wings of a hovering bird.—William Boyd
  Also see Flitted, Quivered.

Folded up

Folded up like a carpenter's ruler.—Stephen Longstreet
Folded up like a parasol.—T. C. Boyle

Followed

Followed like a comet tail.—Thomas Carlyle
Followed like a child after the pied piper.—O. Henry
Followed like a dog.—Zane Grey
Followed like a flock of sheep.
Followed like a pack of dogs after a bitch in heat.—George Garrett
Followed like a shadow.
Followed like a thirsty bloodhound.—T. S. Arthur
Followed like a toy after a two-year-old.
Followed like buzzards after a gut-wagon.

Fond

Fond as a cat is of milk.
Fond as a miser is of his gold.
Fond as hounds are of running after foxes.—Thomas Hood

Foolish

Foolish as judging a horse by its harness.

Foolish as to flash a roll of bills before a lawyer.
Foolish as to scratch one's head with a firebrand.
Foolish as to talk of color to a blind man.
Also see Dumb, Silly, Simple, Stupid.

Forgotten

Forgotten as a child's old toys. —Stephen King
Forgotten as a dead man out of mind. —*Old Testament*
Forgotten like a dead tree. —Derek Robinson
Forgotten like a dream. —Emma Marshall
Forgotten like an almanac out of date. —M. De LaBruyere
Forgotten like spilt wine. —A. C. Swinburne

Forlorn

Forlorn as a dying duck in a thunderstorm.
Forlorn as a lost and motherless child. —Margaret Mitchell
Forlorn as a melting snowman. —James E. Knowles
Forlorn like autumn waiting for the snow. —John Greenleaf Whittier
Also see Friendless, Helpless, Lonely, Sad.

Formal

Formal as a Quaker. —George P. Morris
Formal as a stockbroker. —George MacDonald Fraser
Formal and stilted as Chinese theater. —C. L. Skelton

Fornicated

Fornicated like rabbits.
Fornicated like wild beasts. —Robert R. McCammon
Also see Randy, Rutted.

Fought

Fought like a bull in a tether.
Fought like a bulldog.
Fought like a cock.— Richard Congreve
Fought like a demon. —Victor Appleton
Fought like a dog.
Fought like a pagan who defends his religion. —Stephen Crane
Fought like a tigress defending her young.
Fought like a wounded puma. —George F. Will
Fought like an irrepressible demon. —H. S. Commager
Fought like badgers. —Richard Harding Davis
Fought like cats and dogs.
Fought like demons.
Fought like devils. —William Shakespeare
Fought like hell roosters. —Stephen King
Fought like Kilkenny cats. —*Brewer's*
Fought like lions wanting food. —William Shakespeare
Fought like mad or drunk. —Samuel Butler
Fought like one boxer and his punching bag. —Erica Jong
Fought like siblings.

Fought like tigers.
Fought like two hellcats.
Fought like two old maids.
    Also see Bickered.

Fragile
Fragile as a kite.
Fragile as a lily.
Fragile as a newborn babe.
Fragile as an egg.
    Also see Frail, Helpless, Powerless, Weak.

Fragrant
Fragrant as a rose.
Fragrant as lilacs.—William M. Thackeray
Fragrant as the breath of an angel.—Oliver Wendell Holmes
About as fragrant as a cotton picker's armpit.
About as fragrant as a pigsty.
    Also see Smelled.

Frail
Frail as a box kite.
Frail as a lily.
Frail as a swallow.—Wilbur Smith
Frail as a young tree in a tornado.—Robert R. McCammon
    Also see Fragile, Helpless, Weak.

Free
Free as a bird.—Thomas Hardy
Free as a bird sprung from a cage.
Free as a breeze, free like a bird in the woodland wild, free like a gypsy, free
    like a child.—Oscar Hammerstein, *Oklahoma*
Free as a butterfly.—W. H. Hudson
Free as a cloud.—George Garrett
Free as a fly.
Free as a gift.
Free as a lark.
Free as a sea gull.—Gary Jennings
Free as an eagle.—John Keats
Free as air.—Alexander Pope
Free as nature first made man.—John Dryden
Free as the breeze.—Francis Scott Key
Free as the sun.—William Wordsworth
Free as the wind.—Thomas Chatterton
Free as water.—W. Levingston Comfort

Fresh
Fresh as a bridegroom.—William Shakespeare
Fresh as a crisp head of lettuce.
Fresh as a daisy.—Leo Tolstoy

Fresh as a lark.
Fresh as a new-baked loaf of bread.
Fresh as a newborn.
Fresh as a newborn turd. —*Partridge's*
Fresh as a peach. —Johann Goethe
Fresh as a rose. —Geoffrey Chaucer
Fresh as an egg from the farm.
Fresh as an orchard apple. —George Meredith
Fresh as butter from the churn.
Fresh as dew. —Honore de Balzac
Fresh as flowers in May.
Fresh as night air. —Stephen R. Donaldson
Fresh as new paint.
Fresh as rainwater.
Fresh as spring. —Coventry Patmore
Fresh as the month of May. —Geoffrey Chaucer
Fresh as the morning air. —C.M.S. McLellen
Fresh as tomorrow. —James G. Huneker
Fresh as wind-dried laundry.
Fresh and rosy as an English milkmaid. —F. Hopkinson Smith

Friendless
Friendless as a dentist.
Friendless as a leper.
Friendless as Frankenstein.
> *Also see* Alone, Forlorn, Helpless, Lonely.

Friendly
Friendly as a politician on election day.
Friendly as a puppy. —Bettina Von Hutten
Friendly as a Tenth Avenue whore.
Friendly as weavers. —Mark Twain.
About as friendly as a shark with a toothache.
> *Also see* Amiable, Cordial, Kind.

Frightened
Frightened as a criminal just under arrest. —T. S. Arthur
Frightened as a rabbit caught in a trap.
Frightened as though he had suddenly found himself at the edge of a
    precipice. —Honore de Balzac
> *Also see* Anxious, Scared.

Frigid
Frigid as a cave.
Frigid as a flowing spring.
Frigid as an iceberg.
Frigid as an icebox.
> *Also see* Cold, Cool.

Frisky

Frisky as a colt.—Geoffrey Chaucer
Frisky as a kitten.
   Also see Played.

Frugal

Frugal as a beggar's child.—Ralph Waldo Emerson
Frugal as a poor farmer's wife.—George Garrett
   Also see Cheap, Tight.

Frustrated

Frustrated as a cat covering up shit on a concrete sidewalk.
Frustrated as a fart in a bottle.
Frustrated as being between a dog and a fire hydrant.
Frustrated as being between a rock and a hard place.
Frustrating as cleaning a window with a mudball.—William Pearson

Full (often referring to a drunk)

Full as a bed tick in a mattress.—Stephen King
Full as a bus on a wet Sunday.—Augustus Mayhew
Full as a dog tick.
Full as a fat bear cub.—Peter Jenkins
Full as a fat man.—Peter Jenkins
Full as a lord.
Full as a river at flood level.
Full as an egg.—John Gay
Full as the summer rose.—James Thomson
Full of holes as a colander.—Robert Louis Stevenson
Full of money as a miser's stocking.—Augustus Mayhew
Full of shit as a Christmas goose.
Full of shit as a cranberry merchant.
Full of shit as a cholera submarine.
Full of spirit as the month of May.—William Shakespeare
   Also see Tight.

Fumbled around

Fumbled around like a blind man in an alley.
Fumbled around like a sleepwalker in a strange room.
Fumbled around like a drunk in a dark bar.
   Also see Stumbled.

Fun

Fun as a bag of snakes at an Avon party.
Fun as a barrel of monkeys.
Fun as a baseball game.—Peter Jenkins
Fun as a five-alarm fire.—Stephen King
Fun as a hot fudge enema.
Fun as a gopher in soft dirt.—Labarge
Fun as a puppy in a hydrant factory.
Fun as a Sunday school picnic.

Fun as treeing a coon.
About as much fun as a flat tire.
About as much fun as a jab in the ass with a sharp stick.
About as much fun as a Methodist service.—George MacDonald Fraser
About as much fun as a mudpack.—Thomas Thompson
About as much fun as a vacation in a Soviet prison.—Dean R. Koontz
About as much fun as a wait in a proctologist's office.
About as much fun as cleaning out the attic.—Robert R. McCammon
About as much fun as grocery shopping.
About as much fun as kissing your sister.
About as much fun as listening to a hinge squeak.
About as much fun as slamming your dick in a door.
About as much fun as standing in the rain.
About as much fun as washing a dog.
About as much fun as watching trees grow.
    Also see Exciting.

Funny
Funny as a clown.
About as funny as a bubble gum machine in a lockjaw ward.
    —Jim McCorkle
About as funny as a fart in a space suit.
About as funny as a funeral in a snowstorm.
About as funny as a wooden leg.—George Ade
About as funny as Ex-lax in a diarrhea ward.
About as funny as gangrene.
About as funny as the gout.

Furious
Furious as a bitch when she has lost her puppies.—Vabrugh
Furious as a favored child balked at its wish.—Lord Byron
Furious as a hunt.—George Garrett
Furious as a wounded bull in an arena.—Alexandre Dumas
Furious as the wind.—Thomas Otway
    Also see Mad.

Fussed
Fussed like a hen with one chick.—Margaret Mitchell
Fussed like a worried mother.
Fussy as a boy with a new bride.
Fussy as a nursery maid.

Futile
Futile as curing crabs by setting your shorts on fire.
Futile as turning back the hands of a clock.
    Also see Useless.

Game
Game as a badger.
Game as a fighting cock.
Game as a lion.
Game as a terrier.—George MacDonald Fraser
Game as a hornet.—Alfred Henry Lewis

Gaped
Gaped like a satyr.—George MacDonald Fraser
Gaped like a stuck pig.—John Gay
Gaped like an oyster.
   Also see Gazed, Open, Stared, Wide, Yawned.

Garrulous
Garrulous as a cage of monkeys.—Douglas C. Jones
Garrulous as an old maid.
Garrulous as parrots.—Phoebe Gray

Gasped
Gasped like a beached fish.
Gasped like a fish newly taken from the water.—Edward Eggleston
Gasped like a frog in drought.—Charles Kingsley
Gasped like a leaky engine.—George MacDonald Fraser
Gasped like a netted fish.—Stephen King
Gasped like a salmon on the bank.—George MacDonald Fraser
Gasped like a winded runner.—Stephen King
   Also see Breathed, Panted, Puffed, Wheezed.

Gathered
Gathered like ants.
Gathered like wasps around a jam jar.—Patrick McGinley
   Also see Huddled together.

Gaudy

Gaudy as a butterfly.—William Hazlitt
Gaudy as a harlequin's jacket.—William M. Thackeray
Gaudy as an ape's rump.—Cormac McCarthy
Gaudy as the king's jewelry.
    Also see Bright, Tacky.

Gaunt

Gaunt as a grave.—William Shakespeare
Gaunt as a greyhound.—John Ray
Gaunt as a rail fence.—Tom Wicker
Gaunt as a skeleton.
Gaunt as a stick.—Stephen R. Donaldson
Gaunt as icons of hunger.
Gaunt and taut as a dried mummy.—Ferrol Sams
    Also see Bony, Skinny.

Gay

Gay as a butterfly.—Charles Dickens
Gay as a lark.—La Fontaine
    Also see Happy, Merry.

Gazed

Gazed like a cow.—George MacDonald Fraser
Gazed like boxers before a bout.
    Also see Gaped, Stared.

Gentle

Gentle as a child.—Thomas Hardy
Gentle as a cradled babe.—William Shakespeare
Gentle as a fawn.
Gentle as a feather's stroke.—George Eliot
Gentle as a lamb.—Alice Cary
Gentle as a lover's sighs.—Claudian
Gentle as a pigeon's sound.—Stephen Vincent Benét
Gentle as a turtledove.—R. D. Blackmore
Gentle as sleep.—Lord De Tabley
Gentle as surf on a sandy shore.—Phoebe Gray
Gentle and sweet like a dove.—Mark Twain
Gently as a spider attaching its thread.—Honore de Balzac
Gently like a dog with a quail in its teeth.
    Also see Mild, Smooth.

Ghastly

Ghastly as a laugh in hell.—Thomas Hardy
Ghastly as a smile on a maniac's face.
    Also see Ugly.

Giddy

Giddy as a drunken man.—Charles Dickens
Giddy as a schoolgirl.

Giggled

Giggled like a housemaid.—Doris Leslie
Giggled like a schoolgirl.—Margaret Truman
Also see Laughed.

Glad

Glad as children that come from school.—George Gascoigne
Glad as the skylark's earliest song.—Letitia E. Landon
Also see Cheerful, Gay, Happy, Merry.

Glared

Glared like a bear disturbed in its sleep.—Douglas C. Jones
Glared like a mad thing.—George MacDonald Fraser
Glared at each other like motorists with tangled cars.—Stephen King
Also see Leered.

Gleamed

Gleamed like a bugle.—Robert Houston
Gleamed like a naked sword.
Gleamed like a rising harvest moon.
Gleamed like an angry lion's eye.—Oscar Wilde
Gleamed like gold.—Philander C. Johnson

Glistened

Glistened like a jewel.—Rex Beach
Glistened like a star.—Emma Lazarus
Glistened like coal rubbed in oil.—Rikki Ducornet
Glistened like the dews of morn.—Henry W. Longfellow
Also see Glossy, Lustrous.

Gloomy

Gloomy as a graveyard on a wet Sunday.
Gloomy as a robbed tomb.
Also see Dismal, Glum, Sad, Unhappy.

Glossy

Glossy as a panther's pelt.—Wilbur Smith
Glossy as a shark's tooth.—Arlo Bates
Glossy as wax.—William Dieter
Also see Lustrous, Polished, Shined.

Glowed

Glowed like a blacksmith's forge.
Glowed like a kiln.
Glowed like a lamp.—Stephen King
Glowed like a neon sign.
Glowed like molten iron.
Glowed like sunshine in honey.—Rosemary H. Jarman
Also see Shined.

Glum
Glum as an oyster.
Glum as an undertaker.—William M. Thackeray
  Also see Dismal, Sad, Unhappy.

Go together
Go together like beer and nuts.
Go together like doughnuts and coffee.
Go together like duck and green peas.
Go together like fish and chips.—Hugh McLeave
Go together like ham and ,eggs.
Go together like love and marriage.
Go together like Mutt and Jeff.
Go together like salt and pepper.
Go together like twin brothers.—T. S. Arthur
  Also see Alike, Similar.

Gold
Gold as bread.—Margaret Mitchell
Gold as ripe wheat.

Golden
Golden as the fruits of autumn.
Golden as the sun.—Philip J. Bailey
Golden as sunlight.—Gustave Flaubert

Gone
Gone as a shadow.—R. D. Blackmore
Gone like a fresh breeze.—George Garrett
Gone like a furious gust of black wind.—William Faulkner
Gone like a morning dream, or like a pile of clouds.—William Wordsworth
Gone like a fart in a whirlwind.—John Madson
Gone like an arrow from a bow.—Emma Marshall
Gone like coins spilled in a gutter.—Anthony Forrest
Gone like dreams that we forget.—William Wordsworth
Gone like fog on a mountain.—Lee Smith
Gone like smoke dissolved in air.—Aaron Hill
Gone like tenants that quit without warning.—Oliver Wendell Holmes
Gone like the wind.—Peter Jenkins
  Also see Disappeared, Vanished.

Gone astray
Gone astray like a horny drunk in a smoky tavern at midnight.
Gone astray like a lost sheep.—*Old Testament*

Good
Good as a feast.
Good as a lifetime railroad pass.—Thomas Thompson
Good as a pie.
Good as gold.—Charles Dickens

Good as his word.—Thomas Hardy
Good as snuff and not half as dusty.

Gossip

Gossip, like ennui, is born of idleness.—Ninon De Lenclos
Gossipped as freely as fishwives.—Anthony Forrest
Far and wide the tale was told, like a snowball growing while it rolled.
    —John Greeleaf Whittier
Fond of gossip as an old woman.—Ivan Turgenev
Stories, like dragons, are hard to kill. If the snake does not, the tale runs
    still.—John Greenleaf Whittier
He told tall tales out of school like a child.—Honore de Balzac

Graceful

Graceful as a bird in flight.
Graceful as a cat.—William M. Raine
Graceful as a deer.
Graceful as a deer on the run.—Tom Wicker
Graceful as a fawn.—Rex Beach
About as graceful as an elephant on roller skates.
About as graceful as an escaping ox.—Dudly Pope
About as graceful as an old man on rollerblades.

Gracious

Gracious as a medieval queen.—Thomas Heywood
Gracious as the morn.—Victor Hugo

Grand

Grand as Barbarossa's beard.
Grand as a Greek statue.—Robert Browning
Grand as the passion felt but never spoken.—Tracy Robinson

Grating

Grating as fingernails on a blackboard.
Grating as a sawblade under the file.—Henrik Ibsen
Grating as shards of broken crockery.—Stephen King

Grave

Grave as a judge.—*Poor Robin's Almanack*
Grave as a mourning hearse.
Grave as an eye dwelling on blood.—George Meredith

Gray

Gray as a banker's vest.—Stephen King
Gray as a dead lake.—T. C. Boyle
Gray as death.—Alfred Alcorn
Gray as March ice.—Stephen King
Gray as slate.
Gray and impassive as a monument.—Tom Wicker

Great

Great as an emperor.—John Gay

Great as God.
Also see Large.

Greedy
Greedy as a fox in a henhouse.
Greedy as a hog.
Also see Selfish, Tight.

Green
Green as a gourd. —John Inzer
Green as an emerald.
Green as frog feathers. —Ivan Doig
Green as goose shit.
Green as grass. —Jeffrey Farnol
Green as peestains in an Irishman's underwear. —Stephen King
Green as poison.
Green as scared shit. —Alfred Alcorn
Green as the Amazon. —Ivan Doig
Green as the frozen essence of emeralds. —Stephen R. Donaldson
Green as the sea.

Gregarious
Gregarious as a flock of geese.
Gregarious as cattle.
Gregarious as seals. —Cecelia Holland

Grew
Grew like a weed. —Phoebe Gray
Grew like Jimson weed in a pile of compost.
Grew like the summer grass. —William Shakespeare
Grew like Topsy. —Harriet Beecher Stowe
Grew like weeds on a neglected tomb. —Percy B. Shelley
Grew up like a wild onion. —Robert R. McCammon
Also see Flourished, Thrived.

Grim
Grim as a hangman. —George MacDonald Fraser
Grim as a judge.
Grim as the Swiss Guard. —Robert Browning
Grim as death.
Also see Ominous, Threatening.

Grimaced
Grimaced like a sow in labor.
Also see Winced.

Grinned
Grinned like a baboon.
Grinned like a basket of chips. —Francis Grose
Grinned like a black bear in heat. —T. C. Boyle
Grinned like a cat eating papaws.

Grinned like a Cheshire cat.
Grinned like a Christian holding four aces. —Ivan Doig
Grinned like a dog with a bone. —George Garrett
Grinned like a gargoyle. —George MacDonald Fraser
Grinned like a greeted boy. —John Updike
Grinned like a horse collar. —Ferrol Sams
Grinned like a jackass eating cockleburs. —Robert Houston
Grinned like a jack-o'-lantern. —Robert Houston
Grinned like a man caught stealing gumdrops from a baby. —Phoebe Gray
Grinned like a mule eating briars.
Grinned like a mule shitting razor blades.
Grinned like a pair of toads on a stream bank. —Owen Ulph
Grinned like a possum eating green persimmons.
Grinned like a skunk eating cabbage.
Grinned like a skunk eating garlic.
Grinned like a well-fed fox.
Grinned and nodded like a mouthful of tenpenny nails. —Richard Bachman
Grinned and nodded like a toy duck. —Jack Matthews
    Also see Smiled.

Gripped
Gripped like a bear trap. —Peter Jenkins
Gripped like a pit bull on a chuck roast. —A. Whitney Brown
Gripped like a vice.
Gripped like iron.
Gripped like steel. —Frederic S. Isham
He gripped the armrests of his seat like a cat on a roller coaster.
    —Robert R. McCammon
    Also see Clung, Held.

Groaned
Groaned like a dying horse. —William Ward
Groaned like a rusty winch. —Owen Ulph
Groaned like an old man with arthritis.

Growled
Growled like a bear.
Growled like a dog at an intruder's pant leg. —T. C. Boyle
Growled like a two-man saw. —T. C. Boyle

Grunted
Grunted like a hungry bear.
Grunted like a pig under a tub. —John Lyly
Grunted like a startled warthog. —Stephen King

Guilty
Guilty as a priest in a whorehouse. —Mario Puzo
Guilty as Cain. —Margaret Mitchell
Guilty as homemade sin.

Haggled

Haggled like a fishwife.
Haggled like an apple-wife. —Robert Louis Stevenson
Haggled like Arabs in a bazaar. —William Pearson
    Also see Bickered, Fought.

Hair

Hair as blond as a chorus girl's. —M. M. Kaye
Hair as curly as a watch spring. —Frederic S. Isham
Hair as gold as ripe barley in the sun. —George Garrett
Hair as stiff as broom straw. —Thomas Thompson
Hair as white and thick as a bristle brush. —Robert R. McCammon
Hair as white as snow. —Lewis Carroll
Hair as wild as a horse's tail. —Margaret Mitchell
Hair crept like dry moss from under the brim of his hat.
Hair cropped close as a cannon ball. —Rosemary H. Jarman
Hair like a bunch of carrots. —Doris Leslie
Hair like an amber wreath. —Samuel Minturn Peck
Hair like cornsilk. —Joan Samson
Hair like moldy hay. —Alfred Noyes
Hair like spilled barley. —T. C. Boyle
Hair like spun glass. —Emma Marshall
Hair like threads of gold. —Scottish ballad
Hair like weeds. —Maurice Hewett
Hair looked like an exploded can of tomato soup.
Hair shined like burnished silver. —Howard Spring
Hair stood out like a scared cat's. —Olive Ann Burns
Hair tangled as a basket of snakes. —Lawrence Sanders
Hair tangled like a golden halo. —Lee Smith
Hair was soft and silvery like the gray mist of the river in the morning.
    —Harold Bell Wright

Hair whiteheaded as a mountain. —Thomas Hardy
Blond hair like a spill of golden flowers. —Robert R. McCammon

Hairy

Hairy as a gorilla in a racoon coat.
Hairy as a highland cow. —George Garrett
Hairy as a mastodon. —Joseph Conrad
Hairy as an ape.

Hand

Hand as clammy as a wet fish.
Hand felt like a bundle of dry sticks in a bag. —George MacDonald Fraser
Hand felt like hardwood with the bark on. —James Sherburn
Hand like a bale of cotton with knuckles. —Arthur Baer
Hand like a bird's claw. —George MacDonald Fraser
Hand like a ham. —Stephen Vincent Benet
Hand like a hand of providence. —Mark Twain
Hand like a side of beef. —Tristan Jones
Hand wet and cold like something fished out of a pond. —T. C. Boyle
Hands as big as hams. —Margaret Mitchell
Hands as cold as ice.
Hands as inanimate as gloves. —Craig Thomas
Hands as rough as nutmeg graters. —Howard Spring
Hands big like the claws of a crab. —Guy de Maupassant
Hands like a bunch of bananas. —R. F. Outcault
Hands like anvils.
Hands like beached fish. —Stephen King
Hands like elephant ears. —Arthur Baer
Hands like pale gloves filled with wet sand.
Hands like pitchforks. —*Arabian Nights*
Hands like rugged bark. —Thomas Hood
Hands like shovels. —John Harris
Hands yellow and waxy like a dead man's. —Margaret Mitchell

Handshake

Handshake like a gloveful of shit.
Handshake like a water pump.
Handshake like it was a pump handle.

Handsome

Handsome as a god. —Henri Troyat
Handsome as a hackman's hat. —Sydney Munden
Handsome as a new stake rope on a thirty-dollar pony. —O. Henry
Handsome as a picture. —Mark Twain
Handsome as a set of solid gold teeth. —Rex Beach
Handsome as a blooded stallion. —Margaret Mitchell
About as handsome as a turnip.
  Also see Attractive.

Handy

Handy as a corkscrew in Kentucky.—J. P. Wilson
Handy as a poker in hell.
Handy as a pouch on a kangaroo.
Handy as a shirt pocket.
About as handy as a bale of hay in a garage.
About as handy as a pig with a musket.
About as handy as a wooden ship in a bottle.
About as handy as an umbrella for a fish.
    Also see Functional, Practical.

Happiness

Happiness is as a butterfly, which when pursued, is always beyond our grasp,
    but which, if you will sit down quietly, may alight upon you.
    —Nathaniel Hawthorne
Happiness is like a newly minted coin, it loses its shine the more it is used.
    —George MacDonald Fraser
Happiness is like a refreshing stream, it flows from heart to heart in endless
    circulation.—Henry Grove
Happiness is like a sunbeam, which the least shadow intercepts.
    —Chinese proverb
Happiness is like manna; it is to be gathered in grains, and enjoyed every
    day.—Tyron Edwards
Happiness is like potato salad, spread it and you've got a picnic.
The rays of happiness, like those of light, are colorless when unbroken.
    —Henry W. Longfellow

Happy

Happy as a baby with its first ice cream cone.
Happy as a bastard on Father's Day.
Happy as a bird in the spring.—William Blake
Happy as a boy at a baseball game.
Happy as a boy with a slingshot in a heaven of greenhouses.
Happy as a bug.—Mark Twain
Happy as a butterfly in a garden full of sunshine and flowers.
    —Louisa May Alcott
Happy as a cat that sees cream.
Happy as a child.—William Wordsworth
Happy as a child in a sandbox.
Happy as a cherrystone clam.—George Garrett
Happy as a clam.
Happy as a clam at high tide.
Happy as a clam at high water.
Happy as a clam in the mud at high water.
Happy as a dead pig in the sunshine.
Happy as a dog with a bone.
Happy as a dog with five tails.
Happy as a dinner bell.—Josh Billings

Happy as a duck in water.
Happy as a fish in water.—Victor Cherbuliez
Happy as a fly in a molasses factory.
Happy as a girl with her dance card full.—Richard Harding Davis
Happy as a gnat in a dog's hind end.
Happy as a gopher in soft ground.
Happy as a high-water clam.—John Gould
Happy as a hog in new slop.
Happy as a june bug.
Happy as a kid in a candy store.
Happy as a kid with a new astronaut suit.
Happy as a king.—John Gay
Happy as a lark.—Anne Brontë
Happy as a lizard on a sun-washed rock.—Dean R. Koontz
Happy as a lord.—Victor Hugo
Happy as a lottery winner.
Happy as a lover.—William Wordsworth
Happy as a maypole.—R. D. Blackmore
Happy as a new millionaire.—Margaret Mitchell
Happy as a pardoned life prisoner.
Happy as a pig eating pancakes.
Happy as a pig in clover.
Happy as a pig in mud.
Happy as a pig in shit.
Happy as a pig in swill.—Robert Lewis Taylor
Happy as a poor man with a bag of gold.—Dinah M. Mulock
Happy as a possum up a persimmon tree.
Happy as a priest at a wedding.—George Moore
Happy as a raccoon in a smokehouse.
Happy as a reprieved thief.—Honore de Balzac
Happy as a schoolgirl going home for the holidays.
    —Guy de Maupassant
Happy as a smiling mule in a blackberry patch.
Happy as a turtledove.
Happy as a wave that dances on the sea.
Happy as a weasel full of hen meat.—"Fred Allen" radio show
Happy as a whore on Saturday night.
Happy as children come from school.—George Gascoigne
Happy as the sunlight.—Thomas Ashe
Happy as two lovers.—F. Hopkinson Smith
Happy and thoughtless as an apple on a tree.—George Garrett
About as happy as a duck in Arizona.
    Also see Cheerful, Gay, Merry.

Hard

Hard as a baked brick.—George Garrett
Hard as a barren stepmother's slap.
Hard as a breastplate.—Bernard Cornwell

Hard as a brick.

Hard as a brick bat.

Hard as a bullet.

Hard as a cannonball. —Wilbur Smith

Hard as a club. —Keith Korman

Hard as a cricket ball.

Hard as a curling stone. —George MacDonald Fraser

Hard as a diamond. —J.R.R. Tolkien

Hard as a file. —Zane Grey

Hard as a first sergeant.

Hard as a hailstone.

Hard as a harlot's smile.

Hard as a hickory nut.

Hard as a millstone. —T. S. Arthur

Hard as a nail.

Hard as a nut.

Hard as pavement. —Rex Beach

Hard as a piece of nether millstone. —*Old Testament*

Hard as a pine knot. —James K. Pauling

Hard as a poor man's pecker. —H. Allen Smith

Hard as a rock.

Hard as a silver dollar. —Dashiell Hammett

Hard as a stone. —T. C. Boyle

Hard as a whore's heart. —Wilbur Smith

Hard as an egg at Easter. —Vincent S. Lean

Hard as an IRS auditor's heart. —Elain Viets, *St. Louis Post Dispatch*

Hard as cement. —Howard Spring

Hard as dried leather. —Robert R. McCammon

Hard as flint. —John Gay

Hard as granite. —William M. Raine

Hard as iron. —Thomas Lodge

Hard as marble.

Hard as nails.

Hard as oak.

Hard as Pharaoh's heart. —Charles E. Van Loan

Hard as rock candy. —Margaret Mitchell

Hard as stone. —John Gay

Hard as tap dancing in a swamp.

Hard as the devil's hangnails. —H. Allen Smith

Hard as the hinges of hell.

Hard as the palm of a ploughman. —William Shakespeare

Hard as the rocks of Dundee.

Hard as the sidewalks of New York.

Hard as three-week-old bread.

Hard as wire. —John Heywood

Hard and stern as the mountains. —J.R.R. Tolkien

Hard-boiled as a picnic egg.

Hard-hearted as the man on the monument. —Saul Balmuth

Hard (difficult)

Hard as a fly resisting a honey pot.—Margaret Mitchell

Hard as a Greek puzzle.

Hard as being good.

Hard as carrying hell in a sack with a hole in it.—Owen Ulph

Hard as catching a greased pig.

Hard as catching a waiter's eye.—*Reader's Digest*

Hard as catching fog in a bag.

Hard as Chinese arithmetic.

Hard as collecting feathers in a hurricane.—Arthur Baer

Hard as describing the taste of an oyster.—Dan Jenkins

Hard as finding a pearl in a hailstorm.

Hard as finding a pin's head in a carload of hay.

Hard as finding a taxi in Manhattan on a rainy night.

Hard as following a mosquito through a mile of fog.—Harold Bell Wright

Hard as for an empty sack to stand upright.—Benjamin Franklin

Hard as getting back last year's taxes.

Hard as grasping a shadow.

Hard as hammering a nail with an egg.

Hard as having a secret Fourth of July celebration.—John T. McCutcheon

Hard as looking for a needle in a bottle of hay.—Robert Louis Stevenson

Hard as making a silk purse out of a sow's ear.

Hard as making love while standing up in a hammock.

Hard as nailing currant jelly to the wall.

Hard as packing barbed wire in a paper bag.—Phoebe Gray

Hard as paddling a coffin across the ocean with a teaspoon.

Hard as passing a bakery shop with the door open.

Hard as peeing into the wind.

Hard as picking fly shit out of pepper.

Hard as poking a cat out from under the porch with a rope.

Hard as pulling a horse out of quicksand.

Hard as pulling a rooster's teeth.

Hard as pulling a soldier off your sister.—*Partridge's*

Hard as pulling eyeteeth.

Hard as pushing a wheelbarrow with rope handles.

Hard as pushing mud.—Olive Ann Burns

Hard as putting a bandage on an eel.

Hard as putting out a forest fire with a mouthful of spit.

Hard as putting pantyhose on a porcupine.—Hattie Bremseth

Hard as putting socks on an octopus.

Hard as raping a rhinocerous.—John Irving

Hard as riding a greased pig and holding on.

Hard as riveting a nail into a custard pie.

Hard as roping the wind.

Hard as selling iceboxes to Eskimos.

Hard as shaving an egg.

Hard as shoveling snow with a pitchfork.—Owen Ulph

Hard as sneaking dawn past a rooster.—Thomas Thompson

Hard as sorting bobcats in a burning barn.
Hard as sorting fly specks from pepper wearing boxing gloves.
Hard as stacking BB's.
Hard as stacking toothpicks in the wind.
Hard as straightening a dog's tail.
Hard as taking a drink from a fire hose.
Hard as teaching a pig to play the trombone.
Hard as teaching a pig to sing.
Hard as throwing a pork chop past a wolf.
Hard as trying to catch the moon in a bushel basket.—Stephen King
Hard as trying to get blood out of a turnip.—English proverb
Hard as trying to go through a revolving door on skis.—Peter DeVries
Hard as trying to poke a piece of wet spaghetti up a wildcat's ass.
Hard as trying to swallow a doorknob.—Stephen King
Hard as weaving eels.—Ivan Doig
Hard to lose as a flea on a hound dog.
Hard to move as a concrete mattress.
Hard up as a journeyman tinker.—Victor Canning
   Also see Complex, Confused.

Hardy
Hardy as a forest pig.—F. P. Northall
Hardy as a mountain pine.
Hardy as highland heather.—W. Dudgeon
   Also see Fit, Healthy.

Harmless
Harmless as a babe.—William Wordsworth
Harmless as a dove.—*New Testament*
Harmless as a fly.
Harmless as a hymn book.—Mark Twain
Harmless as a little child.—T. S. Arthur
Harmless as a paper tiger.—Chinese proverb
Harmless as a pet rabbit.—Stan Hoig
Harmless as a strawberry festival.
Harmless as a Sunday school picnic.
Harmless as rain.—John Irving
Harmless as the turtle dove.—Patrick Brontë
Harmless as the turtle of the woods.—Thomas Otway
   Also see Innocence, Safe.

Harsh
Harsh as a penny whistle.—T. C. Boyle
Harsh as the bitterness of death.—A. C. Swinburne
Harsh as truth.—William L. Garrison

Hated
Hated like a cat and dog.—Thomas Carlyle
Hated like poison.—Rex Beach

Hateful as a one-eyed parrot.—Margaret Mitchell
   Also see Loathesome.

Head

Head as empty as a pumpkin's.
Head as level as a carpenter's plane.—Stephen King
Head like a peeled onion.
Head like a sieve.
Head throbbed like a rotten tooth.—Stephen King
Head throbbed like an ancient refrigerator.—Derek Robinson
Head was carried like a pagan prince.—Margaret Mitchell
Head went around like a top.—Victor Appleton
Head went up sharply like an animal scenting danger.—Margaret Mitchell
She held her head up like a queen.—Mark Twain

Healthy

Healthy as a dragon.—Chinese proverb
Healthy as a horse.
Healthy as a May hedge in bloom.—Arthur Conan Doyle
Healthy as a May morning.
   Also see Fit, Hardy.

Heart

Heart as big as a whale.
Heart as cold as stone.
Heart as warm as a desert storm.—Ogden Nash
Heart as calloused as a whore's butt.—Michael Deane
Heart banged like a Boy Scout drum.—Derek Robinson
Heart beat like a drum.
Heart beat like a hammer.
Heart beat like a rabbit's.
Heart beat like a sledgehammer.—Robert Louis Stevenson
Heart beat like a trip-hammer.—Zane Grey
Heart beat like the wings of a caged bird.—Robert R. McCammon
Heart fluttered like a bird.—Robert Louis Stevenson
Heart fluttered like the wings of a dying bird.—Doris Leslie
Heart full of sunshine as a hay field.—Josh Billings
Heart is like the sky, a part of heaven, but changes night and day too, like the sky.—Lord Byron
Heart leaped like a trout in a brook.—George Garrett
Heart like a lion.
Heart like lead.—Victor Appleton
Heart pounded like an oil derrick.—James Patterson
Heart-lifting as trumpets.—Stephen R. Donaldson
Heart was thumping like a paddlewheel.—George MacDonald Fraser
My heart wants to beat like the wings of the birds that rise from the lake to the trees.—Oscar Hammerstein, "The Sound of Music"
My man has a heart as hard as a rock dropped in the sea.—W. C. Handy, "St. Louis Blues"

Hearty

Hearty as a handshake. —T. C. Boyle
Hearty as a young dog. —Jack Matthews
Hearty as an oak. —Samuel Foote

Heavy

Heavy as a boarding house dumpling.
Heavy as a bucket of sand.
Heavy as a cannon. —Robert R. McCammon
Heavy as a cold tortilla. —Thelma Strabel
Heavy as a dead elephant.
Heavy as a millstone.
Heavy as a rock.
Heavy as a sack of cement.
Heavy as a tombstone. —Dashiell Hammett
Heavy as a wet wash of bedclothes. —Douglas C. Jones
Heavy as an elephant's balls. —William Dieter
Heavy as bread dough. —Ivan Doig
Heavy as doom.
Heavy as granite.
Heavy as lead. —Thomas Hardy
Heavy as steel.
Heavy as the hand of death. —Charles Dickens
Heavy as the sands of the sea. —*Old Testament*

Held

Held on like a bull terrier. —Abe Martin
Held on like a bulldog. —Margaret Mitchell
Held on like a possum. —Ferrol Sams
Held on like a summer cold. —George Ade
    Also see Clung, Hung.

Help

Helpful as a life raft. —C. L. Skelton.
Helpful as the Salvation Army.
About as much help as a brother-in-law out of work. —Robert L. Hunter
About as much help as a high wind in a prairie fire.

Helpless

Helpless as a baby.
Helpless as a blind man. —William Wordsworth
Helpless as a child. —Robert Service
Helpless as a cod on a fishmonger's slab. —George MacDonald Fraser
Helpless as a dove caught in the coils of a snake. —Harold Bell Wright
Helpless as a kitten up a tree.
Helpless as a lame beggar. —Ouida
Helpless as a plant without water. —F. Hopkinson Smith
Helpless as a puppy. —Jack Matthews

Helpless as a turtle on its back. —O. Henry
Helpless as an infant. —Mary J. Holmes
> *Also see* Powerless, Weak.

Hesitated

Hesitated like a bather about to make his plunge. —Thomas Hardy
Hesitated like a submissive voice of an inferior. —Sir Walter Scott
Hesitant as a recoiling groom. —Douglas C. Jones

High

High as a cat's back at a dog show.
High as a Georgia pine.
High as a giraffe. —Gene Stratton-Porter
High as a giraffe's balls.
High as a goosed gazelle. —James Goldman
High as a hawk's nest. —Robert L. Hunter
High as a kite.
High as a mountain. —Jeffery Farnol
High as a steeple.
High as an elephant's eye. —Oscar Hammerstein, *Oklahoma*
High as heaven. —*Old Testament*
High as hip waders.
High as Lindbergh.
High as steam off a cold cow turd.
High as the first limb on a coconut tree.
High as the flag on the Fourth of July. —Oscar Hammerstein, *South Pacific*
High as the price of gold. —Josh Billings.
High as the second shelf. —John Ehle
High as the sky.
High as the stars. —Thomas Carlyle
> *Also see* Drunk, Tight.

Hips

Hips as big as watermelons. —Robert R. McCammon
Hips like hills of sand. —*Arabian Nights*

Hissed

Hissed like a barrel of snakes. —John Irving
Hissed like a branding iron.
Hissed like a rocket.
Hissed like a snake. —Victor Hugo
Hissed like a steam kettle.
Hissed like a steam valve. —Tom DeHaven
Hissed like a viper. —Sigmund Krasinski

Hit

Hit him like a bolt from the blue.
Hit him like a locomotive.
Hit him like a Mack truck.
Hit him like a slap in the face.
Hit him like a ton of bricks.

Hoarse

Hoarse as a bullfrog.—John Inzer
Hoarse as a crow.—Robert Louis Stevenson
Hoarse as a sidewalk hawker.

Holed up

Holed up like a badger.—Mary Stewart
Holed up like the James Gang.

Hollered

Hollered like a bull moose.—Robert R. McCammon
Hollered like a branded calf.
Hollered like a stuck pig.—Robert Houston
    Also see Bellowed, Hooted, Howled, Screamed, Yelled.

Hollow

Hollow as a gun barrel.
Hollow as a log.
Hollow as an actor's laugh.—Gallet Burgess
Hollow as the soul of an echo.
    Also see Bare, Empty.

Holy

Holy as a Baptist preacher.—Douglas C. Jones
Holy as the Pope.
    Also see Pious.

Homely

Homely as a basket of chips.—*Massachusetts Spy*
Homely as a hedge.
Homely as a horse.—T. C. Boyle
Homely as a mud fence.
Homely as a stump.
Homely as an Idaho potato.—Pete Dexter
Homely as the queen of spades.
    Also see Ugly.

Honest

Honest as a mirror.
Honest as an open book.
Honest as gold teeth.
Honest as steel.—Jack Fuller
Honest as the day is long.
Honest as the skin between his brows.—William Shakespeare
Honest as the sun.—Phoebe Gray
    Also see Reliable, True.

Hooted

Hooted like butchers on a three-day drunk.—T. C. Boyle
Hooted and danced like pardoned criminals.—T. C. Boyle
    Also see Hollered, Yelled.

Horny

Horny as a boar mink in May. —John Madson
Horny as a brass band.
Horny as a horned toad.
Horny as a tomcat. —T. C. Boyle
Horny as a traffic jam on 42nd Street.
Horny as a three-peckered billy goat.
Horny as the town bull. —George MacDonald Fraser
Horny, wild, and crotch-sore as drovers descending on Abilene. —T. C. Boyle
   Also see Fornicated, Hot, Lecherous, Passionate, Randy.

Hot (high temperature, horny, or illegal)

Hot as a bank robber's pistol.
Hot as a basted turkey. —Will Carleton
Hot as a blast furnace.
Hot as a blister. —Ferrol Sams
Hot as a buzzard's crotch.
Hot as a camel saddle.
Hot as a coal.
Hot as a depot stove.
Hot as a fever
Hot as a fire in a pepper mill.
Hot as a fire sale.
Hot as a firecracker.
Hot as a fired-off pistol.
Hot as a four-alarm fire. —H. C. Witmer
Hot as a Fourth of July rocket.
Hot as a half-chewed jalapeno. —Dan Jenkins
Hot as a June bride. —Peter Jenkins
Hot as a kiln.
Hot as a pepper.
Hot as a pistol.
Hot as a poker. —Richard Bachman
Hot as a polar bear at a cookout.
Hot as a pone cake.
Hot as a scalded dog.
Hot as a scorpion's tail.
Hot as a stolen car.
Hot as a summer skunk.
Hot as a sweatband in a fireman's helmet.
Hot as a tar road in Tennessee.
Hot as a two-dollar pistol.
Hot as a volcano.
Hot as a whore at a monks' convention.
Hot as a whore's pillow. —Chuck Yeager
Hot as an Arkansas summer.
Hot as an iron foundry. —T. C. Boyle
Hot as an iron pump handle on a July noon. —Frederick O'Brien

Hot as an oven. —*Old Testament*
Hot as bricks in a kiln.
Hot as coals in a banked stove. —Stephen King
Hot as coals of glowing fire. —William Shakespeare
Hot as fire. —Zane Grey
Hot as fresh milk.
Hot as Georgia asphalt.
Hot as grits on a griddle.
Hot as hades.
Hot as hate. —Hamlin Garland
Hot as hay harvesting. —Brian Melbancke
Hot as hell. —A. C. Swinburne
Hot as hell on a holiday. —Ben Johnson *Chisum*
Hot as hellfire. —John Dryden
Hot as hell's half acre.
Hot as hell's kitchen.
Hot as high school love.
Hot as molten lead. —William Shakespeare
Hot as mustard.
Hot as nine acres of onions.
Hot as satan.
Hot as teenage love.
Hot as the bottom of a kettle.
Hot as the hinges of hell.
Hot as the inside of a motorman's glove in July.
Hot and sticky as Calcutta. —George MacDonald Fraser
Hot and windless as a furnace room. —Cecelia Holland
    Also see Warm, Horny.

Hovered
Hovered like a hummingbird.
Hovered like a moth around a flame.
Hovered like a moth intoxicated with light. —John Galsworthy
Hovered like a surgical student.
Hovered like a worried bank examiner. —R. F. Delderfield

Howled
Howled like a banshee.
Howled like a cat in heat. —T. C. Boyle
Howled like a hurt cat. —Stephen King
Howled like a thousand demons. —George Eliot
Howled like a wild beast. —Rudyard Kipling
Howled like a wolf. —Charles Dickens
Howled like hounds.
    Also see Bellowed, Hollered, Shrieked, Yelled.

Huddled together
Huddled together like sheep. —Edward Eggleston

Huddled together like survivors packed on a raft. —Anthony Forrest
   Also see Gathered, Hung together.

Humble

Humble as a grateful almsman.
Humble as a Jesuit to his superior. —Samuel Butler
Humble as a lamb. —Alexander Barclay
   Also see Meek, Modest.

Hummed

Hummed like a beehive.
Hummed like a cobbler.
Hummed like a hive of bees. —Joaquin Miller
Hummed like a hive of newly disturbed bees. —Margaret Mitchell
Hummed like a well-oiled engine. —James Sherburn
Hummed like a virgin in a choir.
   Also see Buzzed.

Hung

Hung in the air like a date on a calendar. —Dan Jenkins
Hung in the air like the last bars of a concerto. —Stefen Kanfer
Hung like a stuck pig. —George MacDonald Fraser
Hung like a tail. —George Meredith
Hung like an icicle on a Dutchman's beard. —William Shakespeare
Hung limply like a sock. —Wilbur Smith
Hung on like a summer cold.
Hung on like warts on a toad.
Hung over him like a pall. —Frederic S. Isham
Hung over him like a thundercloud. —Robert Louis Stevenson
   Also see Clung, Held.

Hung (anatomy)

Hung like a hamster.
Hung like a horse.
Hung like Trigger.

Hung together

Hung together like a bee on a honeysuckle vine.
Hung together like a pack of horse thieves. —James Jones
Hung together like vultures guarding a carcass. —D. Giardina
Hung together like burrs. —John Ray
Hung together like bats in a steeple. —Robert Louis Stevenson
Hung together like summer pig manure.

Hungry

Hungry as a badger.
Hungry as a bear.
Hungry as a bitch wolf. —Stephen Longstreet
Hungry as a church mouse.
Hungry as a dog.
Hungry as a horse.

Hungry as a hound.
Hungry as a hunter.—Charles Lamb
Hungry as a lion.—Jeffery Farnol
Hungry as a polecat.
Hungry as a prairie fire.—Frank Waters
Hungry as a tiger.—Jeffery Farnol
Hungry as a tired hound.—*The Christmas Prince*
Hungry as a winter wolf.—Samuel T. Coleridge
Hungry as a wolf.
Hungry as a working mule.—Tom Wicker
Hungry as if it were the last day of Lent.—Henri Murger
Hungry as two bears in a cave.
   Also see Appetite, Ate.

Hunted
Hunted like a fox.
Hunted like a stag.
Hunted like an escaped prisoner.
   Also see Searched.

Hurried
Hurried as if catching a train.—Frederic S. Isham
Hurried like one who had always a multiplicity of tasks on hand.
   —Charlotte Brontë
   Also see Fast, Flew, Off, Swift, Took off, Went.

Hurt
Hurt like a fiery razor.—George MacDonald Fraser
Hurt like a hose clamp on a hemorrhoid.
Hurt like a mule's kick.—Erskine Caldwell
Hurt like a stubbed toe.
Hurt like a toothache.
Hurt like a wound.—Ivan Doig
Hurt like an earache.—Tom Wicker
Hurt like torture.
   Also see Ached, Pain, Sore.

Idle

Idle as a December wind in a dumbwaiter shaft.—Don Marquis
Idle as a summer noon.—Omar Khayam
Idle as an anvil.
Idle and mean as a collier's whelp.—Rudyard Kipling
Idleness is like a disease that must be combated.—Samuel Johnson
Idleness is like the nightmare; the moment you begin to stir yourself you shake
   it off.—*Punch*, 1853
   Also see Impassive, Inert, Lazy, Lifeless.

Ignorant

Ignorant as a child.—Henry David Thoreau
Ignorant as dirt.—William Shakespeare
   Also see Dumb, Stupid.

Illusive

Illusive as a dream.
Illusive as a shadow.—Zane Grey

Immaculate

Immaculate as a sheet of white paper.—Samuel Foote
Immaculate as an angel.
Immaculate as fresh snow.—T. N. Page
   Also see Clean.

Immense

Immense as Texas.
Immense as the oceans.
Immense as the sea.—A. C. Swinburne
   Also see Big, Large, Vast.

Immobile

Immobile as a sphinx's face.
Immobile as an iron lawn jockey.—James Jones

Immobile as granite markers in a city park.—Douglas C. Jones
Immobile as stone.—Douglas C. Jones
   Also see Firm, Fixed, Immovable, Stiff.

Immortal

Immortal as a tomcat.
Immortal as the stars.—Matilde Blind
Immortal as the sun.—Arthur Symons
   Also see Eternal.

Immovable

Immovable as a block of granite.—Mark Twain
Immovable as a setter at the scent.—O. Henry
Immovable as soldiers in a painting.—Tom Wicker
   Also see Firm, Fixed, Immobile, Rigid.

Impartial

Impartial as bullets in a battle.
Impartial as a jury.
Impartial as the grave.—Rudyard Kipling
   Also see Honest.

Impassive

Impassive as a mannequin.—Charles McCarry
Impassive as a stone.—Lee Smith
Impassive as a weasel with a rat in its mouth.—T. C. Boyle
Impassive as an Anglican congregation.
   Also see Idle, Inert, Lifeless.

Impatient

Impatient as a boy.—Sigmund Krasinski
Impatient as a bull at a gate.
Impatient as a hound waiting for the hunt to begin.—James Sherburn
Impatient as a hungry infant.—Sydney Munden
   Also see Anxious, Nervous.

Impenetrable

Impenetrable as chaos.—Stephen R. Donaldson
Impenetrable as deaf ears.
Impenetrable as granite.—Ouida
Impenetrable as rhinoceri.—Ouida
Impenetrable as rock.—Mark Twain

Impersonal

Impersonal as a cyclone.
Impersonal as doom.—Charles Willeford

Impossible

Impossible as counting waves.
Impossible as having your cake and eating it too.
Impossible as for a lawyer to feel compassion gratis.
Impossible as scratching your ear with your elbow.

Impossible as selling your cow and expecting to have the milk too.
  —Dutch proverb

Independent

Independent as a bird.
Independent as a Gypsy in his caravan.
Independent as a hog on ice.
Independent as the moon.—Ivan Doig
  Also see Personal, Privacy.

Indifferent

Indifferent as if he was ordering up eggs.—Mark Twain
Indifferent as thunder.—Jack Fuller
  Also see Aloof, Arrogant, Cool, Remote.

Indistinct

Indistinct as language uttered in a dream.—William Cowper
Indistinct as water is in water.—William Shakespeare
  Also see Faint, Pale.

Individual

Individual as a fingerprint.—Stephen King
Individual as a signature.
  Also see Personal, Privacy.

Inert

Inert as a drowned rat.—Howard Jacobson
Inert as stone.
  Also see Idle, Impassive, Lifeless.

Inescapable

Inescapable as death.
Inescapable as taxes.
  Also see Inevitable.

Inevitable

Inevitable as a dog at a hydrant.
Inevitable as being born.
Inevitable as death.
Inevitable as taxes.
Inevitable as predestination.
Inevitable as the birds sing.—Harold Bell Wright
  Also see Inescapable.

Inexorable

Inexorable as a grave.
Inexorable as a gravedigger's spade.—Rosemary H. Jarman
  Also see Relentless, Resolute, Unyielding.

Infamous

Infamous as Dillinger.

Infamous as Hitler.
Infamous as hell. —Earl of Rochester

Infectious
Infectious as spider poison.
Infectious as the bite of an adder.

Inflexible
Inflexible as a granite block.
Inflexible as an oak. —Oliver Goldsmith
> *Also see* Contrary, Firm, Fixed, Immobile, Resolute, Stiff, Stubborn, Unyielding.

Informal
Informal as a honky-tonk.
Informal as a Polish wedding.
> *Also see* Casual.

Innocence
Innocence is like an umbrella; when once we've lost it we must never hope to see it again. —*Punch*
Innocent as a choir.
Innocent as a cloistered nun.
Innocent as a babe. —Robert Browning
Innocent as a bluebird on a manure pile. —Ivan Doig
Innocent as a child. —Oliver Goldsmith
Innocent as a devil of two years old. —English proverb
Innocent as a dove.
Innocent as a goddam daisy. —Ivan Doig
Innocent as a lamb.
Innocent as a newborn babe. —Honore de Balzac
Innocent as a ten-year-old.
Innocent as an angel. —Honore de Balzac
Innocent as bedtime stories for children.
Innocent as Mary's little lamb. —Stephen King
Innocent as Snow White.
Innocent as the sweetest babe in heaven. —Thomas Hardy
> *Also see* Pure.

Inoffensive
Inoffensive as a daisy.
Inoffensive as a glass of water. —Victor Hugo
> *Also see* Harmless, Innocence.

Insecure
Insecure as a canary in a high wind.
Insecure as a chicken in a cyclone.

Insensitive
Insensitive as a wood tick. —Richard Bachman

Insensitive as the IRS.
Also see Impassive.

Insignificant
Insignificant as a blank spot on the paper of life.—C. C. Skelton
Insignificant as a fart in a windstorm.
Insignificant as a flea on a lion's hip.—George MacDonald Fraser
Insignificant as a hill of beans.
Insignificant as an empty beer can.
Insignificant as peeing in the Atlantic Ocean.
Also see Pointless.

Insistent
Insistent as a fist.—Stephen R. Donaldson
Insistent as depression.
Insistent as remorse.—Victor Hugo
Also see Persistant.

Inspected
Inspected like a chimpanzee for fleas.
Inspected like a mare at auction.

Intangible
Intangible as a shadow.—Honore de Balzac
Intangible as smoke.—Robert R. McCammon
Intangible as a thought.
Also see Elusive.

Intelligent
Intelligent as a Rhodes scholar.
About as intelligent as a bundle of shawls.—Henry James
Also see Smart.

Intense
Intense as a bulldog.
Intense as life.—Theodore Winthrop.
Intense as a cat following a rolling ball of yarn.—Ira Berkow, *New York Times*
Also see Deep.

Intent
Intent as a cannibal at breakfast.—T. C. Boyle
Intent as a cat.—Mark Twain
Intent as a salesperson.
Also see Serious.

Interest
About as much interest as a hog has in mutual funds.—Stephen King
About as much interest as a donkey has in a player piano.
Also see Exciting.

Intimate

Intimate as a love letter.
Intimate as a stain on a bedsheet.
Intimate as sardines in a can.
Also see Close, Personal, Privacy.

Intricate

Intricate as the inside of a watch.
Intricate as the rings around an onion. —John Goldman

Irish

Irish as Paddy.
Irish as Paddy's pig.
Irish as whiskey in coffee. —Hugh McLeave

Irresistible

Irresistible as a cataclysm. —Stephen R. Donaldson
Irresistible as a rhumba.
Irresistible as chocolate.
Irresistible as the apple in the garden. —James Goldman

Irrevocable

Irrevocable as a haircut. —*Reader's Digest*
Irrevocable as death. —Charlotte Brontë
Irrevocable as paid taxes.

Irritable

Irritable as a tired child.
Irritable as a tired donkey. —D. Giardina
Irritable and depressed as an old dog with boils.

Irritating

Irritating as jock itch.
Irritating as railroad station toilet paper.
Irritating as red underwear to a bull. —Gore Vidal
Irritating as tight shoes.

Isolated

Isolated as an abandoned lighthouse. —Ferrol Sams
Isolated as shipwrecked mariners. —Margaret Mitchell
Also see Desolate, Distant, Far, Remote.

Itched

Itched like hemorrhoids.
Itched like the pox.
Itchy as a barrel of live muskrats.
Itchy as poison ivy.
Also see Irritating.

Jabbed

Jabbed at his heart like a knife thrust.—Margaret Mitchell
Jabbed at his mind like a lightning bolt.—Robert R. McCammon

Jabbered

Jabbered like a camel peddler at a bazaar.—T. C. Boyle
Jabbered like crows.
Jabbered like sparrows.
> *Also see* Babbled, Chattered, Prated.

Jaw

Jaw like a flatiron.—Maurice Hewlett
Jaw like a nutcracker.
Jaw like a vice.
Jaw set like frozen yogurt.—George MacDonald Fraser
Jaws as strong as iron.—Robert Louis Stevenson
Jaws like a rat trap.

Jealous

Jealous as a barren wife.—Richard Congreve
Jealous as a couple of hairdressers.—R. C. Trench
Jealous as a newly marked woman at a ball.—Charles J. Apperley
Jealous as a Spanish miser.—Charles Macklin
Jealous as tomcats.—Gerald Seymour

Jerked

Jerked like a deputation of spastics.—Cormac McCarthy
Jerked like a puppy on a leash.
Jerked like the lid of a boiling pot.—Bliss Carman
Jerked his head up and down like Punch.—George MacDonald Fraser

Jerky

Jerky as a ride on a buckboard.
Jerky as a roller coaster ride.

Jingled
Jingled like a crate of broken crockery. —W. J. Locke
Jingled like Christmas bells.
Jingled like rattling handcuffs. —Ivan S. Cobb

Joy
Joy as simple as the wildflowers. —George Garrett
Joy leaped within me like a trout in a brook. —George Garrett
Joy rises in me like a summer morn. —Samuel T. Coleridge
Joyful as a nest.
Joyful as a salvation. —Tom Wicker
Joyful as flowers when they are filled to the brim with dew.
   Also see Gay, Happy, Merry.

Jumped
Jumped as if he'd been shot. —Louis L'Amour
Jumped like a bird for a berry.
Jumped like a bottle bobbing in the sea. —Robert Adelman
Jumped like a frightened rabbit. —Erskine Caldwell
Jumped like a hen on a hot stove. —Tom Wicker
Jumped like a jerked puppet.
Jumped like a popcorn kernel bursting from a heated pan. —Dean R. Koontz
Jumped like a rabbit diving for its warren.
Jumped like a released jack-in-the-box. —Joan Samson
Jumped like a snap beetle. —Ferrol Sams
Jumped like an old dog that had been kicked. —Stephen King
Jumped like he had a bee up his buns. —Tom Wicker
Jumped like St. Vitus dance. —George MacDonald Fraser
Jumped around like a fairgrounds ride. —Derek Robinson
Jumped around like a toad in a thunderstorm.
Jumped and writhed like a spider on a burning log. —T. C. Boyle
Jumped at it like a trout at a mayfly.
Jumped on it like a dog on a bone.
Jumped on it like a duck on a june bug.
Jumped up like a squirrel from behind the log. —Rudyard Kipling
   Also see Bolted, Leaped, Sprung up.

Jumpy
Jumpy as a cat. —Rudyard Kipling
Jumpy as a cat with a can tied to its tail. —Dean R. Koontz
Jumpy as a cricket. —George MacDonald Fraser
Jumpy as a frog in a frying pan.
Jumpy as a kangaroo on a trampoline.
Jumpy as a kitten. —Doris Leslie
Jumpy as a pea on a drum.
Jumpy as a trampoline man. —Hugh McLeave
Jumpy as a virgin at a prison rodeo. —TV show, "Golden Girls"
   Also see Edgy, Fidgeted, Nervous, Restless, Tense, Uneasy.

Keen

Keen as a hawk. —Thomas Hood
Keen as a razor. —John Gay
Keen as a spear. —Sidney Lanier
Keen as a sword. —Rudyard Kipling
Keen as a sword's edge. —A. C. Swinburne
Keen as a weasel on the scent of a stricken bird. —T. C. Boyle
Keen as hate.
Keen as hunger.
Keen as mustard.
Keen as steel. —Ovid
    Also see Sharp.

Kind

Kind as a lover's kiss. —Laurence Hope
Kind as Christ.
Kind as love. —Richard L. Sheil
Kind as Santa Claus. —Oscar Hammerstein, *South Pacific*
About as kind as Ivan the Terrible. —Donald McCaig
Kindness, like grain, increases by sowing. —English proverb
    Also see Amiable, Cordial.

Kinky

Kinky as a bedspring. —Stephen King
Kinky as a phone cord.
Kinky as Hollywood sex.

Kissed

Kissed like a novice French whore. —George MacDonald Fraser
Kissed like a volcano that's hot. —Elvis Presley and Otis Blackwell,
    "All Shook Up"
Kisses as unctuous as oil. —Francis S. Saltus
Kissing a man without a beard is like eating soup without salt.

When you kissed me I lit up like a four-alarm fire.—I. A. L. Diamond, "Some Like it Hot"

Kneeled

Kneeled like a nymph.—George MacDonald Fraser
Kneeled like the mermaid of Copenhagen.
Knelt like a graceful virgin at her altar rites.—Rex Beach

Knew

Knew him like a brother.
Knew it like a book.
Knew it like the back of his hand.
Knew it like the palm of his hand.—Robert Louis Stevenson

Knocked

Knocked on the door like a storm trooper.
Knocked like a yellowhammer.—Ferrol Sams

Labored

Labored as long as a farmhand at harvest.—George Garrett
Labored like a cotton picker.
Labored like a cow in milk.—George MacDonald Fraser
Labored like a galley slave.
Labored like a madman.
Labored like a thresher.—Beaumont and Fletcher
Labored like a tramp freighter in a heavy sea.—E. D. Price
   Also see Worked.

Laid

Laid down together like the lion and the lamb.—Frederic S. Isham
Laid like a blanket.—Phillip McCutchan
Laid like a drunk in a gutter.
Laid like a wax dummy.
Laid out like a rug.
Laid out like a hog for scalding.—Jack Matthews
Laid there like a turd in a dead eddy.

Large

Large as a cavern.
Large as a log of maple.—"Yankee Doodle"
Large as a sapling.—Stephen R. Donaldson
Large as life.—Zane Grey
Large as life and twice as natural.—G. F. Northall
   Also see Big, Immense, Vast.

Lasted

Lasted like iron.—Oliver Wendell Holmes
Lasted about as long as a case of beer at a teamster's picnic.
Lasted about as long as a keg of cider at a barn raising.—Alfred Henry Lewis
Lasted about as long as a snowball in hades.—William M. Raine

Lasting as the pyramids.—Agnes Repplier
Also see Enduring, Permanent, Stable.

Laughed

Laughed like a demon.—Robert R. McCammon
Laughed like a drain.
Laughed like a fool.
Laughed like a hyena.
Laughed like a loon.
Laughed like a maudlin fool.—Zane Grey
Laughed like he had feathers in his shoes.
Laughed like knives grating against a whetstone.—T. C. Boyle
Laughed like Woody Woodpecker.
Laughter flew like sparks.—Robert R. McCammon
Her laughter was like the tinkle of silver bells.—Rex Beach

Lawless

Lawless as the town bull.
Lawless as the sea or wind.—Edmund Waller
Lawless as the storming wind.—William Wilkie

Lazy

Lazy as a day in June.
Lazy as a fat cat.
Lazy as a hound dog.
Lazy as a lobster.
Lazy as a panther stretching in the sun.—Margaret Mitchell
Lazy as a Sunday morning.
Lazy as a toad at the bottom of a well.
Lazy as a toad in a damp hole.—Owen Ulph
Lazy as a village clock.—Marcel Proust
Lazy as an old cat.—George Garrett
Lazy as Joe the marine, who laid down his musket to sneeze.
Lazy as Ludlam's dog that leaned his head against the wall to bark.
	—Thomas Fuller
Lazy as the tinker who laid down his bag to fart.
So lazy he wouldn't pull a soldier off his mother.—*Partridge's*
Also see Idle, Inert, Lifeless.

Leaks

Leaked like a mule pissing on granite.—Owen Ulph
Leaked like a sieve.
The United States government leaks like a rusty tin can.
	—David Brinkley, ABC-TV

Lean

Lean as a bird dying in the snow.—Emile Zola
Lean as a dog in Lent.
Lean as a greyhound.—Peter Jenkins
Lean as a lance.

Lean as a lantern.—William Langland
Lean as a lath.—Thomas Heywood
Lean as a lizard.—James Smith
Lean as a rake.—John Gay
Lean as a sapling.—Keith Korman
Lean as a skeleton.—Thomas Shadwell
Lean as a snake.
Lean as a walking stick.—Robert Bausch
Lean as a whipcord.—Norman Mailer
Lean and thin as a fallen leaf.—George Garrett
     Also see Bony, Gaunt, Skinny, Slender, Thin.

Leaned

Leaned like a drunk against a lamppost.—Ivan Doig
Leaned like a man on a hillside.
Leaned on him like a wounded man.—George Garrett

Leaped

Leaped like a dancer in a show.—John Ehle
Leaped like a hart [stag].—Howard Spring
Leaped like a shot from a gun.—Phoebe Gray
Leaped like a shot rabbit.—R. D. Blackmore
Leaped like a slice of bread from a toaster.
Leaped like spawning salmon at a waterfall.
Leaped like a spring released.—John Updike
Leaped like a stung whippet.—George MacDonald Fraser
Leaped like a trout in May.—Rudyard Kipling
Leaped like a young rabbit.—Gary Jennings
     Also see Bolted, Jumped, Sprung up.

Lecherous

Lecherous as a billy goat.
Lecherous as a ferret.
Lecherous as a mink.
Lecherous as a monkey.—William Shakespeare
Lecherous as a sparrow.—Rosemary H. Jarman
     Also see Amorous, Horny, Passionate, Randy.

Leered

Leered at me with eyes askance like a seducer.—Friedrich Nietzsche
Leered like a satyr.—William M. Thackeray
     Also see Glared.

Left

Left like a beaten army.
Left like a castaway on a rock.
Left like a wet rag.
Left like rats deserting a sinking ship.—Doris Leslie
     Also see Went off, Went out.

. . . .
Legs
Legs as sweet as a preacher's dream. —Ivan Doig
Legs braced like stone columns. —Rex Beach
Legs felt like two lengths of rope. —George Garrett
Legs like Betty Grable.
Legs like broomsticks. —Ferrol Sams
Legs like hourglasses.
Legs like jelly.
Legs like piano legs.
Legs like rubber.
Legs like stilts.
Legs like the siding slats of a tobacco shed. —John Updike
Legs looked like they were full of doorknobs.
Legs numb as in a nightmare. —Margaret Mitchell
Legs worked like hard-driven pistons. —Margaret Mitchell
Ankles and calves thick as young trees. —Robert R. McCammon
Shins as thin as a pair of penholders. —Robert W. Chambers

Lengthy
Lengthy as a lord mayor's show. —Howard Spring
Lengthy as a Fidel Castro speech.
> *Also see* Long.

Liberal
Liberal as a man helping himself to strawberry jam. —Anthony Forrest
Liberal as the air. —William Shakespeare
> *Also see* Free.

Lied
Lied like a butcher's dog.
Lied like a carnival barker. —Robert Bausch
Lied like a charlatan. —Honore de Balzac
Lied like a dog.
Lied like a gas meter. —Harold Brighouse
Lied like a rug.
Lied like a fortune teller.
Lied like a truth. —William Shakespeare
Lied like an auctioneer.
Lied like old people fuck. —Richard Bachman
> *Also see* Crooked, Deceitful, Dishonest.

Lifeless
Lifeless as a collapsed rubber ball.
Lifeless as a park bench bum. —John Irwin
Lifeless as a rag doll. —Vincent Bugliosi
Lifeless as a string of dead fish. —G. K. Chesterton
Lifeless as a wig. —James Sherburn
Lifeless as the grave.
> *Also see* Idle, Inert.

Light

Light as a balloon.—Thomas Hardy
Light as a bundle of air.—Cecelia Holland
Light as a cat's tread.—William M. Raine
Light as a cobweb.—R. D. Blackmore
Light as a cork.—Henry James
Light as a drum.—John Gay
Light as a falling leaf.—Tom Wicker
Light as a feather.—Sophocles
Light as a fly.
Light as a ghost.—Ivan Doig
Light as a leaf.
Light as a monkey.—Ernest Hemingway
Light as a nymph.—Francoise Chandernagor
Light as a puffball of seed.—George Garrett
Light as a sack of feathers.
Light as a snowflake.—Austin Dobson
Light as air.—Henry Fielding
Light as an aspen leaf.
Light as dandelion down.—Philip H. Savage
Light as down.
Light as fairy footsteps.—Evan McCall
Light as gossamer.—Thomas Carlyle
Light as milkweed.—T. C. Boyle
Light as morning cobwebs on the grass.—Austin Dobson
Light as the singing bird that wings the air.—Alfred Tennyson
Light as the spider's silken lair.
Light as the spray that disperses.—A. C. Swinburne
Light as thistledown.
Light as whippped cream.
Light-footed as a hare.—H. H. Boyesen
Lighthearted as a boy.—Richard Hovey
Light on her feet as a mockingbird.—Tom Wicker

Limber

Limber as a dishrag.
Limber as a watch chain.
About as limber as a hole in an anvil.—Owen Ulph
About as limber as a rail spike.
About as limber as a steel fence post.
    Also see Lithe, Supple.

Limp

Limp as a bag of oats.—Elbert Hubbard
Limp as a bath towel.
Limp as a boned fish.—J.R.R. Tolkien
Limp as a chewed rag.—Rudyard Kipling
Limp as a day-old fish.—Cecelia Holland
Limp as a dishrag.

Limp as a fileted fish.—Lawrence Sanders
Limp as a glove.
Limp as a rag.
Limp as a rag doll.
Limp as a wet noodle.
    Also see Loose, Soft, Supple.

Limped
Limped like a charity ward in action.—T. C. Boyle
Limped like a man with the gout.
Limped like a sore-footed soldier.

Lingered
Lingered like a bailiff.—Charles Dickens
Lingered like a skunk's odor.
Lingered like a toothache.
Lingered like an echoing gong.—James Jones
Lingered like an old faith.
Lingered like an old melody.
Lingered like an unloved guest.—Percy B. Shelley
Lingered like hopeless love without despair.—Rufus Dawes

Lips
Lips as wide as a Patton tank.—Robert R. McCammon
Lips as white as a dead man's.—Howard Jacobson
Lips like maraschino cherries.
Lips red as a rose.—Geoffrey Chaucer
Lips so warm and sweet like wine.—Andy Razaf, "Stompin' at the Savoy"
His lips felt as big as a goose-down pillow.—Robert R. McCammon
    Also see Face.

Listened
Listened like a dove that listens to its mate alone.—C. G. Rossetti
Listened like a turkey for the mating call.

Lit up
Lit up like a ballroom.—T. C. Boyle
Lit up like a carnival ride.—Robert Bausch
Lit up like a cathedral.
Lit up like a Christmas tree.
Lit up like a 50-watter with 12 volts on the filament.
Lit up like a firefly.
Lit up like a lantern.
Lit up like a lighthouse.
Lit up like a prison yard.—Jill McCorkle
Lit up like a skyscraper.
Lit up like a store window.
Lit up like Broadway.
Lit up like high mass.
Lit up like Main Street.

Lit up like the star of Bethlehem.
Lit up like Times Square.

Lithe

Lithe as a feather duster. —Gelett Burgess
Lithe as a panther. —Zane Grey
Lithe as a snake.
Lithe as a willow. —Richard Hovey
Lithe as a young dog. —George Garrett
    Also see Flexible, Supple.

Lived

Lived like a fortunate heir. —George Garrett
Lived like a hermit in a cave. —Lee Smith
Lived like a king.
Lived like a lord.
Lived like fighting cocks.

Lively

Lively as a cow on roller skates.
Lively as a cricket.
Lively as a smiling day. —Aaron Hill
Lively as a squirrel. —Oliver Wendell Holmes
Lively as fire. —Robert Bridges
    Also see Agile, Nimble, Spry.

Loathsome

Loathsome as a nest of scorpions. —Rosemary H. Jarman
Loathsome as a toad. —William Shakespeare
    Also see Hated.

Locked

Locked like a vault. —T. C. Boyle
Locked up tight as a chastity belt.
Locked up tight as virgins in a boarding school. —Ferrol Sams

Lonely

Lone as an eagle's nest. —Letitia E. Landon
Lonely as a bachelor looking at Niagara Falls in June. —Arthur Baer
Lonely as a cloud. —William Wordsworth
Lonely as a deserted ship.
Lonely as a duck in the desert.
Lonely as a petunia in an onion patch.
Lonely as a scarecrow in a field of stubble.
Lonely as a stone. —Joseph Heller
Lonely as a tomb. —Ferrol Sams
Lonely as a well-fed flea in a laboratory. —Nicholas Salaman
Lonely as a wordless song. —John Ehle
Lonely as an owl hoot. —Anthony Forrest
Lonely as Sunday. —Mark Twain
Lonesome as a dog in a pound.

Lonesome as a forgotten child.—F. Scott Fitzgerald
Lonesome as a freckle in Pittsburgh.
Lonesome as a walnut rolling in a barrel.—Edna Ferber
Lonesome as an abandoned dog.—Owen Ulph
   Also see Alone, Forlorn.

Long

Long as a day without bread.
Long as a Devonshire lane which has no turning.
Long as a lawsuit.—Thomas Dekker
Long as a Lenten sermon.—James P. Jacobson
Long as a sick man's drug bill.—Rex Beach
Long as a snake's liver.
Long as a Thanksgiving sermon.—*Bartlett's*
Long as a woodman's axe.—Lawrence Sanders
Long as an obituary.
Long as Count de Grasse's queue.—William Cowper
Long as death.— Elizabeth B. Browning
Long as Kelsy's nose.—Stephen Longstreet
Long as one's arm.
Long as religious instructions.—Nicholas Salaman
Long as the bell rope on a freight train.
Long and slender like a cat's elbow.—Thomas Fuller
Long as a coon's age.
Long as a dog's age.
Long as a month of Sundays.
Long ago as when Big Ben was a wristwatch.
Long ago as when Nellie had her operation.
Long ago as when Pontius was a pilot.—*Partridge's*
   Also see Lengthy.

Looked (appearance)

Looked like a bad day in Bangladesh in monsoon season.
Looked like a bad stretch of nine-mile road.—Darcy O'Brien
Looked like a billy goat in stays.
Looked like a calf waiting for the butcher.—Margaret Mitchell
Looked like a car wreck.—Havilah Babcock
Looked like a chap who says his prayers in a cold bath every day.
   —George MacDonald Fraser
Looked like a chicken with a wrung neck.—James Sherburn
Looked like a child who just got caught raiding the jam jar.
Looked like a deflated bulldog.—Derek Robinson
Looked like a drowned cat.—Victor Appleton
Looked like a drowned mouse.
Looked like a fugitive from a concentration camp.—Richard Bachman
Looked like a guilty child.
Looked like a hound caught slipping a chop from the table.—T. C. Boyle
Looked like a mad artist's hell.—George MacDonald Fraser
Looked like a man in the grip of a deep migraine headache.—Stephen King

Looked like a man who had been punched low.—Stephen King
Looked like a man with one foot in the grave.—Robert Service
Looked like a million dollars.—Victor Appleton
Looked like a ragamuffin.—Margaret Mitchell
Looked like a sick kitten.
Looked like a refugee from a Frankenstein movie.—Stephen King
Looked like a refugee from a midnight fire.—Thomas Thomas
Looked like a used rubber.—Derek Robinson
Looked like a winner in a rigged competition.
Looked like a zombie with a dead battery.—Derek Robinson
Looked like all the sadness in the world.—Lee Smith
Looked like an unemployed undertaker's mute.—George MacDonald Fraser
Looked like an unmade bed.—Paul Harvey
Looked like butter wouldn't melt in his mouth.
Looked like death.
Looked like death warmed over.
Looked like forty miles of bad road.
Looked like he combed his hair with an egg-beater.
Looked like he could hunt bears with a ball bat.
Looked like he had a fight with a barber.—B. Q. Morgan
Looked like he had been chewing tobacco and spitting into the wind.
Looked like he had been kicked by a mule.
Looked like he had been thrown through a barb wire fence.
Looked like he had been run over by a Mack truck.
Looked like he had been washed but never ironed.
Looked like he had escaped from the back tent of a carnival.
Looked like he had just inspected God on parade.
Looked like he had just received a bomb threat.
Looked like he had just stepped out of a band box.
Looked like he walked out of a Goodwill store.
Looked like he was caught between a hawk and a buzzard.—H. Allen Smith
Looked like he was rode hard and put away wet.
Looked like he'd lost his best friend.
Looked like Quasimodo on a bad day.
Looked like Scotch elders at a brothel—George MacDonald Fraser
Looked like shit warmed over.—Jack Matthews
Looked like someone who had spent the night in a bus station.
Looked like something the cat dragged home.—Victor Appleton
Looked like something the dog coughed up.
Looked like something you'd find in a live bait shop.
Looked like the devil.
Looked like the devil's first cousin.—Thomas Jefferson
Looked like the fourth runner-up in a hatchet fight.—Jimmie Dean
Looked like the losing fighter about ten seconds after the ref ended the match
    and awarded the winner a TKO.—Stephen King
Looked like the wrath of God.
Looked like the wreck of the Hesperus.
Looked just like a fly in a pan of milk.—Fannie Flagg

He looked and moved like an elderly gentleman with bowel problems.
—T. C. Boyle

She looked like a malicious Betty Grable. —Truman Capote

She looked like a street just before they put on the asphalt. —George Ade

Looked him/her over

Looked at her like she was some kind of Italian sports car and he was ready
to drive her. —TV show, "Murder She Wrote"

Looked him over like he was a mare at auction. —Tom Wicker

Looked him over like he was for sale. —Pete Dexter

Looked him up and down like a sergeant inspecting the ranks. —George Garrett
Also see Examined it.

Loose

Loose as a goose.

Loose as cossack pantaloons. —Oliver Wendell Holmes

Loose as negligence. —James Cawthorn

Loose as old rags.

Loose as wet string.
Also see Limp.

Lost

Lost as a blind man in a strange alley. —Rikke Ducornet

Lost as a needle in a stack of hay. —Thomas Hood

Lost as an Easter egg.

Lost as truth in the mouth of a liar. —Ian St. James

Lost as yesterday. —Ian St. James

Lost like a ball in tall weeds.

Lost like a river running into an unknown sea.

Lost like a sea captain in a fog.

Lost like a star in day. —Henry Ellison

Lost like autumnal leaves when north winds race. —Richard Congreve

Loud

Loud as a bagpipe. —George Garrett

Loud as a cattle market. —Derek Robinson

Loud as a clap of thunder. —Erskine Caldwell

Loud as a fart in church.

Loud as a harvest thunderstorm. —R. D. Blackmore

Loud as a jackhammer. —Stephen King

Loud as a mill. —William Wordsworth

Loud as a neon cross on a church house. —Thomas Thompson

Loud as a pine knot in a sawmill.

Loud as a cavalry to the charge. —George Meredith

Loud as the blows of a hammer.

Loud as the clank of an ironmonger. —Percy B. Shelley

Loud as the clappers of hell.

Loud as the crack of doom.

Loud as the ocean when a tempest blows. —William Wilkie

Loud as the sea. —Richard Duke

Loud as the voice of an auctioneer.
Loud as thunder.—Sydney Dobell
   Also see Noisy.

Lounged
Lounged like a boy of the South.—Robert Browning
Lounged like a gunslinger.—William Boyd
Lounged like a hemophiliac prince.—T. C. Boyle

Lovely
Lovely as a budding rose.—Robert Southey
Lovely as a prom queen.
Lovely as a violin.—Josephine P. Peabody
Lovely as a white Christmas.
Lovely as love.—Lord Byron
Lovely as spring's first rose.—William Wordsworth
   Also see Fair, Pretty.

Low
Low as a baboon's forehead.—Sydney Munden
Low as a beetle's bellybutton.
Low as a caterpillar's fuzz.
Low as a flat frog in a dry well.
Low as a gopher's basement.
Low as a horse's hoof.—Scottish ballad
Low as a Louisiana mud varmint.—Dan Jenkins
Low as a snake.
Low as a snake in the grass.
Low as a snake's belly.
Low as a snake's belly in a tire tread.
Low as a snake's chin.
Low as a snake's pecker. Robert R. McCammon
Low as a spider break dancing.
Low as hell.—D. G. Rossetti
Low as old rags.—Douglas C. Jones
Low as the grave.
Low as the price of Christmas trees on December 26.
Low as the ring around a Scotchman's bathtub.
Low as the spats on a centipede.
Low as whale shit.
Lowly as a slave.—Charles Tupper
   Also see Dismal, Glum, Humble, Sad.

Loyal
Loyal as a clock.—Phoebe Gray
Loyal as a dog.
Loyal as a dove.
Loyal as an eagle's mate.
   Also see Obedient, Reliable, Steadfast, True.

Lugubrious

Lugubrious as a Methodist preacher reveling in hellfire predictions.
—Bernard Cornwell
Lugubrious as a tombstone.—Rennold Wolf
Also see Gloomy, Glum.

Luminous

Luminous as a lit-up ballroom.—H. DeVere Stacpole
Luminous as a neon beer sign.
Also see Bright, Radiant.

Lumpy

Lumpy as a full diaper.
Lumpy as a sackful of door knobs.

Lurked

Lurked like a carrion crow.
Lurked like a vermin.—John Davidson

Lush

Lush as a rain forest.
Lush as Eden.—Steven Callahan
Also see Luxurious, Rich.

Lustrous

Lustrous as a jewel.—Gary Jennings
Lustrous as agate.—Theophile Gautier
Lustrous as ebony.—William Shakespeare
Lustrous as laughter.—A. C. Swinburne
Lustrous as satin.
Lustrous as silk.
Also see Bright, Brilliant, Glossy, Luminous, Polished, Radiant, Shined.

Luxurious

Luxurious as a cluster of grapes.—William M. Ready
Luxurious as an expensive fur coat.
Also see Lush, Rich.

Mad

Mad as a bear with a sore ass.

Mad as a beaver.

Mad as a beaver with a toothache.—Andy Andrews

Mad as a buck.

Mad as a bull at a five-barred gate.—Margaret Mitchell

Mad as a dervish.—Rex Beach

Mad as a duck with its bill caught in a corn crib.

Mad as a gorilla in heat.—Robert Ludlum

Mad as a gorilla with a hernia.

Mad as a hatter.—Lewis Carroll

Mad as a hen.

Mad as a hornet.—Erskine Caldwell

Mad as a hungry cow grazing on AstroTurf.

Mad as a loon.

Mad as a March hare.—Miguel de Cervantes

Mad as a meat axe.

Mad as a mule chewing on bumblebees.

Mad as a nestful of hornets poked with a stick.

Mad as a rained-on hen.—John Ehle

Mad as a rat in a trap.

Mad as a rattler.

Mad as a rattler ready to strike.—Margaret Mitchell

Mad as a striped adder.

Mad as a turpentined wildcat.—Shelby Foote

Mad as a wasp.—John Skelton

Mad as a wet cat.

Mad as a wet hen.

Mad as a wet mouse.

Mad as a wet spider.

Mad as a wet tomcat.

Mad as an adder.
Mad as hops.
Mad as seven hornets.
Mad as snakes in haying.
Mad as the devil.
Mad as thunder.
    Also see Crazy, Furious, Nutty.

Majestic
Majestic as a statue.
Majestic as Caesar.
Majestic as the Alps.
    Also see Grand, Stately.

Malicious
Malicious as a satyr.
Malicious as Satan.—William M. Thackeray
Malicious as Saul to David.
    Also see Bad, Mean, Spiteful.

Mean
Mean as a badger in a barrel.—Evan S. Connell
Mean as a bear with a sore paw.
Mean as a bear with a sore tail.
Mean as a bull with a jackhandle up his ass.
    —Stephen King
Mean as a copperhead.—Robert Lewis Taylor
Mean as a crab.
Mean as a gamecock.—George MacDonald Fraser
Mean as a hungry snake.—Ferrol Sams
Mean as a junkyard dog.—Jim Croce, "Bad, Bad, Leroy Brown"
Mean as a louse.
Mean as a miser.
Mean as a mule with shoulder galls.—Harold Bell Wright
Mean as a rattlesnake.
Mean as a sick grizzly.
Mean as a snake.—Tom Wicker
Mean as a snake with the shingles.—Stephen King
Mean as a suck-egg dog.
Mean as a tromped-on snake.—H. Allen Smith
Mean as an old bear with a boil on its butt.
Mean as an old snake.—Erskine Caldwell
Mean as an old tomcat.
Mean as cat dirt.—Stephen King
Mean as rusty barbed wire.—Robert R. McCammon
Mean as self-righteousness.—John Ehle
Mean as the devil.
Mean as the man who told his children that Santa Claus was dead.
    Also see Bad, Ferocious, Mad, Ornery.

Meandered

Meandered like a drunk.—T. C. Boyle
Meandered like a lazy brook.—Maurice Hewlett
Meandered like a river.
  Also see Roamed.

Meek

Meek as a bankrupt beggar.—William Shakespeare
Meek as a dove.—George Meredith
Meek as a lamb.
Meek as a Madonna.
Meek as a May day.—Geoffrey Chaucer
Meek as a mouse.
Meek as a Quaker.—*Punch,* 1863
Meek as a saint.—Alexander Pope
Meek as a turtledove.—Robert Blair
Meek as Mary's little lamb.—Stephen King
Meek as May.—Alexander Pope
Meek as Moses.
  Also see Humble, Low, Modest.

Melancholy

Melancholy as a cat.—John Gay
Melancholy as a graveyard on a rainy day.
Melancholy as a Quaker meeting house by moonlight.—*Bartlett's*
Melancholy as an Irish melody.—Bliss Carman
Melancholy as the grave.—Francoise Chandernagor
  Also see Gloomy, Sad, Unhappy.

Melted

Melted like a candle in a bonfire.
Melted like butter on a hot griddle.—Stephen Longstreet
Melted like dissolving spray.—Percy B. Shelley
Melted like wax.—*Old Testament*
Melted like wax dolls.—Shelby Foote
  Also see Disappeared, Vanished.

Merciless

Merciless as a jailkeeper.
Merciless as a male tiger.
Merciless as ambition.—Joseph Joubert
Merciless as Caesar.
Merciless as chance.—Tom Wicker
Merciless as Othello.—Ouida
Merciless as the grave.
Merciless as the IRS.
  Also see Cruel, Mean, Pitiless.

Merry

Merry as a beggar.

Merry as a bridegroom proposing a toast.—T. C. Boyle
Merry as a Christmas tree.—Joseph C. Lincoln
Merry as a cricket.—William Shakespeare
Merry as a fiddler.—*The Christmas Prince*
Merry as a grig.—John Gay
Merry as a harlot.—Cecelia Holland
Merry as a king in his delight.—Robert Greene
Merry as a kitten.—Robert Burns
Merry as a lark.—Walter S. Landor
Merry as a magpie.
Merry as a maid.—John Bunyan
Merry as a maltman.—Scottish proverb
Merry as a mouse in malt.—George Garrett
Merry as a tinker.
Merry as a two-year-old.
Merry as bees in clover.
Merry as flowers in May.
Merry as kittens.
Merry as the month of May.—Barry Cornwall
   Also see Gay, Happy.

Mild

Mild as a dove.—William Shakespeare
Mild as a lamb.—Ambrose Philips
Mild as a maid.—Michael Drayton
Mild as a mother with her child.—Samuel T. Coleridge
Mild as a saint whose errors are forgiven.—William Livingston
Mild as an April eve.—William J. Mickle
Mild as any saint.—Alfred Tennyson
Mild as cottage cheese.—Edna St. Vincent Millay
Mild as goose milk.—Mark Twain
Mild as May.—Alexander Pope
Mild as mother's milk.—Frederic S. Isham
Mild as the hour of the setting sun.—Ossian
Mild as the never wrathful dove.—John Langhoren
Mild and peaceful as Socrates.
   Also see Gentle, Smooth.

Mind

Mind like a cesspool.
Mind like a computer.—Louis L'Amour
Mind like a fist.—Rikki Ducornet
Mind like a lavatory wall with nostalgia scribbled all over it.—Tim Rumsey
Mind like a mouse.—Robert R. McCammon
Mind like a sewer.
Mind like a sink.—Agatha Christie
Mind like a steel trap.
Mind slipped like a mill belt.—John Ehle

Mind was like a cushion, bearing the shape of the last person who sat on it.—Anthony Forrest
Little minds, like weak liquors, are soonest soured.
Old minds are like old horses; you must exercise them if you wish to keep them in working order.—John Adams
Mind about as open as a scared oyster.—Ferrol Sams

Mischievous
Mischievous as a four-year-old boy.
Mischievous as a kitten.
Mischievous as a monkey.—Honore de Balzac
Mischievous as a wicked pixie.

Miserable
Miserable as a horsefly at a dog show.
Miserable as a wet dog shivering dejectedly in a rain-swept alley.—E. D. Price
Miserable as a wet hen.—Rosemary H. Jarman
Miserable as sin.—Francoise Chandernagor
Miserable as the fifth act of a tragedy.
    Also see Forlorn, Pitiful.

Moaned
Moaned like a bedridden grandmother.—T. C. Boyle
Moaned like a dove.
Moaned like a dying hound.—Henry H. Brownell
Moaned like the voice of one who crieth in the wilderness alone.
    —Henry W. Longfellow
    Also see Groaned.

Modest
Modest as a squash.
Modest as a violet.
Modest as justice.—William Shakespeare
Modest and shy as a nun.—William Cullen Bryant
    Also see Humble, Low, Meek.

Monotonous
Monotonous as a windshield wiper.
Monotonous as mutton.—Richard Le Gallienne
Monotonous as the dress of charity children.
Monotonous as the sea.—Richard M. Milnes
    Also see Bored, Dull, Exciting.

Moody
Moody as a poet.—Thomas Shadwell
Moody as a reptile unable to shed its skin.—Michael Doane
Moody as a riverboat whistle.
Moody as an artist.
    Also see Disposition.

Motionless

Motionless as a mime.

Motionless as a model. —Thomas Hardy

Motionless as a pillar of the colonial portico of a mansion in a Kentucky prohibition town. —O. Henry

Motionless as a statue. —Rex Beach

Motionless as an agony of inertia, like a machine that is without power.
     —D. H. Lawrence

Motionless as an animal in a spotlight. —Joan Samson

Motionless as an idol and as grim. —John Greenleaf Whittier

Motionless as stone. —Zane Grey

     Also see Fixed, Immobile, Immovable, Still.

Mouth

Mouth as straight as Bible lines. —Ivan Doig

Mouth agape like a stranded cod. —Nicholas Salaman

Mouth drawn in like a miser's purse. —Emile Zola

Mouth felt like the bottom of ninety bird cages.

Mouth felt stiff with smiles. —Doris Leslie

Mouth hung open like an old hound. —Margaret Mitchell

Mouth like a crack in the pavement. —Sewell Ford

Mouth like a miller's paddle. —John Ehle

Mouth like a padlock. —Graham Greene

Mouth like a pickerel. —Anne E. Perkins

Mouth like a scarlet wound. —W. Somerset Maugham

Mouth like a steel trap. —William M. Raine

Mouth like a whirlpool.

Mouth tasted like he was drinking the hole at the water hole and not the water. —Terry C. Johnston

Mouth like the bottom of a parrot cage. —David Niven

Mouth like the entrance to a fun house. —Stephen King

Mouth like the whale that swallowed a whole fleet. —Thomas Lodge

Mouth moved like a puppet's. —John Updike

Mouth opened like a goldfish's. —William Wingate

Mouth opened like a trunk. —Mark Twain

Mouth thin and straight, like a cut in his face. —Honore de Balzac

Mouth tugged down on one side like a dead man's. —John Updike

Mouth watered like a baby who's seen a nipple. —John Ehle

Cruel red mouth like a venomous flower. —A. C. Swinburne

     Also see Tasted.

Moved

Moved like a cat. —William Haggard

Moved like a man with a bad back and sore feet. —Jack Matthews

Moved like a monster. —Lee Smith

Moved like clockwork.

Moved like his feet were on fire. —Stephen King

Moved like lice were falling off him.

Moved like tar in December.

Moved like the Catholic Church.
Moved like the ocean ready to storm.—Richard Bachman
Moved like the Russian government.
    Also see Fast, Slow.

Muddy
Muddy as a sheepdog.—Henri Murger
Muddy as a mudskipper.

Multiplied
Multiplied like Abraham.—Francois Rabelais
Multiplied like hamsters.
Multiplied like rabbits.
Multiply like the bud of the field.—*Old Testament*
    Also see Bred.

Murmured
Murmured like a hive.—Elizabeth B. Browning
Murmured like a seashell.
Murmurmed like bumblebees.—Tom Wicker

Mute
Mute as a clam.
Mute as a fish.—John Gay
Mute as a funeral procession.
Mute as a stump.—Havilah Babcock
Mute as death.
Mute as fish.
Mute as snow.—Elizabeth B. Browning
    Also see Noiseless, Quiet, Silent, Speechless.

Mysterious
Mysterious as a sphinx.
Mysterious as an echo.—Josh Billings
Mysterious as magic.
Mysterious as voodoo.
Mysterious as twilight.
    Also see Strange.

Naked

Naked as a fish. —Hugh Wiley
Naked as a flower. —Madison Cawein
Naked as a jaybird.
Naked as a needle. —William Langland
Naked as a peeled almond. —Rosemary H. Jarman
Naked as a peeled apple. —Oliver Wendell Holmes
Naked as a plucked chicken.
Naked as a raw oyster. —Irvin S. Cobb
Naked as a shorn sheep.
Naked as a stone.
Naked as a worm. —Alexandre Dumas
Naked as an ape. —Francoise Voltaire
Naked as Adam. —Thomas Ward
Naked as Eve when she ate the apple. —Alfred De Musset
Naked as my nail. —Philip Massinger
Naked as the day he was born. —T. C. Boyle
Naked as the moon. —George Sterling
Naked as the palm of your hand.
Naked as the point of a sword. —George Garrett
Naked and clean as a peeled stick. —John Fuller
    Also see Bare.

Narrow

Narrow as a mobile home.
Narrow as a Pullman car. —Stephen King
Narrow as a schoolgirl across the butt. —Robert Lewis Taylor
Narrow as an icepick. —T. C. Boyle
Narrow as the gate to heaven. —Owen Ulph

Natural

Natural as a baby sucking tit. —Jack Fuller

Natural as a mountain stream.—Beer slogan
Natural as breathing.—T. S. Arthur
Natural as cherry pie.
Natural as childbirth.—Stephen King
Natural as daylight.—Nathaniel Hawthorne
Natural as death.
Natural as dunghill steam.—George Meredith
Natural as eating.—Jeffery Farnol
Natural as the sun rises on Wednesday morning.—Erskine Caldwell
Natural as ticks to a hound dog.—Jack Matthews
Natural as to eat, sleep, and wear a nightcap.—John Ford
Natural as walking.—Jeffery Fornal
Naturally as bees swarm and follow their queen.—Henry David Thoreau
　　Also see Common, Familiar.

Near

Near as dammit is to swearing.
Near as the bark to the tree.—William Camden
Near as the end of one's nose.
Near as the pennies in your pocket.
Near as twilight is to darkness.—Thomas Paine
　　Also see Alike, Close, Similar.

Neat

Neat as a bandbox.
Neat as a cat.—Mark Twain
Neat as a coffin.
Neat as a nail.
Neat as a pin.
Neat as a pinky.
Neat as a postman's knock.—George Meredith
Neat as a spinster's pin.—Douglas C. Jones
Neat as a whistle.
Neat as clockwork.—Stephen R. Donaldson
Neat and bare like a GI's footlocker.—George Garrett
Neat and dustless as a good museum.—George Garrett
Neat and soft as a puff of smoke.—George Garrett
　　Also see Prim, Tidy.

Necessary

Necessary as a handsaw to a carpenter.
Necessary as breathing is to live.
Necessary as water, air, and fire for man's life.
　　Also see Needed, Vital.

Needed

Needed like a car needs gas.
Needed like a flower needs the sun.—Thelma Strabel
Needed like applause for an actor.
Needed like snow for a skiing weekend.

Needed about like a broken neck.
Needed about like a cow needs a blackboard. —Stephen King
Needed about like a dog needs two tails.
Needed about like a dog needs side pockets.
Needed about like a drowning man needs a brick.
Needed about like a fish needs a bicycle.
Needed about like a hole in the head.
Needed about like a kangaroo needs a briefcase.
Needed about like a moose needs a shower cap.
Needed about like a rubber dick. —Stephen King
Needed about like a tomcat needs a marriage license.
Needed about like Custer needed more Indians.
Needed about like I need to take a shit and fall backwards. —Dan Jenkins
    Also see Necessary.

Nervous
Nervous as a bastard at a famly reunion. —Robert H. Lindsey
Nervous as a bee with sore feet.
Nervous as a june bug in a henhouse.
Nervous as a mouse.
Nervous as a setting hen with a fox in the henhouse.
Nervous as a wing bird in cat country.
    Also see Anxious, Edgy, Jumpy, Restless, Tense, Touchy, Uneasy.

Nice
Nice as a nanny.
Nice as a new pin. —T. S. Arthur
Nice as nasty.
Nice as nip.
Nice as pie.

Nimble
Nimble as a bee in a tar barrel.
Nimble as a boy.
Nimble as a cat on a hot back stove.
Nimble as a cat on hot bricks.
Nimble as a cow in a cage.
Nimble as a flyweight. —George MacDonald Fraser
Nimble as a goat. —J.R.R. Tolkien
Nimble as a hare.
Nimble as a juggler. —Cecelia Holland
Nimble as a newly gelded dog.
Nimble as a pig.
Nimble as a tumbler. —Cecelia Holland
Nimble as an eel.
    Also see Agile, Lively, Spry.

Nodded his head
Nodded his head like dunking for apples. —Keith Korman
Nodded his head like a puppet on a string. —Raymond Paul

Noise

Noise like a hammer striking a watermelon.—Robert R. McCammon
Noise like an elephant breaking wind.—Robert R. McCammon
Noise cracked like a whip.—Margaret Mitchell
Also see Noisy, Sound.

Noiseless

Noiseless as a serpent would steal to his ambush.—Mary J. Holmes
Noiseless as a shadow.
Noiseless as the fall of snow.
Also see Quiet, Silent.

Noisy

Noisy as a boiler shop.
Noisy as a cookstove falling down stairs.
Noisy as a creditor's meeting.
Noisy as a flock of blackbirds in migration season.
Noisy as a goose with his head hung in a knothole.
Noisy as a skeleton having a fit on a hardwood floor.
Noisy as a sow at the trough.—Douglas C. Jones
Noisy as an old sow leaving a corn patch with six hounds after it.
Noisy as hell changing shifts.—Ivan Doig
Noisy as the stock exchange.—Augustine Birell
Noisy as the testing room of a bass-drum factory.
Noisy as two mules having a kicking match in a tin barn.
Noisy as two skeletons having a wrestling match on a tin roof.
About as noisy as a cheesecake slowly rising.
Also see Loud, Noise.

Nose

Nose as cold as a lump of ice.—Robert R. McCammon
Nose as large as a dill pickle.
Nose curved like a pistol grip.—Tom Wicker
Nose hooked like a hen's beak.—James Sherburn
Nose like a bird dog.
Nose like a customs inspector.—Phillip McCutchan
Nose like a garden implement.—T. C. Boyle
Nose like a promontory.—Robert Burton
Nose like a rudder.—Anita Mason
Nose like a sausage.
Nose quivered like a rabbit's.—Margaret Mitchell
Nose sharp enough to slice salami.—William Pearson
Nose stuck out like the first joint of a thumb.—Frederick O'Brien
Nose twisted like a rabbit's.—Doris Leslie
He blew his nose like the falling of a tree.—David Grayson
Also see Face.

Nostrils

Nostrils dilated like a deer's that sniffs some distant scent.
—F. Hopkinson Smith

Nostrils like two hairy caverns.
Nostrils opening and shutting like gills.—Mark Twain
Nostrils wiggled like a bunny rabbit.

Numerous
Numerous as leaves of the forest.
Numerous as leaves that strew the autumn gale.—Percy B. Shelley
Numerous as sands.—John Ehle
Numerous as sands upon the ocean.—Philip Freneay
Numerous as the hairs on his head.—Paul Wiggins
Numerous as the stars of heaven.—Richard Dabney
Numerous as the writings of ibid.
Numerous as unsold shares in an over-capitalized mining company.
   —F. C. Griffith

Nutty
Nutty as a fruitcake.
Nutty as a peach orchard boar.
Nutty as a peanut bar.
Nutty as a pet coon.
Nutty as a squirrel.
   Also see Crazy, Mad, Strange.

Obedient
Obedient as a child.
Obedient as a dog.
Obedient as a puppet.—George Meredith
Obedient as a shadow.—Jack D. Bruce
Obedient as a sheep.—Robert Browning
Also see Loyal, True.

Obsolete
Obsolete as a discharged school director.
Obsolete as a mule.
Obsolete as an Edsel.
Also see Old.

Obvious
Obvious as a circus parade.
Obvious as a festering cold sore.—Dean R. Koontz
Obvious as a lighthouse.—Ferral Sams
Obvious as a wooden leg.
Obvious as rat sign in a sugar bowl.
Obvious as stars on a clear night.—Alfred H. Lewis
Obvious as the nose on your face.
Also see Clear, Evident, Plain, Stood out.

Off
Off like a bat out of hell.
Off like a big-assed bird with a tail wind.—James Sherburn
Off like a blue streak.
Off like a bride's nightie.
Off like a case of gunpowder.—Jack Matthews
Off like a dirty shirt.
Off like a dog on the track of a hare.—Shelby Foote
Off like a flash.—Victor Appleton

Off like a flight of ducks. —Jack Matthews
Off like a gazelle.
Off like a ghost at the break of day. —Robert Browning
Off like a hare. —George MacDonald Fraser
Off like a hurdle racer. —George MacDonald Fraser
Off like a prom dress.
Off like a rabbit.
Off like a rat to a drainpipe.
Off like a shot. —R. H. Barham
Off like a sprinter at the sound of the gun. —Stephen King
Off like a stung whippet. —George MacDonald Fraser
Off like a turpentined cat.
Off like a whirlwind. —*Old Testament*
Off like crab-infested shorts.
   Also see Fast, Fled, Hurried, Quick, Ran, Swift, Took off, Went.

Old

Old as Adam.
Old as an itch.
Old as beeswax.
Old as Christendom.
Old as creation.
Old as Diogenes's bunion.
Old as dirt. —Jill McCorkle
Old as Eve.
Old as God. —John Inzer
Old as God's uncle. —T. C. Boyle
Old as history.
Old as Macedonia.
Old as Methuselah.
Old as Methuselah's pecker. —Robert R. McCammon
Old as mountains. —J.R.R. Tolkien
Old as my little finger. —John Day
Old as my tongue and a little older than my teeth.
Old as Paul's Cathedral.
Old as the green earth itself. —Jeffrey Farnol
Old as the hills.
Old as the itch. —Spanish proverb
Old as the pyramids.
Old as the sphinx.
Old as the stars. —Francoise Voltaire
Old as the world. —Gary Jennings
Old as time. —Austin Dobson
Old as water.
Old and mean as time. —Lee Smith
   Also see Obsolete.

Ominous

Ominous as a raised fist. —Tom Wicker

Ominous as a thunderstorm. —Tom Wicker
Ominous as the still before the storm.
   Also see Grim, Threatening.

Open

Open as a pie pan. —Keith Korman
Open as the inn gates to receive guests. —George Gascoigne
Open like an obscene cave.
   Also see Gaped, Wide, Yawned.

Oppressive

Oppressive as foul air. —Charles Dickens
Oppressive as humidity. —Richard Brausch
Oppressive as slavery.
   Also see Dark, Gloomy.

Orderly

Orderly as a clerk. —Norman Mailer
Orderly as a corn crop. —Peter Jenkins
Orderly as the web of some huge spider. —J.R.R. Tolkien
Orderly as veiled nuns. —Honore de Balzac
   Also see Neat, Prim, Systematic, Tidy.

Ornery

Ornery as a cub bear.
Ornery as a mad wasp in a dry gourd.
Ornery as an overloaded pack mule. —Owen Ulph
Ornery as buzzard bait.
   Also see Contrary, Inflexible, Mean, Unyielding.

Out

Out like a blown candle. —Stephen King
Out like a broken bulb.
Out like a dead battery.
Out like a lamp.
Out like a light.
Out like a stunned boxer.

Out of place

Out of place as a dolphin tap dancing. —Peter Jenkins
Out of place as a faro layout in a Sunday school. —Alfred H. Lewis
Out of place as a milk bucket under a bull.
Out of place as a mouse doing a one-step with an elephant.
Out of place as a mouse in a meatloaf.
Out of place as a piano in a kitchen. —Edgar Saltus
Out of place as a white poodle on a coal barge. —Arthur Baer
Out of place as laughing in church. —J. N. Crisp
Out of place as three cheers at a funeral.
   Also see Stood out, Stuck out, Went over.

Paced

Paced like a dog on a chain. —Dudly Pope
Paced back and forth like a caged animal. —Terry Ganey
Paced back and forth like a new father.
 Also see Walked.

Packed

Packed like a whorehouse on payday. —Robert R. McCammon
Packed like bullets in a cartridge box. —Shelby Foote
Packed like cigars in a box.
Packed like fish in a basket. —Rosemary H. Jarman
Packed like herring in a barrel. —Shelby Foote
Packed like puppies in a pregnant poodle.
Packed like leaves in a closed book. —Oliver Wendell Holmes
Packed like nightcrawlers in a tobacco tin. —Owen Ulph
Packed like salt cod in a barrel. —Tom Wicker
Packed like sardines.
 Also see Stuffed.

Painful

Painful as a kick in the balls with an army boot.
Painful as a poke in the eye with a sharp stick.
Painful as a slap in the belly with a wet fish.
Painful as a visit to the dentist. —Guy de Maupassant
Painful as being hung by your thumbs.
Painful as being kicked in your stomach by a horse.
Painful as being staked to an anthill.
Painful as stepping on a rake.
Painful as to visit a dentist. —Guy de Maupassant
 Also see Ached, Hurt, Sore.

Painless

Painless as floating on a cloud.

Painless as a kiss.
Painless as a walk in the sun on an autumn day.
Painless as an afternoon nap.

Pale

Pale as a coffined corpse.—Patrick McGinley
Pale as a corpse.—Victor Hugo
Pale as a ghost.—Alexandre Dumas
Pale as a sheet.—Jeffery Farnol
Pale as a whitewashed wall.—Johann Schiller
Pale as an invalid.—Stephen R. Donaldson
Pale as alabaster.
Pale as candle wax.—Cecelia Holland
Pale as cream.—Sir Walter Scott
Pale as death.—Samuel Butler
Pale as dough.
Pale as fresh milk in a white clay pot.—John Ehle
Pale as goat's milk.
Pale as lead.—Geoffrey Chaucer
Pale as marble.—Mary J. Holmes
Pale as milk.
Pale as paper.—Cecelia Holland
Pale as white wine.—Kenelm Digby
   Also see Faded, Faint, Indistinct, Pallid.

Pallid

Pallid as a corpse.—Thomas Hood
Pallid as a corpse on end.—Thomas Hardy
Pallid as a ghost.—William Wordsworth
Pallid as a gravestone.
   Also see Pale.

Panted

Panted like a bull before business.—George MacDonald Fraser
Panted like a climber.—Elizabeth B. Browning
Panted like a dog.
Panted like a dog on a hot day.—Stephen King
Panted like a dog show in mid-July.—T. C. Boyle
Panted like a horse.
Panted like a long-distance runner.
Panted like a man with a heart condition.—Walter Winward
Panted like a spent dog.
Panted like a spent hound.—Arthur Conan Doyle
Panted like a steam engine.
   Also see Breathed, Gasped, Puffed, Wheezed.

Parted

Parted like a scattered flock before a lion.—Sydney Dobell
Parted like a stone from a sling.—Charles Reade

Parted like Moses parted the Red Sea.
Also see Left, Separate, Went off, Went out.

Passed
Passed like a daydream. —Thomas Moore
Passed like a dream.
Passed like shadows. —Margaret Mitchell
Passed like summer rain. —Tom Wicker
Passed swiftly like a dream. —Margaret Mitchell
Also see Went.

Passionate
Passionate as two minks in a sugar sack.
Passionate as young love.
About as passionate as shredded wheat.
Also see Amorous, Horny, Lecherous, Randy.

Passive
Passive as a bronze Buddha.
Passive as a cat.
Passive as a monument.
Also see Idle, Quiet.

Pathetic
Pathetic as a starving child.
Pathetic as an autumn leaf. —George Moore
Pathetic as an octogenarian messenger boy. —Oscar Wilde
Also see Pitiful.

Patient
Patient as a draft animal.
Patient as a gentle stream. —William Shakespeare
Patient as a matador. —George Garrett
Patient as a prostitute. —James G. Huneker
Patient as a spider weaving a broken web. —Edward Bulwer-Lytton
Patient as an Indian. —Rex Beach
Patient as an old worn horse. —George Meredith
Patient as an undertaker. —T. C. Boyle
Patient as Job.
Patient as the female dove. —William Shakespeare

Peaceful
Peaceful as a baby.
Peaceful as a closed shopping center. —Robert Bausch
Peaceful as a graveyard. —Harold Bell Wright
Peaceful as a hired hand. —James Whitcomb Riley
Peaceful as a London suburb on bank holiday. —*London Chronicle*, 1917
Peaceful as a virgin lake. —James R. Lowell
Peaceful as old age. —William M. Raine
Peaceful as sleep. —Beaumont and Fletcher
Peaceful as Socrates.

Peaceful as the morning.—William Wordsworth
Peaceful as two pups in a basket.—Alfred H. Lewis
About as peaceful as hauling leaky dynamite.—Pete Dexter
    Also see Calm, Composed, Placid, Serene, Tranquil, Unruffled.

Penis

Penis as big as a roasting ear.
Penis as hard as a rock.
Penis as long as a blacksnake.
Penis like a wet sock.—John Irving
Penis stiff as a lightening rod.
Penis stuck up like a fence post.
Penis stood up like a tree.
    Also see Erect, Erection, Hard, Long, Stiff.

Permanent

Permanent as change.
Permanent as marble.—Bayard Taylor
About as permanent as a pile of raked leaves.—P. F. Kluge
    Also see Enduring, Lasted, Stable.

Persistent

Persistent as a bulldog.—Oliver Wendell Holmes
Persistent as a mosquito.
Persistent as a mountain stream.—John Ehle
Persistent as a tick.—Robert R. McCammon
Persistent as an itch.
Persistent as the odor of a swamp.—Evan S. Connell
    Also see Enduring.

Personal

Personal as a fingerprint.
Personal as an autograph.
    Also see Independent, Intimate, Privacy.

Pert

Pert as a pearmonger.—John Gay
Pert as a robin in a birdbath.—Stephen King
    Also see Bold.

Picked off

Picked off like crows on a rail fence.
Picked off like ducks in a pond.
Picked off like hunted coyotes.—William M. Raine

Piled

Piled like sacks of wheat in a grainary.—Henry W. Longfellow
Piled up like fish on a slab.—George MacDonald Fraser
    Also see Stacked.

Pink

Pink as a baby's bottom.

Pink as a petticoat.
Pink as a rose.—Gene Stratton-Porter
Pink as coral.—Doris Leslie
Pink as the lip of a seashell.
Pink and tender as an unhealed scar.—Howard Jacobson

Pious
Pious as a nun.—Ferrol Sams
Pious as a pope.—Thomas Hood
Pious as Deuteronomy recited backward.
   Also see Holy.

Pitiful
Pitiful as a dying duck in a thunderstorm.
Pitiful as a crippled child standing in the rain.
Full of pity like a father speaking to a hurt child.—Margaret Mitchell
   Also see Pathetic.

Pitiless
Pitiless as driving sleet.—John C. Neihardt
Pitiless as Simon Legree.
Pitiless as the grave.—Gerald Massey
   Also see Cruel, Mean, Merciless.

Placid
Placid as a cow chewing her cud.
Placid as a duck pond.
Placid as a large lake.
Placid as a mill pond.
Placid as paradise.—Edwin Arnold
Placid as Socrates.
   Also see Calm, Peaceful, Serene, Tranquil.

Plain
Plain as ABC.
Plain as a barn door.
Plain as a hat rack.
Plain as a pack saddle.
Plain as a pattern on a plate.—Derek Robinson
Plain as a pipe stem.
Plain as a pool table.
Plain as a potato cooked in peas.—Jack Matthews
Plain as a white platter.—Ivan Doig
Plain as an old shoe.—Margaret Mitchell
Plain as day.
Plain as daylight.—F. Hopkinson Smith
Plain as pig tracks.—H. Allen Smith
Plain as pigeon droppings.—Stephen Longstreet
Plain as the nose on your face.
Plain as the sun in heaven.—Thomas B. Macaulay

Plain as the wart on your nose.
Plain as the way to church—William Shakespeare
Plain as the way to the market.—Benjamin Franklin
Plain as truth.—George Chapman
Plain as two and two make four.
Plain as white paper.
> *Also see* Evident, Obvious, Stood out.

Played
Played like a child.
Played like a kid.
Played like a kitten.
Played him like a poker hand from a stacked deck.
Played with it like a cat.—Rosemary H. Jarman

Playful
Playful as a kitten.
Playful as a puppy.
Playful as a rabbit.—George P. Morris
> *Also see* Frisky.

Pleasant
Pleasant as cold lemonade on a hot summer day.
Pleasant as good health.
Pleasant as pie.
> *Also see* Delighted, Happy.

Pleased
Pleased as a basket of chips.
Pleased as a child.—Harold Bell Wright
Pleased as a dog with two tails.
Pleased as a hound with a dish of raw innards.—Owen Ulph
Pleased as Punch.
Pleased as two setters in a wading pool.—Robert Adelman
> *Also see* Contented, Happy, Satisfied.

Plentiful
Plentiful as blackberries.—Edward Bulwer-Lytton
Plentiful as fleas on a dog.
Plentiful as washing on a Monday morning line.—Howard Spring
> *Also see* Abundant.

Plump
Plump as a dumpling.
Plump as a melon.—Steven Callahan
Plump as a partridge.—John Gay
Plump as a pigeon.—B. Q. Morgan
Plump as a puffin.
> *Also see* Fat.

Pointless

Pointless as a pencil stub.
Pointless as a rubber ball.
Pointless as Parcheesi. —John Crosby
Pointless as scratching a wooden leg.
Also see Insignificant.

Poised

Poised as a fashion plate. —Ivan St. James
Poised like a dancer. —Mary Stewart
Poised like a hummingbird hanging in air. —F.W.H. Myers

Polished

Polished like a prize horse. —Stephen Longstreet
Polished like a witch doctor's skull.
Also see Glossy, Lustrous, Shined.

Poor

Poor as a beggar in the street. —T. S. Arthur
Poor as a cab driver in Venice.
Poor as a church mouse.
Poor as a field mouse.
Poor as a fence rail.
Poor as a garter snake. —Ferrol Sams
Poor as a pissant.
Poor as a rat.
Poor as a retired Spanish ensign. —Furtserre
Poor as a sheep new shorn. —George Peele
Poor as Cinderella. —Frederick S. Isham
Poor as gar broth.
Poor as Job. —Shakespeare
Poor as Job's cat.
Poor as Job's turkey. —John Marston
Poor as Lazarus.
Poor as watermelon rinds. —F. Hopkinson Smith
Also see Broke.

Popped

Popped like a balloon.
Popped like chestnuts in a fire.
Popped like corn.

Popped up

Popped up like a broken window shade. —Derek Robinson
Popped up like mushrooms.
Popped up like wildflowers.

Popular

Popular as a fire hydrant at a dog show.
About as popular as a gonococcus with bad breath.
About as popular as a mouse at a suffragette meeting.

About as popular as a porcupine at a balloon factory.
About as popular as pork in a synagogue.
About as popular as wasps.—Owen Ulph

Populous
Populous as a hive.
Populous as an anthill.—Victor Hugo
Populous as Hong Kong.

Potent
Potent as a child on crutches.—Tom DeHaven
Potent as a kick in the head.—T. C. Boyle
Potent as Irish whiskey.
Potent as oblivion.—Stephen R. Donaldson
Potent as white lightning.
    Also see Strong.

Poured
Poured like hourglass sand.
Poured like a fountain.
    Also see Flowed, Rained.

Pouted
Pouted like a disappointed child.—Charlotte Brontë
Pouted like a kicked pup.—Ivan Doig
Her mouth looked like you could hold a dance in it and her lip stuck out like
    the dance floor.

Powerless
Powerless as a stone.—Elizabeth B. Browning
Powerless as an infant.
Powerless as thisteldown in a summer storm.—Doris Leslie
    Also see Helpless, Weak.

Practical
Practical as a paper clip.
Practical as a pocket on a shirt.
Practical as a razor.—Cosmo Hamilton
Practical as a safety pin.
Practical as taking your cat to obedience classes.—Shelby Friedman
    Also see Handy.

Pranced
Pranced like a bean-fed horse.—Rudyard Kipling
Pranced like a pair of cannibals about to eat a victim.—Honore de Balzac
Pranced like a horse.
    Also see Danced, Strutted.

Prated
Prated like a parrot.
Prated like old women at a bridge party.
    Also see Babbled, Chattered, Jabbered.

Prayed

Prayed like a drunk Methodist. —George MacDonald Fraser
Prayed like an angel afire. —Edward Eggleston
Prayed like clockwork.
   Also see Begged.

Precise

Precise as guardsmen. —George MacDonald Fraser
Precise as mathematics.
   Also see Exact.

Predictable

Predictable as a horse going back to its barn. —Richard Bachman
Predictable as the sun will rise.
   Also see Constant, Enduring, Sure.

Preened

Preened like a peacock.
Preened like a teenager before his first prom.

Prepared

Prepared as a bride adorned for her husband. —*New Testament*
Prepared as a Boy Scout.
Prepared as the United States Marines.
   Also see Ready.

Pretty

Pretty as a bald-faced heifer.
Pretty as a drawing in a child's Sunday school workbook. —Stephen King
Pretty as a Dresden shepherdess, and as lifeless. —Anthony Forrest
Pretty as a Georgia peach.
Pretty as a goggle-eyed perch.
Pretty as a government check.
Pretty as a green valley.
Pretty as a little red wagon.
Pretty as a painted wagon. —William M. Raine
Pretty as a new windmill. —Lee Smith
Pretty as a peach. —Wallace Irwin
Pretty as a picture. —Mark Twain
Pretty as a red wagon.
Pretty as a speckled calf. —Patrick Smith
Pretty as a speckled pony.
Pretty as a spotted horse in a daisy pasture.
Pretty as a young widow with her wood cut. —John Ehle
Pretty as springtime. —John Ehle
About as pretty as a gargoyle.
About as pretty as a mud fence.
About as pretty as last year's corpse.
About as pretty as road kill.
   Also see Beautiful, Fair, Lovely.

Prim

Prim as a banker.
Prim as a peeled pine pole.
Prim as a Quaker.—George P. Morris
Prim as an old maid substitute teacher.
Also see Neat, Orderly, Tidy.

Privacy

About as much privacy as a goldfish.—Irvin S. Cobb
About as much privacy as a statue in a park.
About as much privacy as Grand Central Station.
About as much privacy as Yankee Stadium.
Also see Intimate, Personal.

Profane

Profane as a drunk sailor.
Profane as a teamster.—Tom Wicker
Also see Swore.

Profile

Profile as sharp as a cameo.—F. Hopkinson Smith
Profile like the blade of a knife, cold and sharp.—Honore de Balzac
Profile like the edge of a key.—Dave Martin

Protective

Protective as a bulletproof vest.
Protective as a hen with one chick.
Protective as a mother with her children.
Protective as a smoke detector.
Also see Safe, Secure.

Proud

Proud as a boy with a brand new top.—John G. Saxe
Proud as a cock.
Proud as a cock on his own dunghill.—Turkish proverb
Proud as a drunk who walks out of a bar without upsetting anything.
　　—Lawrence Sanders
Proud as a father with a new baby.
Proud as a government mule.
Proud as a hen that got a duck for a chicken.
Proud as a hen with one chick.—B. Lowsley
Proud as a highlander.—Scottish proverb
Proud as a house cat.—Tom Wicker
Proud as a king.
Proud as a lizard with two tails.
Proud as a peacock.—Geoffrey Chaucer
Proud as a raiding horse.—John Lyly
Proud as a whitewashed pig.—P. W. Joyce
Proud as a young bull.—Richard Le Gallienne
Proud as an old turkey gobbler in the spring.—Harold Bell Wright

Proud as Lucifer.
Proud as Lucifer's sister.—George MacDonald Fraser
Proud as Punch.
Proud as the queen of Sheba.

Puffed

Puffed like a blacksmith's chimney.—George Garrett
Puffed like a corncob pipe.
Puffed like a leaky steam pipe.—O. Henry
Puffed like bellows of a blacksmith.
Puffed the briar pipe like a locomotive burning up coals.—Robert R. McCammon
Puffed out like canvas in a sail.
Puffed up like a toad-frog.—Tom Wicker
    Also see Breathed, Gasped, Panted, Wheezed.

Punctual

Punctual as a bride at a wedding.—Honore de Balzac
Punctual as a cuckoo in a Swiss clock.—Edith Wharton
Punctual as a tax collector.—*Punch*, 1862
Punctual as morning.—James Whitcomb Riley

Pure

Pure as a baby's love.—Ray Locke
Pure as a bishop's bathroom.
Pure as a bride's blush.—Coventry Catmore
Pure as a dove.—C. G. Rossetti
Pure as a lily.
Pure as a madonna.
Pure as a mountain spring.—John Ruskin
Pure as a virgin's kiss.
Pure as alabaster.
Pure as angel thoughts.—Thomas Moore
Pure as grace.—William Shakespeare
Pure as heaven.—A. C. Swinburne
Pure as heaven's snowflake.
Pure as Ivory soap.
Pure as New York snow.—From Kim Carnes' song, "Betty Davis Eyes"
Pure as winter snow.—F. A. Fahy
Pure as the driven snow.
Pure as the tears of a saint.—Dean R. Koontz
Pure as the thoughts of infant innocence.
Purer than snow.—*Old Testament*
    Also see Innocence.

Puzzled

Puzzled as an old hen that hatched a duck egg.
Puzzled like a man who has lost his glasses.
Puzzled like a roach trying to crawl downstairs on an escalator.—Arthur Baer

Quaked
Quaked like an aspen leaf.
Quaked like California.
Quaked like mice when the cat is mentioned. —Honore de Balzac
    Also see Quivered, Shook, Trembled.

Queer
Queer as a bug. —Elvis Presley and Otis Blackwell, "All Shook Up"
Queer as a three-dollar bill.
    Also see Mysterious.

Quick
Quick as a bunny.
Quick as a cat.
Quick as a dart. —Johann Goethe
Quick as a dart of flame. —Pearl Buck
Quick as a darted beam of light. —R. D. Blackmore
Quick as a deer. —George Garrett
Quick as a duck on a june bug.
Quick as a flash. —Zane Grey
Quick as a fox.
Quick as a gunslinger's draw. —Stephen King
Quick as a heartbeat. —Robert R. McCammon
Quick as a hiccup.
Quick as a lashing whip. —Dean R. Koontz
Quick as a mad cat.
Quick as a minute. —Robert Houston
Quick as a nun's kiss.
Quick as a panther. —Zane Grey
Quick as a rat. —Charles McCarry
Quick as a rat down a rope.
Quick as a rat up a drainpipe.

Quick as a shell on a pea at a carnival.
Quick as a snake.
Quick as a snap.
Quick as a telegraph key.
Quick as a turpentined cat. —Ferrol Sams
Quick as a wink.
Quick as an acrobat. —Dan Jenkins
Quick as an arrow.
Quick as an echo. —Robert Louis Stevenson
Quick as an eyelid's beat. —Guido Cavalcanti
Quick as chain lightning. —Anne E. Perkins
Quick as dust.
Quick as fingers snapping.
Quick as greased lightning.
Quick as green corn through a new maid. —Robert Frost
Quick as gunpowder.
Quick as hell can scorch a feather.
Quick as light. —Henry Vaughan
Quick as lightning. —Mark Twain
Quick as lightning strikes a tree. —John Ehle
Quick as powder.
Quick as shit through a goose.
Quick as spit. —Jack Matthews
Quick as the flash of a quail's wing.
Quick as the passing of a gnat. —Doris Leslie
Quick as thought. —Robert Louis Stevenson
Quick as you can bat your eye.
Quick as you can gut a trout. —George Garrett
Quick as you can say Jack Robinson.
Quick as you can wink. —Robert Louis Stevenson
Quick as a pig's whistle.
Quick as the twinkling of an eye. —Jeffery Farnol
Quick and nimble as a bear.
Quick and wise as a goat. —George Garrett
    Also see Brief, Fast, Off, Sudden, Swift, Took off.

Quiet
Quiet as a bird with a hawk flying over. —Margaret Mitchell
Quiet as a cat. —Tom DeHaven
Quiet as a cemetery. —Peter Jenkins
Quiet as a chicken laying a square egg.
Quiet as a Christian Science reading room. —Stefan Kanfer
Quiet as a church.
Quiet as a church after the groom farts. —Owen Ulph
Quiet as a church mouse.
Quiet as a furrier factory on Sunday. —David Chandler
Quiet as a graveyard. —Thomas Hardy
Quiet as a held breath. —Robert Houston

Quiet as a lamb.—William Shakespeare
Quiet as a leaf dropping to the ground.—Peter Jenkins
Quiet as a manger scene.
Quiet as a moonbeam.—Elizabeth S. P. Ward
Quiet as a moth.
Quiet as a mouse.—Arsene Houssaye
Quiet as a mouse pissing on cotton.
Quiet as a mouse running on Jell-O.
Quiet as a soap bubble bursting.—Peggy Choate
Quiet as a statue.—W. E. Henley
Quiet as a stone.—John Keats
Quiet as a Sunday morning.—John Ehle
Quiet as a tranquil sky.—Henry W. Longfellow
Quiet as a whore in church.—Dean R. Koontz
Quiet as a widow's grave.—Jack Matthews
Quiet as a wolf.—Douglas C. Jones
Quiet as an eel swimming in oil.—Arthur Baer
Quiet as dreaming trees.
Quiet as the deep woods.—Peter Jenkins
Quiet as the dreams of the deaf.—Jack Matthews
Quiet as the first star coming out.—*New York Times*
Quiet as the lighting of a fly on a feather duster.
Quiet as the surface of some uninhabitable and forbidden planet.—T. C. Boyle
About as quiet as two kittens.
   Also see Calm, Noiseless, Placid, Silent, Still, Tranquil.

Quit
Quit like a sick cat.—William M. Raine
Quit like an old car.

Quivered
Quivered like a bow string.
Quivered like a dish of marmalade in an earthquake.—Arthur Baer
Quivered like a hunted beast.
Quivered like a leaf in the wind.
Quivered like a naked Russian in the snow.—William Davenant
Quivered like a virgin's fan.—George MacDonald Fraser
Quivered like harp strings.—Walter Winward
Quivered like jelly.
Quivered like spasms through a tuning fork.—Ivan Doig
   Also see Quaked, Shook, Trembled.

Radiant

Radiant as a summer sun in morn. —James Whitcomb Riley
Radiant as a tiara of celestial diamonds. —Victor Hugo
Radiant as hope. —Stephen R. Donaldson
    Also see Bright, Brilliant, Luminous, Lustrous, Shined.

Ragged

Ragged as a field gone to seed. —T. C. Boyle
Ragged as a scarecrow. —Thomas Heywood
Ragged as a shard of glass. —Douglas C. Jones
Ragged as Ann and Andy.
Ragged as torn newspaper. —Derek Robinson
    Also see Seedy.

Rained

Rained like a Biblical plague. —T. C. Boyle
Rained like a cow pissing on a flat rock.
Rained like a curtain of beads. —Jack Fuller
Rained like bath time on Noah's ark. —Ivan Doig
Rained like pouring piss out of a boot.
Raindrops rang like marbles on the tin porch roof. —Lee Smith
Randy as a rooster on a manure pile.
    Also see Flowed, Poured.

Raised hell

Raised hell like a weasel in a henhouse. —Feroll Sams
Raised hell like six chiggers dug in well.
    Also see Fought.

Ran

Ran as smoothly as a swift stream. —J.R.R. Tolkien
Ran as swift as pudding would creep. —*Partridge's*
Ran lightly as an Indian. —Margaret Mitchell

155

Ran like a bandit.
Ran like a buck.—H. S. Commager
Ran like a chicken before a dog.—Douglas C. Jones
Ran like a coyote.—Jack Matthews
Ran like a deer.
Ran like a dog after a rabbit.—Gerald Duff
Ran like a dog to the whistle.—Robert Louis Stevenson
Ran like a dog with a can on his tail.—Glendon Swarthout
Ran like a frightened animal.
Ran like a greyhound.
Ran like a hen dodging the axe.—Owen Ulph
Ran like a herd of wild cattle.—H. S. Commager
Ran like a homebound horse.
Ran like a homebound ship.—George MacDonald Fraser
Ran like a hunted deer.—Thomas Hood
Ran like a jackrabbit.
Ran like a madman.
Ran like a pack of scalded dogs.
Ran like a pickpocket with a silk purse.—Anthony Forrest
Ran like a rabbit.
Ran like a rabbit panting for its burrow.—Margaret Mitchell
Ran like a rat in a cage.
Ran like a ruptured pig.
Ran like a scalded cat.—C. L. Skelton
Ran like a scared rabbit.—Harold Bell Wright
Ran like a split streak.—Stephen King
Ran like a striped-assed ape.—James Goldman
Ran like a summer lightning flash.—Anthony C. Deane
Ran like an antelope.—Anthony C. Deane
Ran like an ice wagon.—B. Q. Morgan
Ran like an Olympic half-miler.—J. N. Crisp
Ran like fire through stubble.
Ran like he was going to a fire.
Ran like he was racing the devil to the gates of hell.
Ran like hell.
Ran like hell hounds.—Hamlin Garland
Ran like tallow.—Stephen King
Ran like the devil.
Ran like the devil was on his tail.—Stephen King
Ran like the devil's mill.
Ran like the east wind.
Ran like the village fire brigade.—George MacDonald Fraser
Ran like the wind.—Jeffery Farnol
Ran like water off a duck's back.
Ran like yelping wolves.
Ran around like a chicken with its head cut off.
Ran around like a jackass with its ears cut off.
Ran around like a lower primate with an itch in his testicles.—T. C. Boyle

Ran around like a rocket in a rain barrel.
Ran around like the house was afire.
Ran around and around like a weasel in a blender.
Ran home like a burrowing animal. —C. L. Skelton
Ran the bases like he were hauling William H. Taft. —Heywood Broun
  Also see Fast, Fled, Hurried, Off, Quick, Sped, Took off, Went.

Ran (operated)
Ran like clockwork.
Ran like a fine Swiss watch.
Ran like a Rolls.
Ran like a sewing machine.

Randy
Randy as a bear. —Stephen King
Randy as a mink.
Randy as a monkey.
Randy as a ferret.
  Also see Amorous, Horny, Lecherous, Passionate.

Rare
Rare as a blue moon.
Rare as a cat with wings.
Rare as a cold day in July.
Rare as a dodo. —Robert Louis Stevenson
Rare as a dragon's tooth.
Rare as a fat man in a clothing advertisement. —George S. Kaufman
Rare as a fundamentalist with a sense of humor. —Lois Battle
Rare as a left-handed mustache cup. —Walter P. Eaton
Rare as a man without self-pity. —Stephen Vincent Benet
Rare as a pig flying.
Rare as a pig with wings. —Howard Spring
Rare as a sailor on horseback. —Anthony Hamilton
Rare as a two-door outhouse. —William Dieter
Rare as a whore who gave green stamps. —Judith Krantz
Rare as a unicorn. —James Goldman
Rare as a yellow-fronted mallabird.
Rare as an elephant roosting in a tree. —Margaret Mitchell
Rare as Halley's comet.
Rare as hell freezing over.
Rare as holy water in an Orange lodge.
Rare as lawyers in heaven. —Mark Twain
Rare as rocking-horse shit.
Rare as Sahara rain.
Rare as snow in July. —Lee Smith
Rare as snowflakes in a well-regulated August.
Rare as walking on water.
  Also see Unlikely.

Rattled

Rattled like a collection box.—Anthony Trew
Rattled like a loose bone in a goose's hind end.
Rattled like a Model T.
Rattled like a wheelbarrow.—George MacDonald Fraser
Rattled like seeds in a dry gourd.
Rattled like the milkman.
Rattled like two skeletons.
Rattled on like an amateur shrink.—Owen Ulph

Raucous

Raucous as a Saturday night rodeo.—Robert R. McCammon
Raucous as a stag show.
  Also see Rough.

Read him

Read him like a book.
Read him like a fifty-foot "See Rock City" sign.—Robert R. McCammon
Read his mind like a preacher reads a Bible.—Margaret Mitchell
Read his mind like an old tale he had learned by heart.—George Garrett
Read his thoughts like print.—Robert Louis Stevenson

Readily

Readily as a child takes sweetmeats at Mardi Gras.—Ouida
Readily as he would swat a fly.—George MacDonald Fraser

Ready

Ready as a borrower's cap.—William Shakespeare
Ready as a Boy Scout.
Ready as a cocked pistol.
Ready as a primed cannon.—Thomas Carlyle
Ready as the marines.
  Also see Prepared.

Real

Real as a *New York Times* headline.—Richard Bachman
Real as death.
Real as hunger.
Real as taxes.—Robert A. Heinlen
  Also see True.

Rear end

Rear end as wide as a bank president's desk.—Stephen King
Rear end as wide as an axe handle.—George Garrett
Rear end bulged like a sack of meat.—Ferrol Sams
Rear end like jelly on springs.—Michael Carreck
Rear end looked like two dogs fighting under a blanket.—Richard Bachman
  Also see Behind.

Reassuring

Reassuring as a sheltering wing over a motherless bird.—Louisa May Alcott

• •

Reassuring as parsons and squires.—T. C. Boyle
About as reassuring as dentist with an instruction manual.

Red
Red as a beet.
Red as a brick.
Red as a cardinal.—Leonid Andreyev
Red as a cherry.
Red as a chicken's ass at pokeberry time.—Michele Slung
Red as a fall apple.—John Ehle
Red as a fire engine.
Red as a fox's ass at pokeberry time.
Red as a harlot's lips.—Tom Wicker
Red as a holly berry.
Red as a lobster.—Thomas Nash
Red as a maiden's blush.—Douglas C. Jones
Red as a November sunset.—Anthony Forrest
Red as a radish.
Red as a red wagon.
Red as a robin's breast.
Red as a rooster's comb.
Red as a rose.—Omar Khayam
Red as a ruby.—John Ruskin
Red as a stop sign.
Red as a turkey cock.—*Partridge's*
Red as a vixen.
Red as a whore's stoplight.—Stephen King
Red as blood.—Geoffrey Chaucer
Red as flannel.
Red as Georgia clay.—Margaret Mitchell
Red as Mars.—William Shakespeare
Red as pure heart's blood.—Stephen R. Donaldson
Red as wine.

Refreshing
Refreshing as a dash of cold water in the face.
Refreshing as a drink of cold water to a fever patient.—Edward Eggleston
Refreshing as a well in dry land.—Nigel Tranter
Refreshing as an April shower.—Burma-Shave sign
    Also see Fresh.

Regular
Regular as a faucet.—Dan Jenkins
Regular as a heartbeat.
Regular as an almanac.—Stephen King
Regular as clockwork.
Regular as meals.—Clyde Edgerton
Regular as sunrise.

Regular as the tolling of a bell.
Also see Steady, Sure.

Relaxed

Relaxed as a fat cat.—Clare Francis
Relaxed as an empty glove.—Bonnie May Malody
Relaxed like an old setter by the fireplace.
Also see Rested, Slept.

Relentless

Relentless as a bloodhound.
Relentless as decay.—Joseph Wambaugh
Relentless as fate.
Relentless as fear.—Rosemary H. Jarman
Relentless as the tides.—Tom Wicker
Also see Resolute, Unyielding.

Reliable

Reliable as robins in spring.
Reliable as the swallows returning to Capistrano.
About as reliable as a *Pravda* editorial.—Joseph Wambaugh
Also see Loyal, Steadfast, Sure.

Reluctant

Reluctant as a child forced to dance for spinster aunts.
Reluctant as the steps of a bride to the altar.—Donald G. Mitchell

Remote

Remote as a dream.
Remote as a time before birth.—C. L. Skelton
Remote as paradise.—Bernard Cornwell
Remote as the stars.—Charles L. Moore
Also see Aloof, Distant, Far, Isolated.

Resolute

Resolute as a drunken Irishman.
Resolute as thunder.—John Ford
Also see Firm, Immovable, Inflexible, Relentless.

Responded

Responded like an echo.
Responded like Parlor's dog.
Responded like soldiers to a trumpet's call to arms.—William Pearson

Rested

Rested like an Irish setter before the open fireplace.
Rested like God on Sunday.—Patrick McGinley
Rested peacefully as a night nurse on duty.
About as restful as a bowling alley.
About as restful as a firing line.—George Ade
Also see Relaxed, Slept.

Restless
Restless as a boy.—F. Hopkinson Smith
Restless as a butterfly.—Leigh Hunt
Restless as a dog whose master is absent.—Alexandre Dumas
Restless as a fart in a bottle.
Restless as a four-balled tomcat.
Restless as a gypsy.
Restless as a hen on a hot griddle.
Restless as a man with the itch.
Restless as a riot.—Rex Beach
Restless as a wild beast in a cage.
Restless as a windshield wiper blade.—*Reader's Digest*
Restless as ambition.
Restless as cattle in a pen.
Restless as Hamlet.
Restless as quicksilver.
Restless as the sea.—Alfred Austin
Restless as underfed lions in zoo cages.—Stephen King
    Also see Anxious, Edgy, Fidgeted, Nervous, Tense, Touchy, Uneasy.

Returned
Returned like MacArthur.
Returned like swallows to Capistrano.
    Also see Came back.

Rich
Rich as a cream puff.—Rex Beach
Rich as a drugmaker.—John Ehle
Rich as a king.—Robert Louis Stevenson
Rich as a lord.
Rich as a munition maker.
Rich as Croesus.—Robert Burton
Rich as Midas.
Rich as Rockefeller.
Rich as Squire David.—Song, "Yankee Doodle"
Rich as the mint.
About as rich as a newborn sheep.
    Also see Lush, Luxurious.

Right
Right as a golden guinea.—Rex Beach
Right as a nail.
Right as a ram's horn.
Right as a right angle.
Right as a trivet.
Right as rain.
Right as the bank.
Right as the Church of England.

Right as the town clock.—Benjamin Disraeli
Also see Honest.

Rigid

Rigid as a corpse.—Rosemary H. Jarman
Rigid as a pointer.
Rigid as a rock.
Rigid as a sleepwalker.—Mary Stewart
Rigid as a statue.
Rigid as if chiseled from stone.
Rigid as stone.—James B. Kenyon
Also see Hard, Stiff.

Risky

Risky as putting your head in a lion's mouth.—Victor Appleton
Risky as skating over thin ice.
Risky as waving a red flag at a bull.—Victor Appleton
Also see Dangerous.

Roamed

Roamed like a lost dog.—Rikki Ducornet
Roamed the country like a nomad.—Terry Ganey
Also see Meandered.

Roared

Roared like a battlefield.—John Masefield
Roared like a beast.—Robert R. McCammon
Roared like a bull.—Margaret Mitchell
Roared like a bull calf.—George MacDonald Fraser
Roared like a burning lumberyard.
Roared like a demon in torture.
Roared like a demon possessed.—T. C. Boyle
Roared like a flame that is fanned.—Henry W. Longfellow
Roared like a lion.
Roared like a mad bull.
Roared like an angry sea.
Roared like breakers in the night.—Aubrey De Vere
Roared like surf breaking on rocks.
Roared like the sea.—*Old Testament*
Also see Bellowed, Hollered, Hooted, Howled, Yelled.

Rocked

Rocked like a ship at sea.
Rocked like a mass of jelly that has been invisibly shaken.
    —Hermann Sudermann

Rode a horse

Rode a horse like a bear on a barrel.
Rode a horse like a Polish lancer.—George MacDonald Fraser
Rode a horse like a sack of corn.—Nigel Tranter
Rode a horse like a sack of flour.

Rode a horse like a tick on a hound's back.—Patrick Smith
Rode a horse like he was fetching the midwife.
Rode a horse like he was racing the devil to the gates of hell.—Anthony Forrest

Rolled

Rolled around like a snake in heat.—Umberto Eco
Rolled in like a panzer division.
Rolled in like a wave.—Mark Twain
Rolled in money like pigs in mud.—Thomas Hood
Rolled like a log in a swift river.
Rolled off like dirt off a shovel.—Stephen Longstreet
Rolled off like water off a duck's back.
Rolled over like a happy dog.—Robert R. McCammon
Rolled over like a tumblebug.—Erskine Caldwell
Rolled up like a scroll.—C. G. Rossetti
Rolled up like a window shade.—Stephen King
Also see Came in.

Romantic

About as romantic as a claw hammer.—Derek Robinson
About as romantic as a dead toad.
About as romantic as the Chicago stockyards.—Will Irwin
Also see Fond.

Rose

Rose like a giant.—Emma Marshall
Rose like a kite.—William Cowper
Rose like a leaping ballerina.—Mark Twain
Rose like a phoenix from the fires of time.
Rose like an adder's head.—Robert R. McCammon
Rose like an eagle on the wing.—Thomas Hood
Rose like smoke.—George Garrett
Rose and fell like smoke from a gun.—Richard Hough
Also see Went up.

Rotten

Rotten as a pear.—John Gay
Rotten as a three-day-old dead fish.
Rotten as the gills of an old mushroom.

Rough

Rough as a bear.
Rough as a bearskin.—Robert Heath
Rough as a cob in a country privy.
Rough as a hedge.—Thomas Hardy
Rough as a rat-catcher's dog.—Norman Felton
Rough as a Russian bear.—John Taylor
Rough as hemp.—Thomas Carlyle
Rough as pine lumber with the splinters still on.—Douglas C. Jones

Rough as sandpaper.—John Inzer
 Also see Tough.

Round

Round as a ball.
Round as a balloon.
Round as a brandy cask.—Wilbur Smith
Round as a cannonball.
Round as a circus.
Round as a dish.—Francois Rabelais
Round as a dollar.
Round as a dumpling.
Round as a full moon.
Round as a hoop.—Francois Rabelais
Round as a glass.
Round as a globe.—John Gay
Round as a pearl.
Round as a suet pudding.—Doris Leslie
Round as a tire.—John Irving
Round as a windmill.
Round as the globe.—John Gay

Roused

Roused like a huntsman to the chase.—A. C. Swinburne
Rousing as a bugle.—Ouida
 Also see Exciting.

Rude

Rude as a bear.—Jonathan Swift
Rude as rage.
 Also see Rough.

Runs

Runs like a Deere.—John Deere slogan
Runs like a Rolls.—Rolls Royce slogan

Rushed

Rushed like a flood.—E. H. Plumptre
Rushed like a torrid hurricane.—Thomas Hood
Rushed around like a miniature whirlwind.—Frederic S. Isham
 Also see Off, Ran, Sped, Took off, Went.

Ruthless

Ruthless as Hitler.
Ruthless as the sea.—Maurice Hewlett
 Also see Cruel, Mean, Merciless, Pitiless.

Sacred

Sacred as a temple.
Sacred as churchyard turf.—Eliza Cook
Sacred as Hindu gods.
Also see Holy, Pious.

Sad

Sad as a dead duck in a thunderstorm.—Ian St. James
Sad as a government mule hauling a load of pig iron.
Sad as a monkey's face.—Margaret Mitchell
Sad as a subpoena.
Sad as a wilted daffodil.—George Garrett
Sad as melancholy.—Robert Burton
Sad as night.—William Shakespeare
Sad as raindrops on a grave.—George P. Lathrop
Sad as the last chapters of Job.
Sad as the Last Supper.
Sad as the soul strangled.—A. C. Swinburne
Sad as the wheels of a train standing still.
Sad as twilight.—Gerard Massey
Also see Dismal, Gloomy, Glum, Melancholy, Unhappy.

Safe

Safe as a bank vault.
Safe as a child on its mother's breast.
Safe as a church.
Safe as a church picnic.
Safe as a crow in a gutter.
Safe as a house.
Safe as a mouse in a malt heap.
Safe as a mouse in a mill.
Safe as a mouse in cheese.

Safe as a porch rocker.
Safe as a tombstone under its shell. —Alexander Adam
Safe as an iron chest. —T. S. Arthur
Safe as an old lady in a church. —William M. Raine
Safe as coons up a tree.
Safe as if he were in God's pocket. —William M. Raine
Safe as in bed. —Charles Reade
Safe as in the bank. —Richard Le Gallienne
Safe as sleep.
Safe as the bank.
Safe as the Bank of England. —Edward Bulwer-Lytton
Safe as the bellows.
Safe as the pope in Rome. —H. Allen Smith
About as safe as a cow in the stockyards.
    Also see Protective, Secure.

Sang

Sang like a bellyached hog.
Sang like a bird.
Sang like a bird called the swine. —*Partridge's*
Sang like a choirboy. —H. Block
Sang like a meadowlark.
Sang like a siren. —Francoise Voltaire
Sang like an angel.
Sang like death arguing with the devil. —Ivan Doig
Sang like she stepped in a bear trap.
    Also see Talked.

Sank

Sank like a brick.
Sank like a rock.
Sank like a stone. —*Old Testament*
Sank like a scuba diver. —Sam Koperwas
Sank like the *Bismark*.
Sank like the *Titanic*.

Sat

Sat as tight as a treed coon. —Terry C. Johnston
Sat like a bronze statue of despair. —Louisa May Alcott
Sat like a bump on a log.
Sat like a concert pianist.
Sat like a fart in a trance. —George MacDonald Fraser
Sat like a man on thorns. —Mary Stewart
Sat like a pile of dough. —Lee Smith
Sat like a stone. —Doris Leslie
Sat like a stone in a tomb. —Bob Leuci
Sat like a wax dummy. —Stephen King
Sat like some immovable weight. —T. C. Boyle

Satisfied

Satisfied as a breast-fed baby.

Satisfied as a cat that has been in the cream.—Richard Bachman

Satisfied as a five-turd crap before breakfast.—William Boyd

Satisfying as the look of a minister's wife in a prosperous parish.
—Dean R. Koontz
Also see Contented, Happy, Pleased.

Savage

Savage as a bear with a sore head.

Savage as a meat axe.

Savage as a tiger.

Savage as the heart of a tiger chained.—Edwin Arnold
Also see Ferocious, Fierce, Mean.

Scarce

Scarce as a decent pen in a post office.

Scarce as a Democrat at a Vermont town meeting.—Joseph C. Lincoln

Scarce as a deviled egg after a church picnic.

Scarce as a dolphin tap-dancing.

Scarce as a mare's nest.—Havilah Babcock

Scarce as a mule in the Kentucky Derby.

Scarce as buttons on a goose.—John McDonald

Scarce as feathers on a fish.

Scarce as fish out of water.

Scarce as hard money.—Douglas C. Jones

Scarce as hen's teeth.

Scarce as icewater in hell.

Scarce as money around the stock market.

Scarce as orange plumes on St. Patrick's Day.

Scarce as snake hips.

Scarce as snakes in Ireland.

Scarce as white blackbirds.

Scarce as wolves in the city.—George Garrett
Also see Rare, Unlikely.

Scared

Scared as a child.

Scared as a child at a loud noise.—Margaret Mitchell

Scared as a deer caught in a hunter's light.—Robert R. McCammon

Scared as a fox caught in a trap.—Thomas Thompson

Scared as a jackrabbit.

Scared as a jackrabbit that has heard the howl of the wolf.—Alfred H. Lewis

Scared as a nearsighted cat at a dog pound.—Stephen King

Scared as a turkey in November.

Scared enough to shit nickels.—Stephen King

Scary as a crow in a corn field.
Also see Afraid, Frightened, Nervous.

Scattered

Scattered as a flock.—Elizabeth B. Browning

Scattered as leaves when wild winds blow.—Oliver Wendell Holmes
Scattered as sheep having no shepherd.—*New Testament*
Scattered like a covey of quail.—Gerald Duff
Scattered like a hawk scatters chickens.—George Garrett
Scattered like a madwoman's wash.
Scattered like autumn leaves.—William Pearson
Scattered like bright stars.—Marge Piercy
Scattered like chaff before the wind.
Scattered like chickens before a Mack truck.—Robert R. McCammon
Scattered like confetti.—T. C. Boyle
Scattered like dust in a windstorm.—Evan S. Connell
Scattered like flakes of snow.—Henry W. Longfellow
Scattered like frightened sheep before a storm.—Stephen King
Scattered like lambs who smelled wolves.—Nelson Demille
Scattered like monkey shit.—Dan Jenkins
Scattered like porkchop bones at a Baptist picnic.—A. Whitney Brown
Scattered like quail.—Richard Bachman
Scattered like sheep.
Scattered like wildflowers growing among weeds.—George Garrret
Scattered like wildflowers.
   Also see Dispersed.

Scooted
Scooted like a rodent.—Charles McCarry
Scooted like he was scalded.—Douglas C. Jones

Screamed
Screamed like a banshee.
Screamed like a calf for its mother.—Booth Tarkington
Screamed like a fishwife.
Screamed like a jackrabbit with its head in a vise.
Screamed like a loon.
Screamed like a madwoman.
Screamed like a peacock.—Robert Louis Stevenson
Screamed like a pig under a fence.
Screamed like a poor man at a baptism.—John Ehle
Screamed like a sandstorm in the desert.—T. C. Boyle
Screamed like a shrew.
Screamed like a steamwhistle.
Screamed like a tomcat caught in a hay baler.—John Madson
Screamed like the death of the universe.—T. C. Boyle
Screamed like the devil's baby.
Screamed to high heaven.
   Also see Hollered, Screeched, Shrieked, Yelled.

Screeched
Screeched like a coyote.
Screeched like a hog scenting the butcher's block.—T. C. Boyle
Screeched like a hoot owl.

Screeched like a loon.
Screeched like a wildcat.
   Also see Hollered, Screamed, Shrieked, Squealed, Yelled.

Searched
Searched like a bird dog sniffing game.—Robert R. McCammon
Searched like a Hoover.
   Also see Hunted.

Seared
Seared like a brand.—J. H. Newman
Seared like hot iron.
   Also see Burned.

Secret
Secret as the grave.—Lord Byron
Secret as thought.—Francis Fawkes
Secretive as a Sicilian.—Michael Mewshaw
About as secretive as a cricket.—John Ehle
Secrets are like measles: they take easy and spread easy.—*Bartlett's*
   Also see Covert.

Secure
Secure as a Bible.
Secure as a cradle.
Secure as a fortress.
Secure as a hawk with wind under its wings.—Ivan Doig
Secure as a mouse in China.—William Cowper
Secure as happy yesterdays.—James R. Lowell
Secure as sleep.—William Shakespeare
Secure as the grave.
Secure and surly as a traffic court judge.—Stefen Kanfer
   Also see Protective, Safe.

Seedy
Seedy as a blackberry.
Seedy as a pomegranate.
Seedy as a raspberry.—Alice C. Hegan
Seedy as a tangerine.
   Also see Ragged.

Self-important
Self-important as a man with two car phones.—J. Richards
Self-important as the German General Staff.—P. F. Kluge

Selfish
Selfish as a fox.
Selfish as a hungry dog.
Selfish as a spoiled child.
   Also see Greedy, Stingy, Tight.

Sensitive

Sensitive as a flayed man in a sandstorm.—Shelby Foote
Sensitive as a flower.
Sensitive as a toilet seat.
  Also see Nervous, Tense, Uneasy.

Separate

Separate them one from another as a shepherd divideth his sheep from the
  goats.—*New Testament*
Separated like oil from water.—Rex Beach
  Also see Different, Parted.

Serene

Serene as a graven image.—Mark Twain
Serene as a hermit.—Ivan Doig
Serene as a Quaker's meeting.—James Ralph
Serene as a star in a bright mist.—Honore de Balzac
Serene as a waterfall.
Serene as a woodland pond.
Serene as day.—William Wordsworth
Serene as night.—Lord Byron
Serene as the dawn.—Victor Hugo
Serene and assured as the Bank of England.—T. C. Boyle
  Also see Calm, Peaceful, Placid, Tranquil, Unruffled.

Serious

Serious as a judge.
Serious as a heart attack.
Serious as a hog on ice.—Ferrol Sams
Serious as a philosopher.—Miles P. Andrews
Serious as a pope.—Francisque Sarcey
Serious as a snakebite.
Serious as a stroke.
Serious as a tombstone.—Robert Houston
Serious as an owl.
Serious as cancer.
Serious as if in church.—Emile Zola
Serious as taxes.—George H. Lewis
Serious as the fifth act of a tragedy.—Joseph Jefferson
Serious as the Ten Commandments.—W. B. Yeats
  Also see Intent.

Sexy

About as sexy as a bale of wet hay.—Warren Brown, *The Washington Post*
About as sexy as a side of contaminated pork.
About as sexy as Aunt Minnie's wallpaper.
About as sexy as socks on a rooster.
Sexless as a plucked rooster.—T. C. Boyle
Sexless as an anemic nun.—Sinclair Lewis
  Also see Horny, Passionate, Randy.

Shallow

Shallow as a pan. —Booth Tarkington

Shallow as a pie pan.

Shallow as teenage dreams.

Shallow as time. —Thomas Carlyle

Shameless

Shameless as a dog lifting his leg to a hydrant.

Shameless as a nude statue. —Sydney Munden

Shameless as a pregnant whore.

Shapeless

Shapeless as a bear. —Charles McCarry

Shapeless as a busted sofa.

Shapeless as a rock. —Lee Smith

Shapeless as a shadow. —A. C. Swinburne

Shapeless as an old shoe.

Sharp

Sharp as a bayonet. —Percy B. Shelley

Sharp as a blade. —John Crosby

Sharp as a bloodletter's lancet. —T. C. Boyle

Sharp as a fresh razor blade.

Sharp as a knife.

Sharp as a needle. —John Gay

Sharp as a pin.

Sharp as a rat turd. —Ferrol Sams

Sharp as a razor.

Sharp as a serpent's tooth. —William Shakespeare

Sharp as a ship keel. —J.R.R. Tolkien

Sharp as a spade. —John Irving

Sharp as a steel trap.

Sharp as a stiletto. —Stephen King

Sharp as a tack.

Sharp as a tack but twice as rusty.

Sharp as a tiger's tooth.

Sharp as a two-edged sword. —*Old Testament*

Sharp as a whip. —Joan Samson

Sharp as a whiplash.

Sharp as an awl.

Sharp as an icepick. —Stephen King

Sharp as filed steel. —William Shakespeare

Sharp as frigid night air. —John Irving

Sharp as ice crystals. —Stephen R. Donaldson

Sharp as mustard. —Ogden Nash

Sharp as pepper.

Sharp as the fangs of a rattler.

Sharp as the taste of quinine. —James Sherburne

Sharp as truth. —Victor Hugo

About as sharp as a doorknob.
About as sharp as a mashed potato sandwich.
About as sharp as a spoon.
About as sharp as a wet Kleenex.
About as sharp as an old prune.
About as sharp as marble.
About as sharp as mashed potatoes.
 Also see Keen.

Shattered

Shattered like a walnut shell. —Charles Dickens
Shattered like waves against a rock. —Shelby Foote
Shattering as an earthquake.

Shifty

Shifty as a shithouse rat.
Shifty as the sand.
 Also see Cunning, Sly, Sneaked, Wary, Wily.

Shined

Shined like a bald man's head.
Shined like a dead catfish in the moonlight.
Shined like a diamond in a goat's ass.
Shined like a hubcap in a garbage heap. —Owen Ulph
Shined like a lighthouse.
Shined like a meteor streaming in the wind. —John Milton
Shined like a new hansom cab. —F. Hopkinson Smith
Shined like a new penny.
Shined like a silver dollar.
Shined like a stone under water. —Rosemary H. Jarman
Shined like burnished metal.
Shined like copper coins.
Shined like polished ebony.
Shined like satin.
Shined like sealskin.
Shined like spit on the sidewalk. —Gerald Duff
Shined like the elbows in a miser's suit. —William Pearson
Shined like the sun.
Shining and clear as white stones in a brook. —George Garrett
Shined about like a dried yucca. —William Dieter
 Also see Glossy, Lustrous, Polished.

Shivered

Shivered like a wet dog. —Olive Ann Burns
Shivered like an aspen leaf. —James Smith
Shivered with fear like a thin dog in the cold. —Stephen Vincent Benet
 Also see Shook, Trembled.

Shook

Shook as with a chill. —Margaret Mitchell

Shook like a bad axle.
Shook like a dog pissing peach pits.—Tom Sharp
Shook like a dry palm in a high wind.
Shook like a frightened child.—Rex Beach
Shook like a leaf.—Mark Twain
Shook like a leaf in a twister.—John M. Del Vecchio
Shook like a man with malarial fever.—Alistair MacLean
Shook like a puppy will shake a rag toy.
Shook like a reed.—Howard Spring
Shook like a taut rope.—Robert Louis Stevenson
Shook like a terrier with a rat.—Thomas Hood
Shook like a three-dollar horse.—Robert Adelman
Shook like a wet dishrag.
Shook like an aspen leaf.
Shook like an autumn leaf.—C. G. Rossetti
Shook like aspen leaves in the wind.—Sir Walter Scott
Shook like aspic.—Tom McEwen
Shook like Jell-O on a plate.
Shook like jelly.
Shook like one with a severe cold.—Zane Grey
Shook like sails in a storm.—Margaret Mitchell
Shook like the feeder on a thrashing machine.—Gene Stratton-Porter
Shook like the palsy.—Olive Ann Burns
Shook her head like a dog coming out of the water.—Marge Piercy
Shook it like a dishrag.—Peter Jenkins
     Also see Quaked, Quivered, Trembled.

Shorn
Shorn as Samson.—Charles Tupper
Shorn as sheep.
Shorn like a new marine.

Short
Short as knee high to a barrel of taters.—F. Hopkinson Smith
Short as knee high to a duck.
Short as knee high to a grasshopper.
Short as the life of a wave.—Leonid Andreyev
Short and sweet like an old woman's dance.—Abraham Lincoln
     Also see Small.

Shot
Shot like a bullet from a gun.—Oliver Wendell Holmes
Shot like a dog.—Alfred Noyes
Shot like a partridge.—Robert Louis Stevenson
Shot like a yellow dog.
Shot back like a rally in a tennis match.—T. C. Boyle
Shot out like a piston rod.—Richard Harding Davis
     Also see Off, Took off.

Shrank

Shrank like a beggar in the cold. —J. T. Trowbridge
Shrank like a leaf in the fall. —Eugene Field
Shrank like a puddle in the sun. —Cecelia Holland
Shrank like a rabbit before a snake. —Rex Beach
Also see Shriveled up.

Shrewd

Shrewd as a fox.
Shrewd as a goat. —George Garrett
Shrewd as a moneylender.
Also see Clever, Cunning, Sly.

Shrieked

Shrieked like a banshee.
Shrieked like a constipated banshee. —Robert R. McCammon
Shrieked like a drunk in delirium tremens. —T. C. Boyle
Shrieked like a drunken banshee. —Robert R. McCammon
Shrieked like a razor drawn across a pane of glass. —T. C. Boyle
Shrieked like a screech owl. —Patrick Smith
Shrieked like a viola gone sour. —T. C. Boyle
Shrieked like a wounded yak.
Shrieked like children after an ice cream truck. —LaBarge
Shrieked like trapped birds.
Shrieked like violent birds. —John Irving
Also see Bellowed, Hollered, Howled, Screamed, Squealed, Yelled.

Shriveled up

Shriveled up like a dead puffball. —Rex Beach
Shriveled up like a dry sponge. —Stephen King
Shriveled up like a raisin.
Shriveled up like a worm on a hot stove. —H. L. Mencken
Shriveled up like the pictures of mummies you see in books. —Mark Twain
Shriveled up like the tongue of a hanged man. —Tom McEwen
Also see Shrank, Shrunk.

Shrunk

Shrunk like a crushed snail. —Robert Browning
Shrunken like a navel. —Rosemary H. Jarman
Shrunken like a walnut.
Also see Shrank, Shriveled up.

Shuddered

Shuddered like a man in a fever. —Maurice Hewlett
Shuddered like a mule in fly time. —Ferrol Sams
Shuddered like that of the deer when he sees the hounds again upon his
track. —Victor Hugo
Also see Quaked, Quivered, Shook, Trembled.

Shunned

Shunned as a mole shuns light. —O. Henry

Shunned as a sailor shuns the rocks. —John Dryden
Shunned like a thing accursed. —Robert Service
Shunned like a viper. —Matthew Carey
Shunned like one who farts in an elevator.
Shunned like the plague. —Robert Brownell
　　Also see Avoided it.

Shy
Shy as a blushing bride.
Shy as a blushing virgin. —Wilbur Smith
Shy as a fawn. —Ambrose Philips
Shy as a girl on her first date. —Margaret Mitchell
Shy as a polecat. —Keith Korman
Shy as a sheep.
Shy as a sinner at the gates of heaven. —T. C. Boyle
Shy as a spinster in a short skirt. —Derek Robinson
Shy as a squirrel. —George Meredith
Shy as a wren in the hedgerow. —George Moore
　　Also see Coy, Meek, Modest, Timid.

Sick
Sick as a cat.
Sick as a dog. —Richard Jago
Sick as a dog on grass.
Sick as a horse.
Sick as a rat full of poison bait. —Stephen King
Sick as three dogs. —Mark Childress
　　Also see Ached, Pain.

Sighed
Sighed like a bellows. —Robert R. McCammon
Sighed like a bride.
Sighed like a death rattle. —Jack Fuller
Sighed like a dog that lost his master. —Thomas Lodge
Sighed like a schoolboy who has lost his ABC. —William Shakespeare
Sighed like a zephyr. —Mark Twain
Sighed like an old steam engine.

Silent
Silent as a bird alighting. —Cormac McCarthy
Silent as a butterfly. —Tom Wicker
Silent as a catacomb.
Silent as a church. —Charlotte Brontë
Silent as a cloud. —Jack Matthews
Silent as a corpse. —Percy B. Shelley
Silent as a country churchyard. —Thomas B. Macaulay
Silent as a courtier, voiceless before his queen. —Frederic S. Isham
Silent as a dream. —Evan S. Connell
Silent as a ghost. —Harold Bell Wright
Silent as a mole.

Silent as a mouse.—William Cowper
Silent as a picture.—William Wordsworth
Silent as a post.
Silent as a sleepwalker.—Margaret Mitchell
Silent as a snake.—Jack Fuller
Silent as a stone.
Silent as a stone god.—F. Hopkinson Smith
Silent as a tomb.—Thomas Hardy
Silent as a young tree in a windless night.—J.R.R. Tolkien
Silent as death.
Silent as desolation.—T. S. Arthur
Silent as oblivion.—Ivan Doig
Silent as snow falls on the earth.—Chinese proverb
Silent as the grave.—Johann Schiller
Silent as the "P" in swimming.
Silent as the pictures on the wall.—Henry W. Longfellow
Silent as the sphinx.
Silent as the tombs of Egypt.—Lewis W. Green
Silent as thieves.
Silent as thought.—Pierre Beranger
About as silent as schoolboys.
    Also see Mute, Noiseless, Quiet, Speechless, Still.

Silly
Silly as a goose.
Silly as a tipsy widow.—George MacDonald Fraser
Silly as an old maid at a marriage.—Richard Congreve
Silly as the pot calling the kettle black.
    Also see Foolish, Stupid.

Similar
Similar as jumping jacks.—Frederick S. Isham
Similar as two eggs.—William Shakespeare
Similar as two peas in a pod.
About as alike as an apple to an oyster.
    Also see Alike, Go together.

Similes
Similes are a good deal like Ford cars; you can get a good one secondhand and fix it
    up so you can't recognize it yourself—but everybody else can.—*New York Post*
Similes are like songs of love/they much describe/hey nothing prove.
    —Matthew Prior
Similes in each dull line, like glowworms in the dark should shine.
    —Edward Moore

Simple
Simple as a child.—Honore de Balzac
Simple as a kiss under the mistletoe.
Simple as a schoolboy's logic.

Simple as earth.
Simple as pie.
Simple as tit-tat-toe, three-in-a-row. —Mark Twain
   Also see Easy.

Sizzled
Sizzled like hamburger on the griddle.
Sizzled like sidemeat. —Tom Wicker
Sizzled like strips of bacon.

Skin
Skin as smooth as a satin muff.
Skin as smooth as silk. —John Gay
Skin as tan as toffee ice cream. —Dean R. Koontz
Skin as white and smooth as wax. —Lawrence Sanders
Skin like cream.
Skin like ice cream, like toasted-almond ice cream. —T. C. Boyle
Skin like milk. —Rex Beach
Skin like old parchment. —Douglas C. Jones
Skin like old silk. —Richard Bachman
Skin like rhinoceros hide. —Doris Leslie
Skin like silk. —*Arabian Nights*
Skin hung about him like an old lady's loose gown. —William Shakespeare
Skin hung on his bones like an old suit much too large for him.
   —W. Somerset Maugham
Skin smelled like fresh cotton. —John Updike
Skin that looked like green old cheese. —Margaret Mitchell
Skin the color of ripe grapefruit. —T. C. Boyle
Skin yellow like old parchment. —Bernard Cornwell
Her skin had a startlingly fine texture, like flour when you dip your hand into
   it. —John Updike

Skinny
Skinny as a fence post. —George Garrett
Skinny as a flute. —Elisabeth Ogilvie
Skinny as a greyhound.
Skinny as a snake.
Skinny as a sparrow. —Anne Tyler
Skinny as a worm.
   Also see Bony, Gaunt, Lean, Slender, Thin.

Skittered
Skittered like a stone on ice. —Donald McCaig
Skittered like a waterbug. —Douglas C. Jones
Skittered like bugs on the water. —Lee Smith

Skulked
Skulked like a coward.
Skulked like a coyote. —Douglas C. Jones
Skulked like a shivering dog. —A. C. Swinburne

Skulked like something wild.—Peter Bowman
    Also see Sneaked.

Sky

Sky as clear as blue glass.—Doris Leslie
Sky as dark as armour.—Rosemary H. Jarman
Sky pressed down like a weight.—T. C. Boyle
Sky was pale and smudged like a dirty sheet.—George Garrett
Starless sky as dark and thick as ink.—Emile Zola

Sleek

Sleek as a fat cat.
Sleek as a hide.—Lawrence Sanders
Sleek as a jet fighter plane.
Sleek as a mouse.—John Gay
Sleek as a sealskin.—Stephen King
Sleek as a sports car.
Sleek as a stag beetle.—Nicholas Salaman
Sleek as a torpedo.—Donald McCaig
Sleek as a wet otter.—Paige Mitchell
Sleek as an eel.
Sleek as corn silk.
Sleek and smug as a full-bellied shark.—T. C. Boyle

Slender

Slender as a flower stem.—Arthur S. Hardy
Slender as a knife.—Rosemary H. Jarman
Slender as a reed.
    Also see Bony, Lean, Skinny.

Slept

Slept like a brick.—Stephen King
Slept like a baby.
Slept like a child.—Frederic S. Isham
Slept like a cocked pistol.—Emile Zola
Slept like a corpse.
Slept like a dead man.—Mark Twain
Slept like a dog.
Slept like a drugged princess.—T. C. Boyle
Slept like a full dog by the fire.—George Garrett
Slept like a hound in the shade.—Owen Ulph
Slept like a hound under the front porch.
Slept like a log of wood.—Robert Louis Stevenson
Slept like a mouse.—Havilah Babcock
Slept like a night watchman.
Slept like a rock.
Slept like a stone.—Ralph Waldo Emerson
Slept like a stone at the bottom of the sea.—John Irving
Slept like a top.—John Gay
Slept like a train in a roundhouse.—John Ehle

Slept like a tree.—Robert Louis Stevenson
Slept like an alderman.—Jeffery Farnol
Slept like an on-duty deputy.—H. Allen Smith
Slept like death.—Zane Grey
Slept like wood, hollowed and fallen over.—Michael Doane
    Also see Relaxed, Rested.

Slick

Slick as a damp grip.—Dan Jenkins
Slick as a goat's butt.—Tom Wicker
Slick as a greased pig.
Slick as a gut.
Slick as a hog on ice.—James Sherburn
Slick as a minnow's lip.
Slick as a mole's face.
Slick as a snake.
Slick as a tallow candle.—Tom Wicker
Slick as a whistle.
Slick as deer guts on a doorknob.
Slick as frog hair.—Movie, *The Steel Cowboy*
Slick as glass.
Slick as goose grease.—Ferrol Sams
Slick as grease.—Gene Stratton-Porter
Slick as greased lightning.
Slick as hog guts on a doorknob.
Slick as owl shit.—John Inzer
Slick as snot on a brass door knob.
Slick as spit on a gold tooth.
Slick as squirrel guts on a brass doorknob.
Slick as warm owl shit.—Stephen King
Slick as wet paint.—George MacDonald Fraser
Slick as whale shit in an ice flow.
    Also see Slippery.

Slimy

Slimy as a snail.—Tabitha King
Slimy as a snake.
Slimy as an eel.
Slimy as fish guts.

Slipped

Slipped away like a cur when someone throws a stone at it.
    —George MacDonald Fraser
Slipped away like steam from a kettle.—Keith Korman
Slipped in like a cat.
Slipped out of his grasp like a bar of soap.
Slipped out of his grasp like a trout.—Charles McCarry

Slippery

Slippery as a greased pig.

Slippery as a wet tile floor.
Slippery as an eel.
Slippery as an eel dipped in lard.
Slippery as an eel's skin. —Wilbur Smith
Slippery as ice. —Theodore Watts-Dunton
    Also see Slick.

Slithered
Slithered like a harem dancer.
Slithered like a rattler. —George MacDonald Fraser
Slithered like a snake.

Slow
Slow as a barge on a reef. —Robert Houston
Slow as a cow with a full bag. —Glendon Swarthout
Slow as a cow's tail. —Debbie Fellenz
Slow as a crocodile. —Robert Houston
Slow as a herd of turtles in a cloud of clay.
Slow as a man in debt. —Elizabeth B. Browning
Slow as a mud turtle. —B. Q. Morgan
Slow as a municipal decision. —Derek Robinson
Slow as a plumber going for his tools.
Slow as a postal worker on Valium.
Slow as a river eroding rock. —Stephen King
Slow as a sexton ringing the village bell when the evening sun is low.
    —Henry W. Longfellow
Slow as a snail. —Robert Louis Stevenson
Slow as a snail with rheumatism.
Slow as a three-toed sloth. —T. C. Boyle
Slow as a subway at rush hour.
Slow as a swamp turtle.
Slow as a tortoise.
Slow as a worm. —Rudyard Kipling
Slow as an arthritic old man. —Peter Jenkins
Slow as an inchworm on an autumn leaf.
Slow as an old woman.
Slow as an overstuffed possum. —Owen Ulph
Slow as Christmas. —Robert Houston
Slow as city workers. —Pete Dexter
Slow as cold molasses running uphill.
Slow as cream rising on last year's buttermilk.
Slow as flowing oil. —Cecelia Holland
Slow as going backward. —Olive Ann Burns
Slow as grass growing. —Tom Wicker
Slow as judgment. —Robert Houston
Slow as molasses in winter.
Slow as smoke off a manure pile.
Slow as the drift of continents. —T. C. Boyle
Slow as the last drops squeezed from a lemon. —Patrick McGinley

Slow as the second coming. —Ivan Doig
Slow as the seven-year itch.
Slow as the wrath of Christ. —Ivan Doig
Slow as warm molasses. —Robert R. McCammon

Slurped
Slurped like a dog.
Slurped like an old man eating chowder. —Stephen King
Slurped like grandpa sipping coffee from a saucer.

Sly
Sly as a fox.
Sly as a hungry coyote.
Sly as a submarine.
    Also see Cunning, Sneaked, Wary, Wily.

Small
Small as a bee's knee.
Small as a eunuch's prospects.
Small as a flea bite.
Small as street sparrows.
Small as the little end of nothing. —John S. Farmer
Small as the point of a fine needle.
    Also see Short.

Smart
Smart as a carrot.
Smart as a cricket. —Shelby Foote
Smart as a keg of dictionaries. —Owen Ulph
Smart as a new-scraped carrot.
Smart as a pin.
Smart as a sack of rutabagas. —Joseph Wambaugh
Smart as a steel trap.
Smart as a treeful of owls. —H. Allen Smith
Smart as a whip.
Smart as a whiplash.
Smart as a whistle.
Smart as an outhouse mouse. —Owen Ulph
Smart as chain lightning. —Anne E. Perkins
Smart as forty crickets.
Smart as paint. —Robert Louis Stevenson
    Also see Intelligent.

Smelled
Smelled like a buzzard's breath. —Mark Twain
Smelled like a Chinese privy. —Stephen Longstreet
Smelled like a dead camel. —George MacDonald Fraser
Smelled like a distillery. —TV show, "Phillip Marlow, Private Eye"
Smelled like a fertilizer factory on a July afternoon.
Smelled like a French whore.

Smelled like a gorilla's armpit.
Smelled like a perfume factory.
Smelled like a pigsty.
Smelled like a rose.
Smelled like a twenty-hole privy.
Smelled like a whiskey bottle.
Smelled like an embalmer's bag.
Smelled like fifty million dead cigars.—J. D. Salinger
Smelled like Finnegan's goat.
Smelled like guts in a hogshead.—Stephen King
Smelled like it would choke a dog.—Mark Childress
Smelled like something dead.—James Sherburn
Smelled like something dead a week.—Lee Smith
Smelled like something the cat dragged in.
Smelled like the Ganges at low tide.
Smelled like the glowing sunshine.—Serbian ballad
Smelled like the old socks of a thousand putrified mummies.—Tom McEwen
Smelled like twenty pounds of shit in a ten-pound bag.—Richard Bachman
   Also see Fragrant, Stank.

Smile

Smile as broad as a barn door.—Loup Durand
Smile as cold as a deacon's watchchain.—Stephen King
Smile as cold as a polar bear's feet.—Eugene O'Neill
Smile as sweet as flowers.—A. C. Swinburne
Smile as wide and toothy as a death's-head.—Ferrol Sams
Smiled like a brewer's horse.—James Howell
Smiled like a butcher's dog.—Charles Willeford
Smiled like a cherub.—Richard Hovey
Smiled like a crazy man.—Michael Doane
Smiled like a friendly wolf.
Smiled like a happy crocodile.
Smiled like a horny angel.—James Wilcox
Smiled like a hyena.
Smiled like a lizard.—Richard Bachman
Smiled like a politician.—Tom DeHaven
Smiled like a skull.
Smiled like a snake in the Garden of Eden.—Robert R. McCammon
Smiled like a swordfish.
Smiled like Mona Lisa.
Smiled like the face of Buddha.—Lafcadio Hearn
Smiled like three dollars' worth of popcorn.
Smiled like when you heave a brickbat in a mud puddle.—Mark Twain
   Also see Grinned.

Smoked

Smoked like a chimney.—R. H. Barham
Smoked like a furnace.—Erskine Caldwell
Smoked like a kiln.—Robert Louis Stevenson

Smoked like a 1956 DeSoto.—Adam L. Gordon
Smoked like a steam engine.—Richard Bachman
Smoky as an Irish hut.—James Howell

Smooth

Smooth as a baby's bottom.
Smooth as a bed sheet.—Derek Robinson
Smooth as a billiard table.—Anthony Hamilton
Smooth as a car salesman.
Smooth as a dancer.
Smooth as a doorknob.
Smooth as a gun barrel.—Rex Beach
Smooth as a mountain stream.—Beer slogan
Smooth as a new laid egg.—Charles Dickens
Smooth as a perfect peach.
Smooth as a pickerel.
Smooth as a poker table.
Smooth as a pool table.
Smooth as a putting green.—James Wilcox
Smooth as a salt lick.—T. C. Boyle
Smooth as a schoolmarm's thigh.
Smooth as a spoon.
Smooth as calm water.—Douglas C. Jones
Smooth as corn silk.
Smooth as cream in a churn.—James Sherburn
Smooth as glass.—John Gay
Smooth as goat's cheese.—Cecelia Holland
Smooth as ice.—Thomas Heywood
Smooth as ivory.—Jeffery Farnol
Smooth as kidskin.—Ivan Doig
Smooth as polished jewelry.—Max Crawford
Smooth as sanded oak.—Douglas C. Jones
Smooth as satin.—Burma-Shave sign
Smooth as silk.
Smooth as suede.
Smooth as the inside of a young girl's thigh.—Dan Jenkins
Smooth as the northern plains.—Robert R. McCammon
Smooth as the palm of one's hand.
Smooth as the surface of a pebble.—Joseph Addison
Smooth as tile.—T. C. Boyle
Smooth as velvet.—Charles Reade
Smooth and shiny as a marble floor.—James Goldman
Smooth and shiny as the face of a spade.—William Dieter
About as smooth as a junior high school band.
    Also see Gentle, Mild.

Snapped

Snapped at it like a fish at bait.—Douglas C. Jones
Snapped at it like a trout at a fly.—George MacDonald Fraser

Snapped at the bait like a carp at bad cheese. —William Dieter
Snapped like a barnyard dog. —Tom Wicker
Snapped like a fiddle string.
Snapped like a mad dog. —George Eliot
Snapped like a stick.
Snapped like a straw. —Jeffery Farnol
Snapped like a twig.
Snapped like firecrackers.

Sneaked

Sneaked away like a well-whipped cur. —Harold Bell Wright
Sneaked like a cat burglar.
Sneaked like a viper. —George MacDonald Fraser
Sneaky as a cat.
Sneaky as a snake in the grass. —M. M. Kaye
Sneaky as an egg-sucking dog.
    Also see Cunning, Sly, Wily.

Snored

Snored like a blowfly hunting a fresh turd. —Owen Ulph
Snored like a gristmill. —T. C. Boyle
Snored like a horse.
Snored like a pig in the sun.
Snored like a walrus.
Snored like the rattle of autumn leaves. —Lee Smith
    Also see Drowsy.

Snorted

Snorted like a buffalo. —Lewis Carroll
Snorted like a bull in heat.
Snorted like a horse. —William Shakespeare
Snorted like an asthmatic horse. —William Pearson

Snug

Snug as a bug in a rug. —Benjamin Franklin
Snug as a duck in a ditch.
Snug as a parson. —Gustave Flaubert
Snug as a pig in pea straw. —Richard Davenport
Snug as figures in a glass paperweight.
Snug as the yolk in an egg. —Henrik Ibsen
    Also see Comfortable.

Sober

Sober as a buck shad.
Sober as a church.
Sober as a clock.
Sober as a cloud.
Sober as a coroner inspecting a corpse. —Amelie Rives
Sober as a deacon. —F. Hopkinson Smith
Sober as a hangman. —George Garrett

Sober as a hymn.—W. E. Henley
Sober as a judge.—Henry Fielding
Sober as a powderhorn.
Sober as a prairie dog in a cold rain.
Sober as a priest.—Rosemary H. Jarman
Sober as a shoemaker.
Sober as a stump.—Robert Houston
Sober as a vicar.—John G. Saxe
Sober as an ice cream soda on a New Year's Eve.
Sober as an owl.—Phoebe Gray
Sober as the skies.—Bret Harte
Sobering as a dash of cold water in the face.
     Also see Serious, Solemn.

Soft
Soft as a baby's butt.
Soft as a bird's nest.—Margaret Mitchell
Soft as a cloud looks.—Gary Jennings
Soft as a fat cat.
Soft as a featherbed.—T. C. Boyle
Soft as a government job.
Soft as a grape.—Joan Samson
Soft as a kitten's ear.—Neckwear slogan
Soft as a lady's glove.
Soft as a marshmallow.
Soft as a mother's kiss.—Elizabeth B. Browning
Soft as a mouse's ear.
Soft as a pillow.—W. B. Rands
Soft as a prayer.—Ernest Dowson
Soft as a rose petal.—Harold Bell Wright
Soft as a sleeping cat.—Theocritus
Soft as a zephyr's kiss.—David Garrick
Soft as air.—William Shakespeare
Soft as angel's wings.—James Whitcomb Riley
Soft as baby clothes.—Lee Smith
Soft as butter.
Soft as butter in the sun.—William Pearson
Soft as cheese.—John Irving
Soft as dove's down.—William Shakespeare
Soft as fleece.—Stephen Vincent Benet
Soft as footsteps in a dream.—T. C. Boyle
Soft as lips that laugh.—A. C. Swinburne
Soft as love.—William Falconer
Soft as moonlight.—J.R.R. Tolkien
Soft as mush.—Mark Twain
Soft as peach fuzz.
Soft as Pillsbury dough.
Soft as pity.—George D. Sofatey

Soft as pudding.
Soft as rain.—Oliver Wendell Holmes
Soft as satin.—William M. Thackeray
Soft as sifted flower.—Mark Childress
Soft as silk.—John Gay
Soft as swan's down.—Oliver Wendell Holmes
Soft as the dawn.—Samuel Lover
Soft as the morning dew.
Soft as the murmur's of a virgin's sigh.
Soft as the sound of doves in flight.—Robert R. McCammon
Soft as the voice of an angel.—Alice Hawthorne, "Whispering Hope"
Soft as velvet.—Gene Stratton-Porter
Soft as wool.—Robert Burton
Soft as young down.—William Shakespeare
Softly as a butterfly alighting on a flower.—Francis Grierson
    Also see Gentle, Mild.

Sold

Sold like fur coats to Hawaiians.
Sold like hotcakes.
Sold like ice skates in the Congo.
Sold like ice boxes in Alaska.
Sold like lemonade at a track meet.—T. C. Boyle

Solemn

Solemn as a bird.—Stephen R. Donaldson
Solemn as a dying man.—Maurice Hewlett
Solemn as a funeral procession.
Solemn as a judge.
Solemn as a man in church.—Tom Clancy
Solemn as a soldier going to the front.—Norman Mailer
Solemn as a tombstone.
Solemn as an Eskimo.—Richard Bachman
Solemn as an orphan at a family picnic.—Lois Battle
Solemn as an owl.
Solemn as organ music.
Solemn as the swearing in of an inspector of weights and measures.
Solemn and virtuous as deacons at a funeral.—Richard Taylor
    Also see Serious, Sober.

Solid

Solid as a bag of ballast.—F. Hopkinson Smith
Solid as a brick.—George Bernard Shaw
Solid as a gravestone.
Solid as a rock.
Solid as a sod house.—Alfred Henry Lewis
Solid as a stone wall.—Robert R. McCammon
Solid as a tank.
Solid as a totem pole.—Noel Behn

Solid as a tree trunk.—Tom Wicker
Solid as brass.
Solid as Dutch cheese.—F. Hopkinson Smith
Solid as marble.—Stephen R. Donaldson
Solid as the pyramids.—Brander Matthews
Solid as the Rock of Gibraltar.
Solid and squat as a Mayan temple.—Ferrol Sams
   Also see Firm.

Solitary

Solitary as a hermitage.—C. L. Skelton
Solitary as a tomb.—Victor Hugo
   Also see Alone, Lonely.

Soothing

Soothing as a father's arm.—Peter Jenkins
Soothing as a lotion.
Soothing as a massage.
Soothing as a mother's hand.
Soothing as a virgin's kiss.
Soothing as a warm bath.
   Also see Calm, Comfortable.

Sore

Sore as a boil.
Sore as a crab.
Sore as a flea on an iron dog.
Sore as a porcupine with ingrown quills.—Arthur Baer
Sore as a stubbed toe.
Sore as a wet nurse's nipple.
Sore as an ingrown toenail.
   Also see Ached, Mad, Painful, Sick.

Sought after

Sought after like a man who broke out of jail.
Sought after like Bonnie and Clyde.
Sought after like Dillinger.
Sought after like Jesse James.
Sought after like John Wilkes Booth.

Sounded

Sounded like a battle royal.
Sounded like a butter knife in a garbage disposal.—H. Allen Smith
Sounded like a distressed cat.
Sounded like a thousand demons banging anvils in hell.
   —George MacDonald Fraser
Sounded like a wet cloth slapped on stone.—George MacDonald Fraser
   Also see Noise.

Sour

Sour as a pickle.

Sour as a pickle taster's piss.
Sour as a rotten orange.—John McCarthy
Soured like milk in a thunderstorm.—Rex Beach

Sparkled

Sparkled like a diamond.
Sparkled like a garden after a shower.—Willa Cather
Sparkled like the morning dew.
    Also see Glistened, Shined.

Speckled

Speckled as a spotted hound.—Owen Ulph
Speckled like a guinea hen.—Erskine Caldwell

Sped

Sped like a homing pigeon.—Hamlin Garland
Sped like a house afire.
Sped like a shot.
Sped like a streak.
Sped like greased lightning.
    Also see Flew, Hurried, Ran, Went.

Speechless

Speechless as a mummy.
Speechless as a stone.—Elizabeth B. Browning
    Also see Mute, Silent.

Speedy

About as speedy as a post office worker.
About as speedy as a snail.
About as speedy as a steamroller.—George Ade
About as speedy as a turtle.
    Also see Fast, Fleeting, Flew, Quick, Swift, Took off, Went.

Spent money

Spent money like a clipper hand in port.—George MacDonald Fraser
Spent money like a doctor.
Spent money like a drunk duke on his birthday.
Spent money like a drunken sailor.
Spent money like a lord in Parliament.—Robert Louis Stevenson
Spent money like it had been left to him.—Rex Beach
Spent money like manhole covers.
Spent money like pouring it down a rat hole.—Margaret Mitchell
Spent money like throwing it out the window.—Thomas Hardy

Spied

Spied like a Peeping Tom.
Spied like a varmint.—Tom Wicker
Spied like the CIA.

Spineless

Spineless as a chocolate eclair.

Spineless as a jellyfish.
Spineless as an amoeba.
>   *Also see* Helpless, Weak.

Spit
Spit like a cobra.
Spit like a tobacco chewer.
Spit like an angry cat.—Margaret Mitchell

Spiteful
Spiteful as a ferret.—Max Hennessey
Spiteful as a monkey.—Honore de Balzac
Spiteful as an old maid.
>   *Also see* Hated, Malicious, Mean.

Spoke
Spoke like a book.—Robert Louis Stevenson
Spoke like a church elder to the town drunk.
Spoke like a father to a hurt child.—Margaret Mitchell
>   *Also see* Talked.

Spotted
Spotted like a coach dog.—Rex Beach
Spotted like a leopard.
Spotted like a pair of dice.

Sprang
Sprang from his chair like a schoolboy at the tap of the teacher's dismissing
>   bell.—Harold Bell Wright
Sprang like a jack-in-the-box.
Sprang like a switchblade.
Sprang like a tiger.—Ridley Wills
Sprang like Russian tumblers.—T. C. Boyle
Sprang up like dandelions after a spring shower.
Sprang upon him like a tiger upon a lamb.
>   *Also see* Bolted, Jumped, Leaped, Sprung up.

Sprawled
Sprawled like a discarded rag doll.—Douglas C. Jones
Sprawled like a rolled drunk.

Spread
Spread like a contagion.—Mary R. Rhinehard
Spread like a fungus.—Max Hennessey
Spread like a grassfire whipped by wind.
Spread like a lie.
Spread like a slow balm.—Victor Canning
Spread like cancer.
Spread like fire.—Edward Bulwer-Lytton
Spread like fire among dry stubble.—T. S. Arthur
Spread like fire in broom sedge.—Erskine Caldwell

Spread like fire on a parched plain.—Bernard Cornwell
Spread like floodwater.
Spread like gossip.
Spread like gypsy moths in June.—Joan Samson
Spread like ivy.
Spread like lightning.—Victor Appleton
Spread like measles in a country school.
Spread like oil on still water.—Douglas C. Jones
Spread like scandal after a sewing bee.—William Sage
Spread like wildfire.

Sprouted
Sprouted like a clinging vine.—T. C. Boyle
Sprouted like dandelions.
Sprouted like weeds on a cow pie.
Sprouted like wildflowers.
   Also see Flourished, Grew, Thrived.

Sprung up
Sprung up like Jack's beanstalk.—Thomas Hardy
Sprung up like wildflowers.
   Also see Bolted, Jumped, Sprang, Sprouted.

Spry
Spry as a bad wildcat.—Jack London
Spry as a cat.—Anne E. Perkins
Spry as a cricket.
Spry as a fox.
Spry as a goat.—Mary Stewart
Spry as a gray squirrel.
Spry as a sparrow.
Spry as an old yellow tomcat.
   Also see Agile, Lively, Nimble.

Square
Square as a boxing ring.
Square as a brick.—F. Hopkinson Smith
Square as a child's block.
Square as a chimney.
Square as a die.—Rex Beach

Squeaked
Squeaked like a rusty hinge.
Squeaked like a startled mouse.—George MacDonald Fraser
Squeaked like a village of tree toads.—Jack Matthews
Squeaked like an angry mouse.—Mary Stewart

Squealed
Squealed like a child at play.
Squealed like a drunken fishwife.—Rex Beach
Squealed like a sow farrowing a litter of broken glass.—John Madson

Squealed like a steam whistle.
Squealed like a stuck pig.
Squealed like an accordian.
Squealed like pigs at a slaughter.
   Also see Screamed, Screeched, Shrieked.

Squeezed
Squeezed like an orange.
Squeezed like an accordian.

Squirmed
Squirmed like a child in church.
Squirmed like a dog with a flea on its ass.
Squirmed like a schoolboy undergoing maternal inspection.
   —Harold Bell Wright
Squirmed like a worm in hot ashes.

Stable
Stable as earth.—Thomas Blacklock
Stable as the hills.—Lewis H. Green
   Also see Enduring, Firm, Lasted, Resolute, Steadfast.

Stacked
Stacked like a brick outhouse.
Stacked like a truckload of melons.—Owen Ulph
Stacked like canned goods in a supermarket.
Stacked like slices of bread.—Mary Stewart
   Also see Piled.

Staggered
Staggered like a child learning to walk.
Staggered like a drunken man.—*Old Testament*
   Also see Paced, Walked.

Stale
Stale as last week's bread.
Stale as old beer.
Stale as the butt of a dead cigar.—Rudyard Kipling
Stale as yesterday's newspaper.
   Also see Obsolete.

Stalked
Stalked like a cat on the prowl.
Stalked like a heron.—Rosemary H. Jarman
Stalked like a hunter.
   Also see Followed, Pursued.

Stank
Stank like a bobcat in heat.—Stephen King
Stank like a city sewer.—Jack Matthews
Stank like a church.
Stank like a dead skunk in the road.

Stank like a polecat.
Stank like a sewer.
Stank like a sick swamp. —Jack Matthews
Stank like a weasel fart.
Stank like a wet dog.
Stank like old cheese.
Also see Fragrant, Smelled.

Stared

Stared like a bird staring at a snake.
Stared like a dead pig. —Francios Rabelais
Stared like a fakir in a trance.
Stared like a glass eye.
Stared like a hen stares at the duck she has hatched. —Thomas Hardy
Stared like a hypnotized rabbit. —M. M. Kaye
Stared like a lunatic over the asylum wall. —Tristan Jones
Stared like a mad bull.
Stared like a man turned to stone. —Robert Louis Stevenson
Stared like a poisoned pig. —Benjamin Franklin
Stared like a stuck pig. —John Gay
Stared like a wooden saint. —George Eliot
Stared like an idiot.
Stared like he was staring at a bleeding statue. —T. C. Boyle
Stared like one dazed.
Stared like one stunned.
Stared like the eyes of a carp.
Also see Gaped, Gazed.

Stately

Stately as a king. —Walter Thornbury
Stately as a queen. —William M. Thackeray
Stately as a Victorian mansion.
Also see Grand, Majestic.

Steadfast

Steadfast as a principle. —John Keats
Steadfast as a sentry.
Steadfast as a wall. —Geoffrey Chaucer
Steadfast as the sun. —Thomas Carlyle
Also see Firm, Loyal, Reliable, Strong, True.

Steady

Steady as a church.
Steady as a clock.
Steady as a hay wagon. —Juan Valera
Steady as a mill. —Mark Twain
Steady as a rock.
Steady as a rock in a frozen brook. —Stephen King
Steady as a surgeon's hand.
Steady as an old plow horse.

. . . .

Steady as an ox.
Steady as an undertaker. —F. Hopkinson Smith
Steady as granite.
Steady as shore lights in a storm.
Steady as steel. —Robert Louis Stevenson
Steady as the throb of an engine.
Steady as the stare of a glass eye.
Steady as time.
Steady and reliable as tested steel.
 Also see Composed, Steadfast, Unruffled.

Stern

Stern as a chaperone.
Stern as a Lutheran preacher.
Stern as a nun. —Tom DeHaven
Stern as death. —Robert Service
Stern as fate. —Robert Service
Stern as stone. —J.R.R. Tolkien

Sticky

Sticky as cockleburrs.
Sticky as fly paper.

Stiff

Stiff as a board. —Zane Grey
Stiff as a dead body. —Jonathan Dickinson
Stiff as a fence post. —T. C. Boyle
Stiff as a five-day corpse.
Stiff as a frozen fish.
Stiff as a frozen statue.
Stiff as a handspike. —Robert Louis Stevenson
Stiff as a mean dog's tail.
Stiff as a plank.
Stiff as a poker.
Stiff as a post. —Lee Smith
Stiff as a ramrod. —Charles J. Lever
Stiff as a ram's horn. —Thomas Hardy
Stiff as a shingle. —Robert Lewis Taylor
Stiff as a side of meat. —Ivan Doig
Stiff as a stone. —John Ruskin
Stiff as a tombstone. —T. C. Boyle
Stiff as a twig. —George Garrett
Stiff as a wax dummy.
Stiff as butchers' meat. —Anthony Forrest
Stiff as frozen leather. —Bernard Cornwell
Stiff as glass. —Robert Bausch
Stiff as leather.
Stiff as Paddy's father when he was nine days dead.
Stiff as salt-dried rope.

• •

Stiff as wood.—Mary Stewart
Stiffened like a dog on point.
About as stiff as boiled spaghetti.
    Also see Firm, Rigid.

Still

Still as a cairn.—Stephen R. Donaldson
Still as a churchyard at midnight.
Still as a corpse.
Still as a graveyard.—O. Henry
Still as a king's mummy in a catacomb.—Gustave Flaubert
Still as a little old owl.—Lee Smith
Still as a monument.
Still as a mouse.—Mark Twain
Still as a picture.—John Greeleaf Whittier
Still as a pool.
Still as a portrait.
Still as a rock.—Mark Twain
Still as a rock on a mud flat.
Still as a saint.—Michael Doane
Still as a statue.—Fernan Cabellero
Still as a stump.—Gary Jennings
Still as a sunning crocodile.
Still as a tomb.—Harold Bell Wright
Still as a tombstone.—Homer
Still as a windless bush.—Rosemary H. Jarman
Still as an idol.—John Greenleaf Whittier
Still as death.—Robert Louis Stevenson
Still as lake water.—Mary Stewart
Still as Lot's wife.—Ivan Doig
Still as Sabbath day.—Shelby Foote
Still as stone.—*Old Testament*
Still as the grave.—William Shakespeare
Still as the moment before creation.—Anita Mason
Still as water in a jar.—Cecelia Holland
Still like Sunday.—Mark Twain
    Also see Calm, Noiseless, Placid, Quiet, Serene.

Stirred up

Stirred up like a nest of hornets.
Stirred up like a stepped-on anthill.—George Garrett
Stirred up like the top of a drum.—James Whitcomb Riley
Stirred up like the trumpet's call to strife.—John Greenleaf Whittier
    Also see Roused.

Stood

Stood as still as a great dark stone.—Lee Smith
Stood as still as the angel of death.—Lee Smith
Stood as straight and firm as a stone wall.—Tom Wicker

Stood as straight as a lamppost. —Howard Spring
Stood as straight as a pine sapling. —Rex Beach
Stood as straight as an Indian. —Lee Smith
Stood as straight as soldiers at attention.
Stood like a great oak tree.
Stood like a grotesque statue. —Robert R. McCammon
Stood like a lump.
Stood like a patient ox. —Stephen King
Stood like a pyramid. —Emma Marshall
Stood like a rock. —Zane Grey
Stood like a sentinel under inspection. —George Meredith
Stood like a sparrow in a cow turd. —George Garrett
Stood like a statue. —Zane Grey
Stood like a stud bull.
Stood like a watchful hawk.
Stood like a wax dummy.
Stood like a wet dog. —Janusz Glowacki
Stood like a wooden man. —Rex Beach

Stood out
Stood out like a beacon. —Sidney Sheldon
Stood out like a broken nose. —Jack Matthews
Stood out like a bull snake in a bathtub.
Stood out like a fried egg stain on a full dress vest. —Arthur Baer
Stood out like a giraffe in the back seat of a Volkswagen.
Stood out like a goose in chicken soup. —Owen Ulph
Stood out like a kangaroo pushing a shopping cart. —William Pearson
Stood out like a kingpin in a bowling alley.
Stood out like a lightning bug. —Mark Twain
Stood out like a picture in a magazine. —Lee Smith
Stood out like a salesman in a white suit. —Ivan Doig
Stood out like a sore thumb.
Stood out like a sore thumb at an amateur piano contest.
Stood out like a statue.
Stood out like an unzipped fly.
Stood out like the pyramids.
Stood out like virgins at the gates of hell. —Elizabeth Adler
Also see Attracted, Evident, Obvious, Out of place, Plain.

Stout
Stout as a miller's waistcoat.
Stout as a mule.
Stout as a war-horse. —George Garrett
Stout as an oak. —Peter Jenkins
Also see Strong.

Straight
Straight as a beeline.
Straight as a beggar can spit. —Rudyard Kipling

Straight as a bolt from a crossbow sped. —Mark Twain
Straight as a candle. —Hans Christian Anderson
Straight as a crow flies. —Charles Dickens
Straight as a dart. —Pilpay
Straight as a deck seam.
Straight as a fishing line.
Straight as a gun barrel. —Harold Bell Wright
Straight as a homing bird. —Gene Stratton-Porter
Straight as a lamppost. —Howard Spring
Straight as a lance.
Straight as a line. —Thomas Hardy
Straight as a loon's leg. —Joseph Smith, Jr.
Straight as a pine sapling. —Rex Beach
Straight as a plank. —F. Hopkinson Smith
Straight as a plumb line.
Straight as a poplar. —Charlotte Brontë
Straight as a ramrod. —William M. Raine
Straight as a reed. —Frederic S. Isham
Straight as a rule. —John Bunyan
Straight as a ruler.
Straight as a sapling. —Doris Leslie
Straight as a Sioux chief. —Booker T. Washington
Straight as a shingle.
Straight as a shot. —Jack Fuller
Straight as a slat. —Robert Lewis Taylor
Straight as a soldier.
Straight as a spear. —Nathaniel Lee
Straight as a string. —Mark Twain
Straight as a yardstick.
Straight as a young poplar. —Jeffery Farnol
Straight as a young tree. —Howard Spring
Straight as an arrow. —Edward Bulwer-Lytton
Straight as an ironing board. —Robert Houston
Straight as fence wire. —Ivan Doig
Straight as the backbone of a herring.
Straight as the crow flies.
Straight as the flight of the dove. —George Meredith
Straight as the part in a bartender's hair. —Glendon Swarthout
Straight as thin icicles. —Owen Ulph
Straight as virtue. —John Crosby
    Also see Erect, Upright.

Strange

Strange as a dreamer's mad images. —Percy B. Shelley
Strange as a one-legged dance. —John Ehle
Strange as a wedding without a bridegroom.
Strange as death. —Elizabeth B. Browning

Strange as snow in July.
   Also see Mysterious, Rare.

Stricken
Stricken like a child approached by a mean dog.
Stricken like a rabbit confronted by a fox.

Strong
Strong as a beer-wagon horse.—Stephen Longstreet
Strong as a bull.—Thomas Carlyle
Strong as a cart horse.—M. M. Kaye
Strong as a Flanders mare.
Strong as a garlic milkshake.
Strong as a giant.—Jeffery Farnol
Strong as a horse.
Strong as a lion.—Francis Fawkes
Strong as a tractor.—Charles Willeford
Strong as a vice.—Zane Grey
Strong as a white oak stump.
Strong as an acre of garlic.
Strong as an iron chain.—Pilpay
Strong as an oaken staff.—Henry Van Dyke
Strong as an ox.
Strong as Atlas.
Strong as battery acid.
Strong as God.—Friedrich Nietzsche
Strong as granny's corset.
Strong as Hercules.
Strong as homemade soap.
Strong as horseradish.
Strong as iron.—*Old Testament*
Strong as iron bands.—Henry W. Longfellow
Strong as love.—A. C. Swinburne
Strong as mustard.—John Gay
Strong as Pluto's gates.—William Shakespeare
Strong as rawhide.
Strong as Samson.—Francios Rabelais
Strong as steel.
Strong as the wind.—Mary Johnston
Strong as Zeus.—Aeschylus
Strong and solid as the biceps of Hercules.—Robert R. McCammon
   Also see Potent, Stable, Steadfast, Stout, Sturdy.

Struggled
Struggled like a beached trout.—Owen Ulph
Struggled like a beast in a trap.—Harold Bell Wright
Struggled like a fish on a line.
Struggled like a flower toward heaven.
Struggled like an old lawyer between two fees.—Richard Congreve

Strutted

Strutted like a bantam.
Strutted like a banty rooster.
Strutted like a berserk ostrich. —Bernie Miklasz, *St. Louis Post-Dispatch*
Strutted like a cock o' the walk.
Strutted like a crow. —Tobias G. Smollett
Strutted like a duchess. —George MacDonald Fraser
Strutted like a new churchwarden. —Thomas Adams
Strutted like a peacock.
Strutted like a thespian.
    Also see Danced, Pranced, Swaggered and strutted, Walked.

Stubborn

Stubborn as a child.
Stubborn as a cross-eyed mule.
Stubborn as a mule.
Stubborn as a mule refusing baptism. —Stephen Longstreet
Stubborn as a stuck door.
    Also see Contrary, Inflexible, Resolute, Unyielding.

Stuck

Stuck like a bad smell.
Stuck like a barnacle.
Stuck like a burr.
Stuck like a coat of paint. —Lewis W. Green
Stuck like a cocklebur.
Stuck like a cocklebur to a sheep's coat.
Stuck like a country postmaster to his office. —Artemus Ward
Stuck like a fly in molasses.
Stuck like a horse leech's daughter.
Stuck like a knife. —Dan Jenkins
Stuck like a leech. —R. D. Blackmore
Stuck like a pincushion.
Stuck like a postage stamp.
Stuck like a shadow.
Stuck like a wet shirt.
Stuck like a tick.
Stuck like a tick on a hound's back. —Patrick Smith
Stuck like a tick to a sheep's back. —Maurice Hewlett
Stuck like flypaper.
Stuck like glue.
Stuck like gum under a movie seat.
Stuck like shipwrecked mariners on a rock. —J. M. Barrie
Stuck like the paper to the wall.
Stuck tighter than a poor relation.
Stuck together like an Italian family.
Stuck together like sand burrs. —John Gay

Stuck out

Stuck out like a cockroach on a wedding cake.—Stephen King
Stuck out like a sore thumb.
Stuck out like a wooden leg.
Stuck out like bad teeth.—Mark Childress
   Also see Evident, Obvious, Out of place, Stood out, Went over.

Stuffed

Stuffed like a Christmas goose.—Anthony Forrest
Stuffed like a roasting chicken.
Stuffed like a Thanksgiving turkey.
   Also see Packed.

Stumbled

Stumbled like fat sheep.—Stephen Crane
Stumbled around like a blind dog in a meat market.
Stumbled around like a sleepwalker in a strange town.—Jack Matthews
   Also see Fell.

Stung

Stung like a bee in the warm core of a rose.—Ouida
Stung like a frozen lash.—Robert Service
Stung like a gallinipper.
Stung like a hive of angry bees.—George Garrett
Stung like a scorpion.—Osmani proverb
Stung like a serpent.—Robert Burton
Stung like an adder.—*Old Testment*
Stung like bees unhived.—Robert Browning
Stung like ice.
Stung like scorn.—Thomas Hardy

Stunned

Stunned as if a good boxer had just caught him with a startling left hook and
   a stultifying right.—Norman Mailer
Stunned like a knocked-down boxer in the first round.

Stupid

Stupid as a Berkshire hog.—George MacDonald Fraser
Stupid as a coot.—Frank Cowan
Stupid as a loon.
Stupid as a post.—Clement Robinson
Stupid as a tree.
Stupid as a stone.—Robert Browning
Stupid as an excuse.
   Also see Dense, Dumb, Foolish, Ignorant, Thick.

Sturdy

Sturdy as a stud.
Sturdy as a wild-ass colt.—William Cowper
Sturdy as an oak.
   Also see Strong.

Stuttered
Stuttered like a boy caught with his hand in the cookie jar.
Stuttered like a cement mixer.
Stuttered like a cracked record.

Sublime
Sublime as a kiss.
Sublime as heaven.—William Thompson
Sublime as love.

Subtle
Subtle as failing of the sight.—C. L. Hildreth
About as subtle as a bass drum.
About as subtle as a dead pig.—T. Wright
About as subtle as a fire engine.
About as subtle as a government mule.
About as subtle as a nun.
About as subtle as a parade.
About as subtle as a slamming door.
About as subtle as a sledgehammer.
About as subtle as an earthquake.
About as subtle as an elephant at a Tupperware party.
About as subtle as tapping a pile driver.—Channing Pollack
About as subtle as two cymbals dropped down the stairs.—Michael Doane

Sudden
Sudden as a cyclone touching down from a clear blue sky.—Stephen Wright
Sudden as a fart.
Sudden as a massacre.—Mark Twain.
Sudden as an April shower.
Sudden as an assassin's dagger.—Walter Winward
Sudden as lightning.—Ben Jonson
Sudden as the bursting of a flood that had long been held back by a dike.
    —J.R.R. Tolkien
Sudden as the single bark of a dog.—T. C. Boyle
Sudden as thunder out of a clear sky.—Robert Louis Stevenson
Sudden and swift as a raging cyclone.
    Also see Abrupt, Quick.

Suffered
Suffered like a shot soldier.
Suffered like a wounded deer.
Suffered like an animal dying in a trap.—Margaret Mitchell
    Also see Hurt.

Superfluous
Superfluous as a fifth wheel.
Superfluous as a Gideon's Bible at the Ritz.—F. Scott Fitzgerald
Superfluous as an echo.

Superfluous as to light a candle to the sun.—Robert South
Also see Needed.

Superstitious
Superstitious as a sailor.
Superstitious as an Alabama swamp witch.
Superstitious as voodoo.

Supple
Supple as a buggy whip.—George Jean Nathan
Supple as a glove.
Supple as a tobacco pouch.—Honore de Balzac
Supple as a young dog.—George Garrett
Supple as the necks of a swan.
Also see Limber, Limp.

Supreme
Supreme as a pope.—John Milton
Supreme as God.

Sure
Sure as a brook must have banks.
Sure as a goose goes barefoot.
Sure as a sow has tits.—William Dieter
Sure as a dead man stinks.
Sure as a gin bottle gets empty.—T. C. Boyle
Sure as a gun is iron.—Margaret Mitchell
Sure as a squirrel will climb a tree.
Sure as amen in church.
Sure as an arrow.—Robert R. McCammon
Sure as birth and death.
Sure as comes the postman and the sun.—William M. Thackeray
Sure as day.—William Shakespeare
Sure as day comes.—Erskine Caldwell
Sure as death.—William Shakespeare
Sure as death and taxes.
Sure as Dover stands at Dover.—Thomas Hood
Sure as fire burns.—John Ehle
Sure as fire is hot.—Harold Bell Wright
Sure as fleas bite.
Sure as God made little fishes.
Sure as God made little green apples.—Thomas Hardy
Sure as God sees me.—Robert Louis Stevenson
Sure as God's in heaven.
Sure as gospel.
Sure as grass grows in the field.—Edward Eggleston
Sure as gravity.
Sure as heaven.
Sure as hell.
Sure as linen gets gray.—T. C. Boyle

Sure as night follows day.
Sure as one hand washes the other.
Sure as one's creed.
Sure as preachings.
Sure as rain's got water in it. —William Dieter
Sure as Satan. —Thomas Hardy
Sure as smoke is proof of fire. —Cicero
Sure as snakes crawl.
Sure as summer follows spring.
Sure as taxes.
Sure as the devil's in London. —Henry Fielding
Sure as the fishes swim and the birds do fly. —Gerhart Hauptman
Sure as the leaves will fall in autumn.
Sure as the rising of the morning sun.
Sure as the sun rises on Wednesday morning. —Erskine Caldwell
Sure as the sun shines.
Sure as the sunrise. —Harold Bell Wright
Sure as the world. —Lee Smith
Sure as there's snakes in Virginia.
Sure as thorns in the beds of hell. —Owen Ulph
Sure as two and two makes four.
Sure as you are a foot high. —William M. Raine
Sure as you're alive.
Sure as you're born. —Zane Grey
Sure as you live and breathe.
Surely as water will wet us, as surely as fire will burn. —Rudyard Kipling
Just as sure as you're born. —Mark Twain

Surefooted
Surefooted as a goat. —Ouida
Surefooted as a Grand Canyon donkey.
Surefooted as a mountain goat. —Zane Grey

Surly
Surly as a bear.
Surly as a butcher's dog.
Surly as the night clerk at a cheap hotel.
   Also see Mean, Ornery.

Surprised
Surprised as a kid seeing Santa.
Surprised as a pregnant nun.
Surprised as Dewey.

Suspicious
Suspicious as a cat. —Honore de Balzac
Suspicious as a hairpin in a bachelor's bed.
Suspicious as a virgin nun. —Gerald Seymour
   Also see Wary.

Swaggered and strutted

Swaggered and strutted like a Bronx pimp.
Swaggered and strutted like a crow in the gutter.—George Garrett
Swaggered and strutted like a peacock.
  Also see Strutted, Walked.

Swam

Swam like a duck.—William Shakespeare
Swam like a fish.—Victor Appleton
Swam like an otter.
Swam about like a rock.
Swam about like a stone.—Robert Louis Stevenson

Swarmed

Swarmed like a fair.—Johann Schiller
Swarmed like an anthill.
Swarmed like ants.
Swarmed like bees.—Lewis W. Green
Swarmed like bees around a hive.—Margaret Mitchell
Swarmed like beetles.—Doris Leslie
Swarmed like Comanches around a wagon train.—Robert R. McCammon
Swarmed like gnats.
Swarmed like hornets.
Swarmed like locusts.
Swarmed like roaches in Arizona.

Swayed

Swayed like a bird on a twig.—Arnold Bennett
Swayed like a charmed cobra.—Jim Dodge
Swayed like a drunken man.—Mary Stewart
Swayed like a man at sea.—Jack Matthews
Swayed like a snake about to strike.—T. C. Boyle
Swayed like an elephant.
Swayed like dancers.—Wilbur Smith

Sweated

Sweated like a field hand.
Sweated like a horny sailor.—Derek Robinson
Sweated like a mule.—Tom Wicker
Sweated like a New York waiter.—David Letterman
Sweated like a pig.—Stephen King
Sweated like a plow hand.—Erskine Caldwell
Sweated like a swamp rat.—Norman Mailer
Sweated like a trooper.
Sweated like old cheese.—Derek Robinson
Sweated like two mules.—Jack Matthews

Sweet

Sweet as a candy-dipper's handshake.
Sweet as a church alto.—Thomas Thompson

Sweet as a daisy. —F. Hopkinson Smith
Sweet as a girl graduate.
Sweet as a June breeze in a hay field.
Sweet as a maiden's dream of love. —John Greenleaf Whittier
Sweet as a marshmallow.
Sweet as a puppy. —Jack Matthews
Sweet as a rose. —John Gay
Sweet as strawberry shortcake.
Sweet as a stump-roped cow.
Sweet as a sugarplum.
Sweet as a Vidalia onion.
Sweet as a violet. —John Ford
Sweet as an angel's dreams.
Sweet as apple cider. —Eddie Leonard
Sweet as first love. —Gerald Massey
Sweet as forgiveness. —A. C. Swinburne
Sweet as fresh berries and cream. —James Sherburn
Sweet as honey. —*New Testament*
Sweet as love. —John Keats
Sweet as new wine. —John Baret
Sweet as peaches and cream.
Sweet as pie.
Sweet as rest. —A. C. Swinburne
Sweet as showers on dry hills. —J.R.R. Tolkien
Sweet as sugar.
Sweet as the ecstasy of reconciliation. —Doris Leslie
Sweet as the roses of May.
Sweet as the shepherd's pipe upon the mountains. —Thomas Otway
Sweet as the smile of spring.
Sweet as the sound of a bell. —Zane Grey
Sweet and calm as a sister's kiss. —P. J. Bailey
Sweet and yeasty as new-baked bread. —George Garrett
    Also see Charming, Pleasant.

Swelled up
Swelled up like a balloon.
Swelled up like a blacksmith's bellows. —Victor Hugo
Swelled up like a gobbler. —Margaret Mitchell
Swelled up like a gourd.
Swelled up like a melon.
Swelled up like a mushroom.
Swelled up like a poisoned pup. —Gene Stratton-Porter
Swelled up like a sail by the sea breeze. —Gustave Flaubert
Swelled up like a summer sausage. —Stephen King
Swelled up like a toad.
Swelled up like a tumor. —Ralph Waldo Emerson
Swelled up like a turkey gobbler.
Swelled up like an angry hen ruffling her feathers.

Swelled up like an inner tube.
Swelled up like an old tire with too much air in it.—Stephen King
Swelled up like the bosom of a man set fire.—William Wordsworth
Also see Puffed.

Swept

Swept like leaves before an autumn gale.—William Cullen Bryant
Swept like wildfire.
Swept along like a twig in a millrace.—Richard Hough
Swept along like flecks of foam on a river.—Shelby Foote
Swept the country like a locust swarm.—Ouida
Swept the country like a plague.
Swept through like fire through tender.—Ian St. James
Swept up like roaches.
Swept up like rat droppings.—V. G. Bortin

Swift

Swift as a blow.—Robert Louis Stevenson
Swift as a cat.—Rex Beach
Swift as a flash.—Henry W. Longfellow
Swift as a fox.—Harold Bell Wright
Swift as a greyhound.—Percy B. Shelley
Swift as a panther.—Robert Service
Swift as a lithe sixteen-year-old.—Margaret Mitchell
Swift as a thunderbolt.—Richard Lovelace
Swift as a whirlwind.—Francois Chandernagor
Swift as an arrow.—William Blake
Swift as an eagle.
Swift as light.—Barry Cornwell
Swift as lightning.—William Cowper
Swift as quicksilver.
Swift as sharp scissors in silk.—Rikki Ducornet
Swift as the flowing wind.—J.R.R. Tolkien
Swift as the wind.
Swift as thought.—William Shakespeare
Swift and graceful as a bird.—Jeffery Farnol
Also see Fast, Off, Quick, Took off, Went.

Swore

Swore like a bargee.—Victor Canning
Swore like a costermonger.
Swore like a drunken sailor.
Swore like a drunken tapster.—John Doran
Swore like a drunken tinker.—George Garrett
Swore like a fishwife.
Swore like a fishwoman.—Mark Twain
Swore like a judge.—Jack Matthews
Swore like a longshoreman.
Swore like a lord.—T. Elyot

Swore like a Mississippi pilot.—George MacDonald Fraser
Swore like a mule skinner.
Swore like a pirate.
Swore like a porter.—Thomas B. Macaulay
Swore like a preacher's son.—H. L. Mencken
Swore like a sailor.
Swore like a tartar.—Honore de Balzac
Swore like a teamster.
Swore like a trooper.—Robert Southey
Swore like an army mule skinner.—Margaret Mitchell
Swore like an imp.—Victor Hugo
Swore like an unemployed longshoreman.—Josh Greenfield
Swore like the army in Flanders.—Laurence Sterne

Swung
Swung like a hanged man.
Swung like a pendulum.

Symmetrical
Symmetrical as a circle.
Symmetrical as a picture frame.
Symmetrical as Grecian art.—Margaret Mitchell
Symmetrical as the handles on a vase.—John Updike

Systematic
Systematic as a country cemetery.—James R. Lowell
Systematic as algebra.
Systematic as law.
Systematic as peeling an onion.—William Pearson
   Also see Orderly.

Tacky

Tacky as poor manners.
Tacky as turkey turds.—Paul Hemphill
Also see Cheap, Gaudy.

Tactful

Tactful as a concierge.
Tactful as a matured politician.
Tactful as an ambassador.
About as tactful as a mad rattlesnake.

Talked

Talked like a Baptist preacher making a recruiting speech.—Margaret Mitchell
Talked like a book.—Edward Bulwer-Lytton
Talked like a soda-water bottle just uncorked.—A.S.M. Hutchinson
Talked like an apothecary.
Talked like an old man with a hernia.—George MacDonald Fraser
Talked like he was in his dotage.—Margaret Mitchell
Talked like he was vaccinated with a phonograph needle.
Talked like running water.—A. W. Chambers
Also see Prated.

Tall

Tall as a doorway.—Ivan Doig
Tall as a Georgia pine.
Tall as a maypole.
Tall as a pine.
Tall as a pump handle.—Stephen Longstreet
Tall as a steeple.
Tall as a tree.—Mark Twain
Tall as nine axe handles.
Tall as Robert Pershing Wadlow (world's tallest recorded man, 8' 11.1",
1918–1940).

Tall as the Eiffel Tower.
Tall as the Empire State Building.
Tall and burly as a black oak.—Robert R. McCammon
Tall and thin as a bean pole with the crop picked.—Victor Canning
Tall and thin as a stilt-walker.—Ferrol Sams
   Also see High.

Tantalizing
Tantalizing as a half-remembered tune.
Tantalizing as the last piece of pie.
   Also see Alluring, Appealing, Attractive, Enticing.

Tapered
Tapered like a cone.
Tapered like a lizard's tail.—Oliver Wendell Holmes
Tapered like an icicle.

Tart
Tart as a lemon.
Tart as a sour pickle.
Tart as buttermilk.
Tart as the taste of juniper.—T. C. Boyle
   Also see Sour.

Tasted
Tasted like a hunk of old cold cannibal.—Mark Twain
Tasted like a manure rake.—Stephen King
Tasted like a sumo wrestler's jock strap.
Tasted like a wet dog.
Tasted like a wet sheepdog.
Tasted like a whale suppository.
Tasted like dinosaur vomit.
Tasted like fried monkey vomit.
Tasted like old dead gopher shit.—Stephen King
Tasted like mule piss.—Owen Ulph
Tasted like panther piss.
Tasted like rusty nails.—James Sherburn
Tasted like something you'd sit in to remove a tattoo.—H. Allen Smith
Tasted like stump water.
Tasted like the floor of a bird cage.
Tasted like the sole of a zookeeper's boot.
Tasted like vulture spit.—H. Allen Smith
Tasted like weasel piss.—Keith Korman
Tasted like worm piss.
Tasted like yak shit.
   Also see Mouth, Tongue.

Tattered
Tattered as magazines in a dentist's office.—Stephen King

Tattered like a lumberjack's shirt.
Tattered like an old quilt much used.

Taunted

Taunted him like a baited badger. —Rex Beach
Taunted him like a prostitute.

Taut

Taut as a bowstring. —Robert Louis Stevenson
Taut as a drum head. —H. Allen Smith
Taut as a fiddle. —Robert Louis Stevenson
Taut as a fiddle string. —George MacDonald Fraser
Taut as a guy wire.
Taut as a piano wire. —Peter Straub
Taut as a violin string. —Margaret Truman
Taut as a watch spring. —Graeme Kent
Taut as new-strung barbed wire. —Ferrol Sams
Taut as wet hemp. —Rosemary H. Jarman
    Also see Tense, Tight.

Tedious

Tedious as a long sermon.
Tedious as a twice-told tale. —Homer
Tedious as eating a pomegranate.
Tedious as waiting for a train.
    Also see Tired.

Temper

Temper as explosive as a gun. —Rex Beach
Temper as mild as milk. —Thomas Hardy
Temper like a firecracker.
Temper like a wasp in a bottle.
Temper like a wild dog's. —George MacDonald Fraser
Temper that raged like an oil well ablaze.
    —Bernie Miklasz, *St. Louis Post-Dispatch*
    Also see Mad.

Temporary

Temporary as a haircut.
Temporary as a sunset.
Temporary as a wave.
Temporary as an erection.

Tempting

Tempting as a box of chocolates.
Tempting as Eve without a fig.
    Also see Alluring, Appealing, Attractive, Enticing, Tantalizing.

Tenacious

Tenacious as a bulldog.
Tenacious as a recurring dream.

Tenacious as a terrier.—Vincent Bugliosi
  Also see Resolute, Stubborn, Unyielding.

Tender

Tender as a baby's fingers—Stephen Wright
Tender as a chick.—John Gay
Tender as a memory.
Tender as a mother's heart.—Rick Roethler
About as tender as a judge's heart.
  Also see Kind, Soft.

Tense

Tense as a ball of wire.—John Irving
Tense as a cat.—Clare Francis
Tense as a fiddle string.—John Crosby
Tense as a string drawn tight.—John Ehle
Tense as an "E" string.—George MacDonald Fraser
Tense as rigor mortis.—Tom Wicker
Tense as wire.—A. C. Swinburne
  Also see Anxious, Edgy, Fidgeted, Nervous, Restless, Taut, Uneasy.

Terrible

Terrible as a bad marriage.
Terrible as death.
Terrible as the curse of a dead man's eye.
  Also see Mean.

Thick (close together)

Thick as a mist.—Percy B. Shelley
Thick as autumnal leaves.—John Milton
Thick as bats on a summer night.—H. S. Commager
Thick as beans in a pod.
Thick as bees.
Thick as bugs on a bumper.
Thick as Egypt's locusts.—John Dryden
Thick as fiddlers in hell.
Thick as fleas on a dog's back.
Thick as fleas on a yard dog.—Tom Wicker
Thick as flies.—F. Hopkinson Smith
Thick as flies around a corpse.—F. Paul Wilson
Thick as flies around a country schoolhouse.
Thick as flies in a barnyard.—Tom Wicker
Thick as fog.
Thick as gnats.—Douglas C. Jones
Thick as gravestones in a city cemetery.—H. S. Commager
Thick as hasty pudding.—Song, "Yankee Doodle"
Thick as herrings in a barrel.
Thick as hickory nuts.—Tom Wicker
Thick as hops.
Thick as huckleberries.

Thick as lawyers in hell.
Thick as molasses.
Thick as mud.
Thick as pea soup.
Thick as peas in a half-bushel.
Thick as peas in a pod.
Thick as pudding.—Joan Samson
Thick as stars above.—George Eliot
Thick as ticks in a mattress.—John Ehle
Thick as wool.—Elizabeth B. Custer
Thick as your aunt Nellie's gravy.—Peter DeVris
Thick like plums in a pudding.—Peter Schneider

Thick (dimension)
Thick as a brick.—C. L. Skelton
Thick as harrow teeth.—Mark Twain
Thick as my arm.—George MacDonald Fraser
Thick as my little finger.—Mark Twain
Thick as Paddy's head.—George MacDonald Fraser
Thick as three planks.—Derek Robinson
Thick as your thigh.
Thick as your thumbnail.—Mark Twain
    Also see Dense, Dumb, Ignorant, Stupid.

Thick (friendly)
Thick as pickpockets.
Thick as thieves.—English proverb
Thick as thieves in bed.
Thick as three in a bed.—Scottish proverb
Thick as two in a basket.
Thick as two peas in a pod.
Thick as two pirates.

Thin
Thin as a bar of homemade soap after a hard day's washing.
Thin as a bean pole.
Thin as a cat's elbow.
Thin as a crane.—Anita Mason
Thin as a cypress.—Tom DeHaven
Thin as a dime.
Thin as a featherless bird.—T. C. Boyle
Thin as a heron's leg.—Stephen King
Thin as a hunger striker.—Peter Schneider
Thin as a husband's alibi.
Thin as a knife.
Thin as a lath.—Arthur Conan Doyle
Thin as a motel wall.
Thin as a pencil.
Thin as a phantom.—Thomas Hardy

Thin as a pumpkin vine.
Thin as a rail.
Thin as a rake.—Havilah Babcock
Thin as a ramrod.—Bernard Cornwell
Thin as a reed.
Thin as a shadow.
Thin as a skinned cat.—Henri Troyat
Thin as a snake.
Thin as a sparrow.—Emily Brontë
Thin as a spider's web.—George Garrett
Thin as a thermometer.
Thin as a vegetarian's cat.
Thin as a vine.—Cecelia Holland
Thin as a wafer.
Thin as a warped stick.—Robert R. McCammon
Thin as a whip.—John Updike
Thin as a whippet.—Tom Wicker
Thin as a wishbone.—Robert Lewis Taylor
Thin as a worn-out dime.—William Pearson
Thin as a young poplar.—Honore de Balzac
Thin as boarding house soup.—Jack Buck
Thin as cut hair.—T. C. Boyle
Thin as fraud.—Percy B. Shelley
Thin as Ghandi.
Thin as hotel toilet paper.
Thin as ice in August.
Thin as newsprint.—Tom Clancy
Thin as poorhouse butter.—Stephen Longstreet
Thin as poorhouse gruel.
Thin as prison soup.—R. F. Delderfield
Thin as the homeopathic soup that was made by boiling the shadow of a pigeon
    that had starved to death.—Abraham Lincoln
Thin as tracing paper.—John Updike
Thin as Twiggy.
Thin as wallpaper.
    Also see Bones, Lean, Skinny.

Thirsty
Thirsty as a camel.
Thirsty as a cross-country runner.
Thirsty as a drunk just released from the hospital.
Thirsty as a dry road.—Cyril Harcourt
Thirsty as a fish.
Thirsty as a goat.—Phoebe Gray
Thirsty as a graven image.—Anne E. Perkins

Thorny
Thorny as a blackberry patch.

Thorny as a cactus.
Thorny as a honey-locust.—Edward Eggleston

Threatening
Threatening as a bank robber.
Threatening as a flame thrower nozzle.—Tristan Jones
Threatening as a lawsuit.
Threatening as legal jargon.
Threatening as a thundercloud.
Threatening as the flu.
Also see Grim, Ominous.

Threw down
Threw down like a bundle of limp rags.
Threw down like a candy bar wrapper.
Threw down like a dead cat.—Tom Wicker
Threw down like a rag doll.
Threw down like an old bubble gum card.
Threw down like yesterday's newspaper.
Also see Dropped.

Thrived
Thrived like dandelions.
Thrived like Johnsongrass.
Thrived like weeds.—Andrew Mavell
Also see Flourished, Grew, Sprouted.

Throbbed
Throbbed like a dying trout.—Owen Ulph
Throbbed like a swollen gum with an abcess in it.—Stephen King
Throbbed like a wounded bird.—Francis Thompson
Throbbed like an ancient refrigerator.—Derek Robinson
Throbbed like the tail of a mean dog.
Also see Ached, Head, Hurt.

Thud
Thud like a dropped casket.
Thud like a drunk on the stairs.—Tom DeHaven
Thud like a drunk who fell off his bar stool.
Also see Fell.

Thunder
Thunder like beer barrels tumbling down stairs.—Ivan Doig
Thunder like the devil bowling.

Tidy
Tidy as a candy shop.
Tidy as an old maid's parlor.

Tidy as spats on a rooster.—Ivan Doig
   Also see Neat, Orderly, Prim.

Tight

Tight as a bowstring.—Edward Bulwer-Lytton
Tight as a brassiere.
Tight as a bull's ass in fly time.
Tight as a corset.
Tight as a cotton clothesline after a rain.—Jim Wright, Texas congressman
Tight as a crossbow.—T. C. Boyle
Tight as a drum.
Tight as a duck's ass.
Tight as a fiddle string.—Derek Robinson
Tight as a fish line.—Ivan Doig
Tight as a gnat's ass.—Ridley Pearson
Tight as a jaybird's ass.
Tight as a jug.—John Inzer
Tight as a lid of a honey jar.
Tight as a lockjawed clam.
Tight as a miser.
Tight as a nun.
Tight as a pickle jar lid.
Tight as a Pullman window.
Tight as a rat's ass.
Tight as a Scotsman's purse.—Tom Wicker
Tight as a size nine shoe on a size twelve foot.
Tight as a stretched wire.—John Ehle
Tight as a ten-day drunk.
Tight as a tick in a hound dog's ear.
Tight as a vise.—Dean R. Koontz
Tight as a watch case.—Anthony Forrest
Tight as an eight-day clock.
Tight as an old man's bowels.—Donald McCaig
Tight as lockjaw.—Tom Wicker
Tight as rawhide.—Robert Lewis Taylor
Tight as the bark on a beech tree.—Edward Eggleston
Tight as the bark on a tree.
Tight as the instep of a chicken.
Tight as the paper on the wall.—Glendon Swarthout
Tight as the skin of a gooseberry.
Tight as the skin on a grape.
Tight as the skin on a sausage.
Tight as the strings of a violin.
   Also see Cheap, Drunk, Taut.

Timid

Timid as a bashful child.
Timid as a child deserted by its nurse.
Timid as a doe.—Robert Noel

Timid as a fawn. —William M. Thackeray
Timid as a mouse.
Timid as a sheep. —Ouida
Timid as a titmouse.
Timid as a wild rabbit. —Margaret Mitchell
Timid as an abused dog.
    Also see Meek, Modest, Shy.

Tired
Tired as a dog. —Gene Stratton-Porter
Tired as a tombstone. —Robert Browning
    Also see Out, Slept.

To and fro
To and fro like a Ping-Pong ball.
To and fro like shuttlecocks.

Tongue
Tongue as rough and heavy as an oriental carpet. —George Garrett
Tongue like a carving knife. —George MacDonald Fraser
Tongue like a filet of raw salmon. —Owen Ulph
Tongue like sawdust. —Doris Leslie
Tongue tasted like a skidmark.
Tongue that flapped like a banner in a fair wind. —George Garrett
    Also see Mouth, Tasted.

Took it
Took it like a hungry fish. —George MacDonald Fraser
Took it like Dewey took Manila.
Took it like Grant took Richmond.
Took it like Schwartzkopf took Kuwait.
Took it like Sherman took Atlanta.

Took off
Took off like a flock of geese when an eagle flies overhead.
Took off like a flock of vultures flushed from a kill. —T. C. Boyle
Took off like a three-year-old at the start of a steeplechase. —T. C. Boyle
    Also see Fast, Fled, Hurried, Off, Ran, Swift, Went.

Took to it
Took to it like a duck to water.
Took to it like a fox takes to chickens. —Jack Matthews
Took to it like a gull to a top wave. —Mary Stewart
Took to it like a retriever to ducks. —Ouida
Took to it like pitch. —Robert Louis Stevenson
    Also see Agreeable, Natural.

Toppled
Toppled like a lightning-struck pine. —Gerald Duff
Toppled like tenpins. —Sidney Sheldon
    Also see Dropped, Felt.

Tossed

Tossed like a driven foam.—Ralph Waldo Emerson
Tossed like a salad.
Tossed around like a cork in a cauldron.
Tossed around like a cork on the waves.—Thomas Hardy
Tossed around like a feather in a whirlwind.
Tossed around like a peanut at sea.
Tossed around like popcorn in a popper.—Margaret Mitchell
Tossed aside like a rag doll.
    Also see Flung.

Touchy

Touchy as a disturbed badger.—Owen Ulph
Touchy as a new blister.—Mark Childress
Touchy as a virgin.—Tom Wicker
Touchy as the gout.
    Also see Anxious, Edgy, Nervous, Tense, Uneasy.

Tough

Tough as a boot.
Tough as a Cape Cod fisherman.—Robert Edgren
Tough as a fast-food steak.
Tough as a fried ham.
Tough as a hickory rail.—Stephen Vincent Benet, describing Lincoln
Tough as a jockey's tail end.
Tough as a lighter knot.
Tough as a marine.
Tough as a mule's mouth.—Stephen Longstreet
Tough as a picnic egg.
Tough as a rat catcher's dog.
Tough as a ten-year-old tennis shoe.
Tough as a thirty-cent steak.
Tough as an old field hand.—Mark Childress
Tough as boiled mother-in-law.—W. C. Fields
Tough as brogans.—Lee Smith
Tough as cactus.—Zane Grey
Tough as dog breath.
Tough as gristle.
Tough as iron.
Tough as lawnmower tires.—Robert R. McCammon
Tough as nails.
Tough as old boot leather.—C. L. Skelton
Tough as old leather.
Tough as old Nick.
Tough as shoe leather.
Tough as teak.—George MacDonald Fraser
    Also see Rough.

Tranquil

Tranquil as a dreamless sleep.—William Wordsworth

Tranquil as a summer sea.—William Wordsworth
Tranquil as Christmas Eve.
Tranquil as night.
About as tranquil as a riot.
About as tranquil as a rodeo.
About as tranquil as a Texas cyclone.
About as tranquil as nursery school.
Also see Calm, Peaceful, Placid, Serene, Unruffled.

Transparent
Transparent as a clear sky.
Transparent as cellophane.—Caryl Rivers
Transparent as glass.
Transparent as spring water.
Also see Clear, Evident, Obvious.

Trapped
Trapped like a bear in a pit.—Victor Hugo
Trapped like a bear in a trap.
Trapped like a cat in a barrel.—Januaz Glowacki
Trapped like a cub in the snow.—Hank Searles
Trapped like a rabbit in its burrow.—Loup Durard
Trapped like a rat.
Trapped like a rat in a cage.
Trapped like flies in a bottle.
Trapped like flies in a web.
Trapped like flies on flypaper.
Also see Caught.

Treated
Treated as devoutly as a Jesuit treats his beads.—Lewis W. Green
Treated like a borrowed lawnmower.
Treated like a dog.
Treated like a king.
Treated like a mule.
Treated like a queen.
Treated like a twig in a sacrificial fire.—Richard Hough
Treated like he was the scum of the earth.—William M. Raine
Treated like dirt.
Treated like shit.

Trembled
Trembled like a frightened child.—C. G. Rossetti
Trembled like a frightened deer seeking a place of refuge.
    —Lewis Carroll
Trembled like a guilty thing surprised.—William Wordsworth
Trembled like a hunted prey.—Thomas Otway
Trembled like a leaf.—Victor Appleton
Trembled like a man with palsy.—J. M. Barrie

Trembled like a rabbit in a snare.—Stephen King
Trembled like a tuning fork.
Trembled like a wet puppy.—James Sherburn
Trembled like an aspen.—Louis L'Amour
Trembled like an aspen leaf.—William Shakespeare
Trembled like the last leaf of autumn.—Derek Robinson
    Also see Quaked, Quivered, Shook.

Tricky
Tricky as a bear.
Tricky as a concierge.
Tricky as a lawyer's convention.—John M. Del Vecchio
Tricky as a magician.
    Also see Clever.

Trivial
Trivial as a parking ticket.
Trivial as a parrot's prate.—William Cowper
Trivial as the giggle of a housemaid.—Henry James

Trotted
Trotted at his heels like a pampered cur.—Doris Leslie
Trotted like a docile dog.—Thelma Strabel
Trotted like a servile footman, all day long.
    —William Shakespeare
    Also see Paced, Ran.

Troublesome
Troublesome as a cornered copperhead.
Troublesome as a law-suit.—Coley Cibber
Troublesome as a monkey.—Thomas Shadwell
Troublesome as a salmon in a dry creek.
Troublesome as a she-bitch with crabs.—Stephen King
Troublesome as a rat-tailed horse tied short in fly time.—Stan Hoig

True
True as a compass.
True as a die.—John Gay
True as a dove.—James Smith
True as a gun.—Ben Jonson
True as a shepherd to his flock.—Lord Byron
True as a stump.—Mark Childress
True as an arrow to its aim.—Francis H. Doyle
True as heaven is true.—Robert Service
True as steel.—Mark Twain
True as the gospel.—John Gay
True as the homing bird flies with its message.—John B. O'Reilly
True as the light.—Thomas Hardy

True as truth.—Madison Cawein
 Also see Honest, Loyal, Obedient, Real, Reliable, Steadfast.

Tucked away
Tucked away like a treasure.—Robert R. McCammon
Tucked away money like a miser.

Tumbled
Tumbled like a sack of stones dropped from a bridge.—T. C. Boyle
Tumbled like a stuffed toy.—Stephen King
Tumbled like bricks from a dump truck.—Derek Robinson
Tumbled like rolling empty barrels down stairs.—Mark Twain
 Also see Dropped, Fell, Stumbled, Toppled.

Tuneless
Tuneless as a bag of wool.—George Eliot
Tuneless as a canary with strep throat.
Tuneless as a guitar with old strings.

Turned
Turned like a windmill sail.—John Greenleaf Whittier
Turned like an ice skater.

Turned down
Turned down like a bedspread.
Turned down like a blind date.
 Also see Twirled.

Twanged
Twanged like a cheap guitar.
Twanged like an ill-tuned fiddle.—Alain Paris

Twirled
Twirled like a ballerina.
Twirled like a dervish.
Twirled like a spinning top.
Twirled like a weather cock in March.
Twirled like a whirligig.
 Also see Whirled.

Twisted
Twisted as an old paint tube.—Fannie Hurst
Twisted like a nest of snakes.—Herman Melville
Twisted like an "S."—John Hood
Twisted like knotted snakes.—Charles Harpur
Twisted like Pebble Beach pines.

Twitched
Twitched like a dog tormented with fleas.—Gary Jennings
Twitched like a landed fish.—George MacDonald Fraser
Twitched like a landed trout.—Stephen King
Twitched like a wagonload of old maids at a hayride.—Ferrol Sams

Ugly

Ugly as a baboon.
Ugly as a ball of dried blood. —Pete Dexter
Ugly as a bear. —William Shakespeare
Ugly as a buffalo's ass.
Ugly as a demon king.
Ugly as a gargoyle.
Ugly as a hairless monkey. —Margaret Mitchell
Ugly as a haystack in January.
Ugly as a mud fence. —Zane Grey
Ugly as a mud fence daubed with tadpoles.
Ugly as a mudhen.
Ugly as a rubber crutch.
Ugly as a scarecrow.
Ugly as a toad.
Ugly as an ape.
Ugly as an old witch.
Ugly as death warmed over.
Ugly as galvanized sin.
Ugly as homemade lye soap.
Ugly as homemade sin. —John Inzer
Ugly as sin.
Ugly as the ass end of a bus.
Ugly as the devil. —Henry Fielding
Ugly as the landscape; dry, rocky and not worth fighting for.
    —P. F. Kluge
    Also see Ghastly, Homely.

Unappetizing

Unappetizing as the heel of a zookeeper's boot.
Unappetizing as the floor of a parrot's cage.

Unblemished

Unblemished as a baby.

Unblemished as the white-robed virgin choir.—William Livingston
Also see Pure, Smooth.

Uncertain
Uncertain as an April sun.—Doris Leslie
Uncertain as the glory of an April day.—William Shakespeare
Uncertain as the weather.

Unchangeable
Unchangeable as regrets.
Unchangeable as the past.
Unchanging as a nation's flag.—George Jean Nathan

Uncomfortable
Uncomfortable as a Baptist in a bordello.—Vincent Bugliosi
Uncomfortable as a hard-backed oak chair.
Uncomfortable as an afterthought.—*Reader's Digest*
Uncomfortable as the Garden of Eden during mosquito season.

Uneasy
Uneasy as a man at a ladies' bridge club meeting.
Uneasy as a pig in a parlor.
Also see Anxious, Edgy, Nervous, Restless, Tense.

Unending
Unending as the changes in weather.
Unending as the river and the stars.—W. E. Henley
Also see Eternal.

Unexpected
Unexpected as a bolt of lightning from a clear blue sky.
Unexpected as a clap of thunder on a clear day.—Jack Matthews
Unexpected as a night assassin.—Rosemary H. Jarman
Unexpected as cuss words in a sermon.—Thomas Thompson
Unexpected as death.—Peter Jenkins
Unexpected as winter thunder.
Unexpected like a bolt out of the blue.—Thomas Carlyle
Also see Abrupt, Sudden, Surprised, Unpredictable.

Unhappy
Unhappy as a gambler who has lost everything.
Unhappy as a proctologist who's lost his rubber gloves.
Unhappy as King Lear.
Also see Dismal, Gloomy, Glum, Sad.

Universal
Universal as children playing.
Universal as seasickness.—George Bernard Shaw

Unlikely
Unlikely as a cat having fondness for the company of mice.—Robert R. McCammon
Unlikely as a mouse falling in love with a cat.
Unlikely as a pig laying eggs.

Unlikely as pigs flying.
Unlikely as teaching an alligator to polka.
Unlikely as Michael Jordan buying elevator shoes.
   Also see Rare.

Unlovely
Unlovely as a rotting animal.
Unlovely as leprosy.
Unlovely as road kill.
Unlovely as the corpse of a man. —Rudyard Kipling
   Also see Homely, Ugly.

Unmanageable
Unmanageable as a flood.
Unmanageable as a fool.
Unmanageable as a spoiled brat.
Unmanageable as an avalanche. —Stephen R. Donaldson

Unmistakable
Unmistakable as an accent.
Unmistakable as foreign clothes. —Henry James
   Also see Real, Sure.

Unpredictable
Unpredictable as a copperhead.
Unpredictable as a hen in a hurricane. —Ivan Doig
Unpredictable as a rutting boar. —Douglas C. Jones
Unpredictable as a storm at sea.
Unpredictable as the weather.
Unpredictable as winter. —Darcy O'Brien
   Also see Surprised, Unexpected.

Unraveled
Unraveled like a ball of yarn.
Unraveled like a whodunit.
Unraveled like a Singapore suit.

Unrestricted
Unrestricted as a flood.
Unrestricted as a tornado.
Unrestricted as the rain. —Mark Twain
   Also see Free.

Unruffled
Unruffled as a great horned owl perched in a dead tree. —Owen Ulph
Unruffled as time. —Edgar Saltas
   Also see Calm, Composed, Peaceful, Serene, Steady, Tranquil.

Unruly
Unruly as a colt.
Unruly as a riot.
Unruly as a two-year-old boy.

Unseasonable
Unseasonable as snow in summer.
Unseasonable as watermelons in January.

Unstable
Unstable as a bucket of dynamite caps.—Jack Matthews
Unstable as propane gas.—Jack Matthews
Unstable as sand running through an hourglass.
Unstable as the waves of the sea.—George Bishop
Unstable as water.—*Old Testament*

Untidy
Untidy as a Bohemian.—Alphonse Daudet
Untidy like a bird of paradise that had been out all night in the rain.
   —Oscar Wilde
   Also see Looked.

Unwelcome
Unwelcome as snow in summer.
Unwelcome as water in a leaking ship.
Unwelcome as water in your shoe.
   Also see Out of place, Went over.

Unwieldy
Unwieldy as a sunk ship.
Unwieldy as Noah's ark.—Shelby Foote
   Also see Awkward, Big.

Unyielding
Unyielding as a cornered bear.
Unyielding as a rock.
Unyielding as steel.
   Also see Immovable, Inflexible, Resolute, Rigid, Stubborn.

Up and down
Up and down like a boat in a storm.—Phillip Sidney
Up and down like a bucket in a well.
Up and down like a chicken drinking.—Leigh Hunt
Up and down like a drawbridge.
Up and down like a fiddler's elbow.
Up and down like a yo-yo.

Upright
Upright as a flagpole.
Upright as a marble column.—Cecelia Holland
Upright as a ninepin.—Honore de Balzac
Upright as a post.
Upright as a ramrod.
Upright as a sentinel.
Upright as a stake.
   Also see Erect, Straight.

Useless

Useless as a bladeless knife without a handle. —Ivan Doig
Useless as a broken cannon. —Rosemary H. Jarman
Useless as a broken feather.
Useless as a button on a hat.
Useless as a comb to a bald man.
Useless as a concrete bicycle. —Arnold Sawislak
Useless as a concrete parachute.
Useless as a dead actor. —Brander Matthews
Useless as a glass eye at a keyhole. —L. Monta Bell
Useless as a gun with no bullets.
Useless as a lamp without a wick.
Useless as a life preserver on a duck.
Useless as a lock without a key. —Anthony Forrest
Useless as a milk bucket under a bull.
Useless as a monkey trying to teach table manners to a bear. —Stephen King
Useless as a rubber crutch.
Useless as a rubber-nosed woodpecker in the Petrified Forest.
Useless as a screen door on a submarine.
Useless as a sucked orange. —John P. Marqund
Useless as a trailer hitch on a Yugo.
Useless as an icebox to an Eskimo.
Useless as barking at a knot in a fence post. —Owen Ulph
Useless as bringing a doctor to a dead man. —Rosemary H. Jarman
Useless as Ex-lax in a dysentery ward.
Useless as gasoline in a fire extinguisher. —H. C. Whitwer
Useless as Kotex in a men's prison. —Robert R. McCammon
Useless as rearranging the deck chairs on the *Titanic*.
Useless as shouting down an empty well. —Vincent Bugliosi
Useless as sights on a musket. —James Goldman
Useless as taking a needle to stop a charging bull.
Useless as talking to a brick wall.
Useless as talking to an empty cat food can. —Stephen King
Useless as talking to the wind. —T. S. Arthur
Useless as the blind leading the blind.
Useless as the fifth wheel on a wagon.
Useless as tits on a boar hog.
Useless as trying to catch the moon in a bushel basket.
Useless as trying to stop the river current with a fish net.
Useless as trying to stop up a rat hole with apple dumplings.
Useless as using a sieve to carry water.
Useless as whispering in the ear of a corpse.
Useless as whistling psalms to a dead horse. —*Bartlett's*
  Also see Futile, Worthless.

Vacillating

Vacillating as a veteran politician.
Vacillating as a windshield wiper. —Harriet Dorian

Vain

Vain as a barnyard cock. —Thelma Strabel
Vain as a girl. —William M. Thackeray
Vain as a peacock. —Zane Grey
Vain as an Etonian duke. —George MacDonald Fraser

Valiant

Valiant as a football hero.
Valiant as a lion. —William Shakespeare
Valiant as Hercules. —William Shakespeare
   Also see Brave, Fearless.

Vanished

Vanished, ghostlike, into air. —Henry W. Longfellow
Vanished like breath upon a mirror. —Vincent Bugliosi
Vanished like a bursted bubble.
Vanished like a cocktail before dinner.
Vanished like a dollar on Saturday night. —Abe Martin
Vanished like a ghost. —Louis L'Amour
Vanished like a ghost at dawn. —Robert R. McCammon
Vanished like a mirage. —T. C. Boyle
Vanished like a pebble in a pond.
Vanished like a pie.
Vanished like a puff of smoke. —Frederic S. Isham
Vanished like a puff of steam. —H. G. Wells
Vanished like a sunbeam. —George Garrett
Vanished like a swift, invisible shadow. —D. H. Lawrence
Vanished like a vision. —Charlotte Brontë
Vanished like beer at a teamsters' picnic.

Vanished like grain before the scythe. —Shelby Foote
Vanished like hailstones. —William Shakespeare
Vanished like rats. —Doris Leslie
Vanished like rats deserting a sinking ship.
Vanished like smoke from Aetna. —William Shakespeare
Vanished like the mist of the morning.
Vanished like tobacco smoke. —Ben Jonson
Vanished, ghostlike, into air. —Henry W. Longfellow
   Also see Disappeared, Melted.

Vast
Vast as China. —Lee Smith
Vast as the Sahara.
Vast as the sea. —Stephen R. Donaldson
   Also see Big, Immense, Large.

Veered
Veered like race cars at Indianapolis.
Veered like waterbugs. —Norman Mailer

Veined
Veined like a relief map of the moon. —T. C. Boyle
Veined like grandma's legs. —Thomas Thompson

Vibrated
Vibrated like a tuning fork. —Stephen King
Vibrated like dishes during an earthquake.
   Also see Quivered, Trembled.

Vicious
Vicious as a dog pack. —Stephen King
Vicious as a hungry Doberman.
Vicious as a pit bull.
   Also see Bad, Mean, Ferocious.

Virtuous
Virtuous as a nun.
Virtuous as a reformed whore. —Rosemary H. Jarman
Virtuous as a saved soul.

Visible
Visible as a glowworm. —Robert Lewis Taylor
Visible as the stars.
Visible as the sun in Montana.
   Also see Obvious, Vivid.

Vital
Vital as air.
Vital as an elixir. —Stephen R. Donaldson

Vital as blood.
Also see Necessary.

Vivid

Vivid as a dream.—William Wordsworth
Vivid as a nightmare.—Stephen R. Donaldson
Vivid as a photograph.
Vivid as eyesight.—William Kennedy
Vivid as language.—Stephen R. Donaldson
Vivid as television.
Also see Clear, Evident, Plain.

Voiceless

Voiceless as silence.
Voiceless as the funeral train.—T. B. Reade
Voiceless as the sphinx.
Voiceless as the tomb.
Also see Mute, Noiseless, Silent, Speechless.

Vomited

Vomited like a freshman.
Vomited like a sailor.—Tom DeHaven

Vulnerable

Vulnerable as a baby.—John Irving
Vulnerable as a baby seal.—Patrick McGinley
Vulnerable as a rabbit in the mown field.—Cecelia Holland
Vulnerable as an insect.—Craig Thomas
Vulnerable as targets on a rifle range.—C. L. Skelton
Also see Bare.

Waddled

Waddled like a duck.
Waddled like an Armenian bride. —Osmani proverb
Waddled like slaphappy wrestlers. —Peter Bowman
   Also see Staggered.

Wailed

Wailed like a bobcat.
Wailed like a children's hopital ward. —John Irving
Wailed like a midnight wind. —Aubrey De Vere
   Also see Blubbered, Cried.

Waist

Waist like a Vienna guardsman. —F. Hopkinson Smith
Waist like an hourglass.
   Also see Fat.

Wakeful

Wakeful as a man with three sparkin'-age daughters. —Louis L'Amour
Wakeful as a sentry on guard.

Walked

Walked like a chicken with frozen toes.
Walked like a convalescent. —Stephen King
Walked like a gunslinger.
Walked like a hen with an egg broke in her.
Walked like a man who knew where he was going.
Walked like a man who was going somewhere. —George MacDonald Fraser
Walked like a mechanical toy.
Walked like an army drill instructor. —Peter Jenkins
Walked like he had a hitch in his get along.
Walked like he had gravel in his shoes. —George Ade
Walked like he was tiptoeing on eggs. —George MacDonald Fraser

Walked like he was too good to touch the ground.—Lee Smith
Walked like his ass was on sideways and he had to crap.—Stephen King
Walked like she had a feather up her ass.
Walked alone like one who has the pestilence.—William Shakespeare
Walked off like a madam bidding her guests good night.—William Shakespeare
I can walk like an ox, run like a fox, swim like an eel, make love like a mad
    bull.—Davy Crockett
    Also see Paced, Staggered, Waddled.

Wandered

Wandered at random, like a dog that has lost the scent.—Francoise Voltaire
Wandered like a milkweed puff.—Gary Jennings
Wandered like an unfettered stream.—Nathaniel Hawthorne
Wandered like Ishmael.—George MacDonald Fraser
    Also see Meandered, Roamed.

Warm

Warm as a hearth bug.—John Ehle
Warm as a mouse in a churn.
Warm as a mouse in cotton.
Warm as a plate of country biscuits.—Peter Jenkins
Warm as a stove.—Laurence Sterne
Warm as a wood cook stove.
Warm as an electric blanket.
Warm as an Eskimo in a pup tent.
Warm as fresh milk in a pail.
Warm as Indian summer.
Warm as Molly's milk.—Dougas C. Jones
Warm as moonlight.—J.R.R. Tolkien
Warm as love.—James Thomson
Warm as sunshine.—William Wordsworth
Warm as the engine room of a steamboat.—Richard Harding Davis
Warm as toast.—John Gay
Warm as wool.—John Peele
Warmed them up like a camp-meeting revival.—Mark Twain
    Also see Hot.

Warming

Warming as a depot stove.
Warming as a fireplace on a winter's eve.
Warming as brandy on a bleak November afternoon.—Lawrence Sanders

Wary

Wary as a blackjack dealer.
Wary as a blind horse.—Thomas Fuller
Wary as a cat at a rat hole.—William M. Raine
Wary as a fox.
Wary as a fox with pups.—Ray Locke
Wary as a young thing that's been caught.—John Ehle
    Also see Alert, Careful, Cautious.

Washed away
Washed away like a sand castle before the surf.
Washed away like duck decoys in a winter flood.
Washed away like makeup on a widow's face. —Thomas Thompson

Watched
Watched like a ferret. —Thomas Harris
Watched like a hawk.
Watched like a hawk-bird. —Lee Smith
Watched like a snake watches a mouse. —George MacDonald Fraser
Watched like a snake watches a rabbit.
Watched like a terrier at a rat's hole. —Charles Kingsley
Watched like one who feared robbins. —William Shakespeare
Watched him like a snake about to spring. —Robert Louis Stevenson
Watched him like a hen with chicks.
Watched like you'd watch a rattlesnake. —Rex Beach

Watchful
Watchful as a dog. —Richard Harding Davis
Watchful as a sentinel.
Watchful as a soldier in battle.
Watchful as the eye of a bird.

Waved
Waved like a juggler with nine plates in the air. —T. C. Boyle
Waved like a red flag at a bull. —C. L. Skelton
Waved like an opera star. —Ferrol Sams
Waved like autumn corn. —Sir Walter Scott

Weak
Weak as a baby.
Weak as a bled calf. —Thomas Hardy
Weak as a cat.
Weak as a child. —Jeffery Farnol
Weak as a drink of water.
Weak as a kitten.
Weak as a moth.
Weak as a newborn colt.
Weak as a reed. —Tom Wicker
Weak as a squeezed-out rag. —Robert R. McCammon
Weak as a stuffed toy. —Stephen King
Weak as dishwater.
Weak as rainwater. —James Sherburn
Weak as water. —*Old Testament*
Weak as yesterday's dreams. —Donald McCaig
   Also see Fragile, Frail, Helpless, Powerless, Spineless.

Weather-beaten
Weather-beaten as a fisherman's oar. —Thomas Wade
Weather-beaten as a stump. —Jack Fuller

Weather-beaten as a windmill.
Weather-beaten as an old barn.
Weather-beaten as rock.—Anita Mason
   Also see Worn.

Welcome
Welcome as a good-natured friend who makes short calls.
Welcome as a kiss.—Lawrence Sanders
Welcome as a long-awaited guest.—Margaret Mitchell
Welcome as a sharp steel file in prison.
Welcome as a raise.
Welcome as an engagement ring to an old maid.
Welcome as drops of rain in the desert.—Rosemary H. Jarman
Welcome as four aces.—Arthur Baer
Welcome as land to sailors long at sea.—Aeschylus
Welcome as the clang of a dinner bell.
Welcome as the flowers of spring.
About as welcome as a box of rattlesnakes.
About as welcome as a bullet.
About as welcome as a car repossessor.—Thomas Thompson
About as welcome as a coal bill in father's Christmas mail.—Frank M. O'Malley
About as welcome as a fart during sex.
About as welcome as a fart in an elevator.
About as welcome as a fart in church.
About as welcome as a plague of locusts.—Margaret Mitchell
About as welcome as a polecat at a picnic.—Charles Henderson
About as welcome as a turd in a punch bowl.
About as welcome as Atilla the Hun.
About as welcome as diphtheria.
About as welcome as dog shit on a new pair of shoes.
About as welcome as the black plague.
About as welcome as water in a leaking ship.

Went
Went like a bomb.
Went like a derby winner in the last furlong.—George MacDonald Fraser
Went like a dose of salts.
Went like a house afire.
Went like a lover to his bride.—Rosemary H. Jarman
Went like a prairie fire.
Want like a rat to a drainpipe.
Went like a shot.
Went like a whale.
Went like blazes.—De Quincy
Went like goose shit through a tin horn.
Went like he was running from hell itself.
Went like shit through a cane break.
Went like the devil.
Went like the hell flies were after him.—William M. Raine

Went like the wind.—Victor Appleton
Went like wildfire.
>   *Also see* Fled, Hurried, Ran, Took off.

Went at it

Went at it like a bull at the gate.—Nigel Tranter
Went at it like a weasel in a henhouse.—Jim Harrison
Went at it like Frederick the Great with a wasp in his pants.
>   —George MacDonald Fraser

Went at it like he was killing snakes.—Rex Beach
Went at it like Trojans.

Went down

Went down like a broom's edge under a mow.—Tom Wicker
Went down like a dead bird.—James Sherburn
Went down like a house of cards.
Went down like a shanghaied sailor—George MacDonald Fraser
Went down like a shot rabbit.

Went for it

Went for it like a charged-up bull.—Olive Ann Burns
Went for it like a starving dog.—Phillip Kimball
Went for it like a steer to salt.—Glendon Swarthout
>   *Also see* Attacked, Charged.

Went off

Went off like a bomb.
Went off like a charge of gunpowder.
Went off like a firecracker.
Went off like a pipe bomb.

Went out

Went out like a candle.—Rex Beach
Went out like a light.
Went out like a pissed-on campfire.

Went over

Went over like a house afire.
Went over like a million bucks.
Went over about like a fart in church.—Ivan Doig
Went over about like a lead balloon.
Went over about like a turd in a punchbowl.
Went over about like a wet firecracker.—Richard Bachman
Went over about like a wet noodle.
Went over about like three cheers at a funeral.
>   *Also see* Popular.

Went through it

Went through it like a dose of salts through a widow woman.
Went through it like a flash of lightning through a gooseberry bush.
>   —Benjamin Webster

Went through it like a fork through Jell-O.
Went through it like a madwoman sorting laundry.
Went through it like a rat through cheese. —George MacDonald Fraser
Went through it like a shot. —Mark Twain
Went through it like an electric current. —T. S. Arthur
Went through it like cheese through a goose. —Stephen King
Went through it like the cannonball express through Schenectady.
Went through it like the grace of heaven through a camp meeting.
Went through it like water through a sieve. —Alexander Barclay

Went up
Went up like a balloon.
Went up like a rocket.
Went up like a sky rocket.
   Also see Rose.

Wept
Wept like a child. —Harold Bell Wright
Wept like a crocodile. —Robert Burton
Wept like a fountain. —A. Gustave Droz
Wept like a girl. —Rex Beach
Wept like a gutter on a rainy day. —Guy de Maupassant
Wept like a wench who has burned her grandma. —William Shakespeare
   Also see Cried.

Wet
Wet as a dog in the rain. —James G. Huneker
Wet as a drowned cat. —Tom Wicker
Wet as a drowned rat. —Thomas Heywood
Wet as a fish.
Wet as a muskrat. —Douglas C. Jones
Wet as Glasgow on Saturday night. —Clare Francis
Wet as water.

Wheezed
Wheezed like a calliope with sore tonsils.
Wheezed like an asthmatic adulterer.
Wheezed like an old door. —John Fuller
Wheezed like an old pump. —George MacDonald Fraser
   Also see Breathed, Gasped, Panted, Puffed.

Whimpered
Whimpered like a cur. —J. A. Symonds
Whimpered like a dog on a doorstep in the rain. —Thelma Strabel
Whimpered like a dog ready to hunt.
Whimpered like a lowing cow. —John Gay
Whimpered like a puppy about to be hit with a rolled-up newspaper for soiling
   the rug. —Margaret Truman
   Also see Cried.

Whirled

Whirled like a puppy on a rope.—Jack Matthews

Whirled like a tornado.—Doris Leslie

Whirled like lightning.—George MacDonald Fraser
  Also see Turned, Twirled.

White

White as a blizzard.—Elain Viets

White as a bone.—Stephen R. Donaldson

White as a candle.—Cormac McCarthy

White as a cotton sheet.—John Ehle

White as a fang.

White as a fish belly.—Mark Twain

White as a ghost.

White as a gull's wing.

White as a haunt.

White as a lace tablecloth.—Gerald Duff

White as a lily.—William Shakespeare

White as a marshmallow.

White as a marshmallow cream.—Jim Dodge

White as a perfect rose.—Rosemary H. Jarman

White as a sheet.—Robert Louis Stevenson

White as a shroud.

White as a snowfield at high noon.—Tabitha King

White as a soul.—Robert Bausch

White as a spook.

White as a Sunday shirt.—Joseph C. Lincoln

White as a swan.—Francois Rabelais

White as a wax candle.

White as a whale's tooth.

White as a zombie.

White as an abbot.

White as an altar sheet.—Robert Bausch

White as an Easter lily.

White as an old bone.—F. W. Beland

White as bleached sand.—Rosemary H. Jarman

White as chalk.—Geoffrey Chaucer

White as communion candles.

White as cotton.

White as Dover chalk.—James Goldman

White as driven snow.—John Lyly

White as flour.

White as fresh milk.

White as goat's milk.—George Garrett

White as Irish linen.—Thomas Hood

White as Italian marble.

White as ivory.

White as new-plucked cotton.

White as paper.
White as pie dough.
White as snow.—Lewis Carroll
White as snow in the sunshine.—J.R.R. Tolkien
White as soap.—Robert Bausch
White as spit in a cottonfield.
White as teeth.—T. C. Boyle
White as terror.
White as the belly of a dead carp.
White as the driven snow.—T. C. Arthur
White as the neck of a swan.—James Lane Allen
White as the light.—*New Testament*
White as walrus ivory.
White as whalebone.
White as winter mist.—Rosemary H. Jarman
White as your handkerchief.—Henry James
White and pure as the falling snow.—Mary J. Holmes
White and secret like a virgin's dream.—Doris Leslie

Wholesome
Wholesome as a big ripe apple.—Phoebe Gray
Wholesome as the morning air.—George Chapman
    Also see Healthy.

Wide
Wide as a barn door.
Wide as a church door.—William Shakespeare
Wide as an axe handle.
Wide as life.—A. C. Swinburne
Wide as the Thames.—T. C. Boyle
Wide as the whole state of Texas.
Wide as the world is wide.
    Also see Broad, Gaped, Open, Yawned.

Wide awake
Wide awake as a treeful of hooty owls.
Wide awake as a weasel.—Robert Lewis Taylor
Wide awake as an old owl with diarrhea.—Stephen King
Wide awake as morning.—Robert Houston
    Also see Alert, Cautious.

Wild
Wild as a buck.
Wild as a bull-pup.—Richard Hovey
Wild as a chased deer.—Thomas Churchyard
Wild as a deer.—Zane Grey
Wild as a forest creature.—Margaret Mitchell
Wild as a gypsy.—Dolores Barnes Wilson
Wild as a hawk.
Wild as a jungle dance.—John Ehle

Wild as a maniac's dream.
Wild as a March hare.
Wild as a mountain lion.
Wild as a snake.
Wild as a tiger.
Wild as a young bull.
Wild as a young horse.
Wild as an antelope. —Zane Grey
Wild as an unbroken horse. —Marie Lowell
Wild as dreams. —Ralph Waldo Emerson
Wild as the devil.
Wild as the waves. —Aubrey De Vere
Wild as the West Texas wind. —Marty Robbins, "El Paso"
Wild as the wind.

Willful
Willful as a mule. —Danish saying
Willful as a prince. —Sir Walter Scott

Willing
Willing as a prostitute on a slow Saturday night.
Willing as a turtle. —John Gay
   Also see Agreeable.

Wily
Wily as an old fox. —Sir Walter Scott
Wily as a collie.
   Also see Cunning, Sly, Sneaked.

Winced
Winced like a nerve touched by a dentist's drill.
Winced like a touched nerve. —Henry James

Windy
Windy as a dog-day in Kansas. —O. Henry
Windy as Chicago.

Wise
Wise as a bishop. —Colley Cibber
Wise as a hooty owl. —Ivan Doig
Wise as a serpent. —*New Testament*
Wise as an owl. —John Keats
Wise as Shakespeare. —Henry David Thoreau
Wise as Solomon.
   Also see Intelligent, Smart.

Withered
Withered as an autumn leaf. —William Collins
Withered as an old stone. —J.R.R. Tolkien
Withered like a rose without light.

Withered and died like a jellyfish washed up on the beach. —T. C. Boyle
Also see Died.

Wobbled
Wobbled like a drunken tailor with two left legs.
Wobbled like an elephant on ice skates.
Wobbled like a sixty-five-year-old man on roller blades.
Wobbled around like a blind dog in a meat house.
Also see Stumbled.

Worked
Worked like a beaver. —Victor Appleton
Worked like a cart horse. —Stephen King
Worked like a charm. —Joan Samson
Worked like a demon.
Worked like a dog. —Rex Beach
Worked like a dog in a meat pot. —Edward Eggleston
Worked like a dray horse.
Worked like a farmhand at harvest.
Worked like a field hand. —Margaret Mitchell
Worked like a fiend. —Harold Bell Wright
Worked like a galley slave.
Worked like a German clock. —George Garrett
Worked like a horse.
Worked like a machine. —Zane Grey
Worked like a madman.
Worked like a miner in a landslide.
Worked like a slave. —Thomas Hardy
Worked like a Trojan.
Worked like a whistle. —Robert Adelman
Worked like clockwork.
Worked like mad. —F. Hopkinson Smith
Worked like one possessed. —Doris Leslie
Worked like the devil for my pay. —Haven Gillespie, song,
    "That Lucky Old Sun"
    Also see Labored.

Worn
Worn as an old harness. —Derek Robinson
Worn as the seat covers of a 1957 Dodge.
    Also see Old, Weather-beaten.

Worthless
Worthless as a bucket of spit.
Worthless as a four-card flush. —Owen Ulph
Worthless as crabgrass. —John McDonald
Worthless as pigsquat. —James Wilcox
Worthless as spit. —Dean R. Koontz

Worthless as withered weeds.—Emily Brontë
Also see Useless.

Wound up

Wound up like a clock spring.
Wound up like a corkscrew.
Wound up like a fiddle string.
Wound up like a kid at Christmas.
Wound up like a top.
Also see Taut, Tense.

Wrinkled

Wrinkled as a raisin.
Wrinkled as a baked apple.—Nikolai V. Gogol
Wrinkled as an old apple.—Francoise Chandernoger
Wrinkled as crushed rice paper.—Malcomb Bosse
Wrinkled as old parchment.—George Eekwood
Wrinkled as used aluminum foil.—Robert Bausch
Wrinkled like a newly plowed field.—Jules Verne
Wrinkled like a ripe fig.—George Garrett
Wrinkled like a walnut.

Writhed

Writhed like a nest of snakes.—Stephen King
Writhed like a snake.—George MacDonald Fraser
Also see Squirmed.

Yawned
Yawned as big as a rain barrel.
Yawned like an English setter by the fireplace.
Yawned like the mouth of a cavern.—John Dennis

Yelled
Yelled like a bear dog on a wildcat's trail.—Robert Lewis Taylor
Yelled like a Comanche.—Margaret Mitchell
Yelled like a drunken Indian.—Robert Lewis Taylor
Yelled like a maniac.—Alexandre Dumas
Yelled like a steam whistle.
Yelled like an Apache after a successful scalping.—Margaret Mitchell
Yelled like the mate on a tramp steamer.—Joseph C. Lincoln
    Also see Bellowed, Hollered, Hooted, Howled, Screamed.

Yellow
Yellow as a cat's eye.
Yellow as a guinea.—Doris Leslie
Yellow as a gourd.—F. Hopkinson Smith
Yellow as an old cur dog.
Yellow as an old molted bird.—Margaret Mitchell
Yellow as canned corn.—Carolyn Wells
Yellow as corn in the sun.—Ouida
Yellow as jaundice.—George Meredith
Yellow as ripe corn.—D. G. Rossetti
Yellow as the Missouri River.—William S. McNutt

Yelped
Yelped like a dog with a hurt leg.—Robert R. McCammon
Yelped like a lost hound.—Margaret Mitchell
Yelped like he was hornet-stung.—Robert R. McCammon

Zigzagged
Zigzagged like a snipe.
Zigzagged like a race car.
Zigzagged like lightning.—Robert Southey

Zip
About as much zip as a wet paper napkin.
About as much zip as a wet potato chip.—Tim Rumsey
About as much zip as road kill.
About as much zip as an inarticulate simile.

Index of Selected Authors